I Blog, Therefore I Am

"Hello world, this is me, I'm a mess, and
I have no idea who I am, sorry."

Book Of Blogs Inc.
Edited by Peter Wojtowicz
www.bookofblogs.org

authorHOUSE™

1663 LIBERTY DRIVE, SUITE 200
BLOOMINGTON, INDIANA 47403
(800) 839-8640
WWW.AUTHORHOUSE.COM

First published by AuthorHouse 04/13/05

ISBN: 1-4208-4352-4 (sc)

Library of Congress Control Number: 2005902933

Printed in the United States of America
Bloomington, Indiana

This book is printed on acid-free paper.

Front Cover Designed By: 360 Grafix; www.360grafix.com

A portion of the proceeds from the sale of this book will be will be given to various educational and teenage charities.

Hello universe.

If I write this, does it really matter? In one hundred years I will be long forgotten, no one will know my name. My life is only a spec in the history of time. Not only that, I am one of billions of specs on this planet. Do I really matter? Do I have a purpose- or I am just wasting my time?

Truly yours,

Dedication:

To my parents, Roman & Bozena, my brothers, Tomasz & Robert, my hetero-life mate Woochy, my brothers from different mothers Greg & Dave and of course my dear Helen.

Thank You

To Adam Carrola and Dr. Drew Pinski, a true inspiration to me and millions of youth across the nation. You two are truly doing God's work. Thank you for giving me this advice several years ago, "The world is your oyster, cause that's ALL the world is."

I would be lost without it.

Blog:

(blŏg) *noun* :

an online diary; a personal chronological log of thoughts published on a Web page; also called Weblog.

Table of Contents

Dedication: vii

Thank You ix

Foreword xxi

He Raped Me 1

What's This World Coming Too? 4

Thanks.. 4

Punishment 5

Saturday 5

Mirror, Mirror on the Wall... 7

Surviving... 8

I Have Enough Sin in me to Damn a Million Souls 9

I'm Quitting 10

Food Fight! 10

Change 11

Scratch Last Post 12

Feel So Empty... 12

Well... 13

Raising Mackenzie 13

Moving 14

Corporate Whore 16

Wow It Has Been A While.. 17

Randomness 17

The.Czar.of.Bombastic. 18

Martin James McGowan... 19

Jungle Fever... 21

Silent Sufferer.. 22

ahhh Shit 24

Lost Love.. 24

Thank you all 25

Belly Space Competition 25

Sex in School Restrooms = Unhygienic 26

Changing Myself.. 27

The More You Ignore Me, The Closer I Get... 28

Mistake 29

Voices in Their Heads.. 29

Me Insecure?... 30

Smokin Cigs...or not?!?!?! 31

Hate Filled Heart 32
Strange feeling 33
And She Killed Herself 33
Sex! 35
The Last Time... 35
Question Yourself! 35
Needing A Life 36
Life Sucks.. 36
Yes... 37
Sex as Golf? 37
Perfection 38
Stupid Things That People Say 38
Porn 39
You Know You're in 2005 When... 40
Letter to Young Man 41
I Heart You Brendan 42
Angry.. 43
Publicity Stunt... 44
Sexy Saturday 45
The Forever Wakefulness of the Week 45
Suicide.. 46
Good Eye Sniper 47
Mood 47
Here Is A Story For You 47
Strokes 48
Tears In Dreams and Life 49
Live Dreams.. Dont Dream Them.. 50
Drastic Mood Change... 51
Tension... And Release... 51
2004 52
Shopping 53
What's Going On With Me? 54
Laughing Like No Tomorrow... 55
Dad.. 56
Perfect World.. 56
Rapist 57
The Real Deal 58
Insomnia.. 58
Finals.. 59
America 59
Why Do I Blog? 60

What Are We Here For? 61

I Miss Her.. 61

Ugh 62

Feeling Human! 62

Last Few Days at NorCal 64

Hug 64

Momz 65

Understanding 66

Feeling Weird 67

Skoo 68

Pics of My Ass 69

You Died at 3:00 p.m. 70

Two Years of Delusion 71

How Can You Live Like That...? 71

Turn Around Life 73

Stray Thoughts 73

Restless 73

Let Me Tell You About My Day... 74

Let Me Be Loved 74

Life is an Experience 75

To see?? To Notice??? The Same Thing?? 75

Tim's 77

Gold Medals and Monkey Slippers 78

Falling From Grace 79

Whatta Bitch 82

This School SUCKS!!! 83

The Phone Call.. 83

Religion Has Become a Coverup 84

I Dunno 85

Office Dilemma 86

STOP IN THE NAME OF LOVE 88

MAKE A MOMENT 89

January.. 89

Hope or Pain 89

Poetry...Written By Me of Course 90

Uniforms?! What the Fuck?! 90

The Real Me (Poem) 91

Fear 92

In the; We Are 92

Top 10 Scariest Thing 92

Ouch 94

sigh 95
Girls and a House Warming Party 95
Sad Story 97
GET A JOB 97
Near Death Experience 99
Cause I Said I Dont Need You Anymore 100
HookUp With Guy At Work 101
Feel So Blue 101
Night of Disaster 101
QUOTE OF THE MONTH 102
Pregnant Lactating Nuns and Worse Deviances 103
High On Life 103
Teacher Edicit 106
Blow Up This Mother Fucker 107
M.A... 108
What a Strange Life 109
WTF 110
It's 1st Time in Blog 111
Butterflies To A Child 111
Keep on Trucking 112
... A Second Spent In Fear 112
My Fault 113
Some Strange Feelings 113
Amongst Us 114
How can Something so Abused be so Purrrfect? 114
Ugh 116
Problems Never Stop 117
Sex in New Orleans 117
You Wanna Fight a Pork Chop? 118
Bad Trisha... 119
Wow! Go figure! 119
Whats a Dickfor? 120
Who's Tired of Being the Good Guy? 120
Darn Economics Teacher 121
To Get Away From You 122
beeedoodeeebooo 123
..pieces.. 124
...balance... 125
Who do we Blog? 125
Around 126
Basics 126

Cards of Life 127
My Dad is in Jail 127
I'm Back... I Don't Know Why... But I Got's Lots To Say This Time... ... 129
Who Saids Men Don't Have A Sesitive Side? 137
Disposal... 137
Crazy Night.. 143
Weekend 143
Derick & Lily.. 144
Bad Weekend 147
Warning 147
Oklahoma 148
Last Resort 148
Someone to Talk To 150
Jumped... 151
My Baby Is Not a Mistake... 151
Emotional 152
U Turn... 153
Cope... 154
Scared 155
Problem 156
Burn.. 157
Yesterday.. 157
Birthday 158
Life Is So Confusing 159
Wishing Plant 159
Up All Night.. 160
BK... 161
Robotripin' 162
Wake & Bake 163
American Porn... 164
Small Town 164
Depressed 166
New Year... 167
3 More Days 167
What to Write?.. 168
I Just Want to Sleep 168
Happiness 169
Your So Gay! 170
New Jersey.. 172
Boom! I Need To Cut 172
Perplexed 172

My Day 173
Home 175
Seeing Red 176
Dad 176
Right Now 176
My Situation 177
Lord 177
King for a Day 178
I Hate Life 178
Piss On You 178
Turkey Break 179
This Pen 182
Diary 183
Life Lesson 183
The Ball Stops Here 184
Where Did I Go Wrong? 185
Guess What? 186
Actions 186
High Ramblings 186
He Told Me He Loved Me 187
Good Day 188
Bad Karma 189
Draft 190
No Reason To Stay 190
Just Me 191
Doves 191
To Helen 192
Ending My Pain 192
My Mother 193
What is Going On With America? 194
You Don't Know 194
Hips 195
Messed Up 195
Dreams 195
Miss Spelled 196
Last Night 197
Job 198
Real 199
I Do 199
Nothing Hurts 199
Never 200

Forehead 201
More Then Enough 201
Grim Reaper 203
Monster Inside 204
Sux 205
Sorting Me Out 206
Fading 207
My Walk With God 209
I Wish 209
4 Days 210
My Apology 211
Unhappy 212
My Day 212
Septum 213
Por Nada 214
Coupons 214
Back Talk 214
Lock 215
Just A Thought 216
How Come 216
Rambling 217
So Cold 217
Why I Do What I Do 218
Fuel 220
A Thing Called Life 220
Man Vs God 221
72 Hours 221
This Morning 224
Tired Of Drama 224
Being Irish 226
What Should I Do? 226
Bags 227
My Thoughts On the USA 227
Ruthlessly Absurd 228
Tweeken 228
Stop The Comments 230
Seeken Employment 230
Drugs Are Funny Things 231
Skin 232
Glowsticks 232
I Hate Myself 233

Can You See My Pain? 233

I Am Stuck 234

Crampy 234

Black Cloud 234

Some Days 235

Digital Bathroom Scale 236

You Rock My World 237

This Can't Be 237

Fuck Food 238

Hi My Name Is 239

Don't Let It Show 242

DARE 243

Maybe Someone Will Read This 244

Turtles 246

Conclusion 247

Acknowledgements 251

Foreword

Inadvertently, everyone reaches a point in life where they must become aware of their true selves in hopes of establishing some kind of purpose and meaning of our life. Unfortunately, this process is inevitable; it is an unalienable angst which every rational being will face.

I was faced with this agony of finding myself and the purpose of my being during my sophomore year in college. I was suddenly plagued with a sense of restlessness as it occurred to me that everything would be changing… soon. My future had managed to creep up on me and I was help responsible of deciding my own fate; life would no longer come with a side of advisors and curriculums. I was the burden of my own self from that point forth, and it was anything but pleasant.

Subsequently, I searched for help through the vast catacombs of the internet, and surprisingly found comfort in a rather interesting phenomenon, blogs. People from all over the world, all walks of life, of all faiths and backgrounds had recorded their most intimate thoughts and experiences in which they invited the rest of the world to view them. While sifting through the sheer number of these online journals, I was shocked to see that each one of these people had issue of their own; whether it was regarding family, friends, fears, anxieties, joys, or angst. I came to realize that I was not alone and others were facing problems much like my own.

I formed the not for profit organization of, Book of Blogs to research this interesting phenomenon. My organization decided to compile the book, "I Blog, Therefore I Am" to bring this phenomenon to the public eye.

Each one of these entries in this book is completely **unedited** and **uncensored**. These logs vary from a whole assortment of topics, some will make you laugh, and some cry and some will completely shock you! These entries are meant to provoke your mind. There is a large amount of controversial material in the following pages that does not necessarily reflect the views and opinions of the author or the staff of Book of Blogs. Proceed at your own risk!

He Raped Me
BitterNothing
May 19, 2004 @ 2:20 am

I never thought of this before,

I hid the truth, he really did rape me

I never considered it rape because I didn't want to believe it, it was force but I went along with it. I thought that if I said no or stop that he would make me do it anyway, at least that's what he had told me.

So please read this and understand that life is a sacred thing and that everyone should be thankful for the life that they have cause you never know what other people are going through so here goes nothing

I was 13 and I feel in love way to fast. I thought if I wasn't with him I would die without him near my side he was 15 and I thought we would be together forever but I was wrong.

We met at a friends house and we began to talk. We clicked like that and we knew there was a spark between us.

So we talked for a long time before I had to go, and I left before we exchanged numbers but he was smart enough to ask his friend for my number. He called so suddenly and he asked me out and I of course said yes. He was so nice and seemed so perfect but then after a few months of dating things changed. I started to hang with my friends more often and he began to call all the time screaming "where are you, who are you with" I never lied to him and he would get mad that I was with my friends instead of him.

I had a life outside of him but he didn't understand that. I had to sneak out to go see him when he wanted me too, I had to call every morning evening and night just to tell him I love him and that I wouldn't leave him. But then it got worse. He stared to push me and throw me into the walls. His words hurt just as much as the physical painhe would scream slut, whore, bitch constantly at me. He would put bruises on my arms and would throw objects at me like books or anything small enough to pick up. He mad scratches on my arms and he choked me just so I would listen to him.

1

He never raped me but all he wanted was sex. He would yell if I didn't give him what he wanted and I figured it was better than him forcing me to do something.

I stayed with him for a year. I was scared to leave him. What would I do without him. I would alone. I told myself that "I don't have a family. I have few friends..where would I go what would I do, I would be nothing again " so I stayed even though I he would hurt me.

He would do things to me in front of his friends and some times I would fight back but I wouldnt win. I would get a few good hits in but he was stronger, bigger and more powerful than I could ever be..

I started doing drug and drinking more often. I even started to cut myself and all he said was that I deserved what I got.When I told him that I was gonna dump him he told me that if I did he would kill himself and that he was sorry and never hurt me again and that he loved me more than anybody in the world.

What was I suppose to do. I didn't know. I was confused and in love with a man who hurts me. I never felt love before so I stayed with him.

But he never stopped. It was the same old Matt and I couldn't take it anymore, so I told him over the phone that it was over.He screamed and yelled and said he's gonna die and I told him that that would be his decision cause to him I was already dead. I meant nothing to him and I will always be nothing to him!

I was scared that he would and come do something to me but he didn't . I thought it was over and that he would leave me alone, but he didn't.

He went around telling people things about me that weren't true, he called me and left messages saying IM gonna die, everytime I saw him he acted like everything was ok and he would flirt with me and ask me out again.

He pretending that we had a great relationship and that he was the best ever.

Did he understand what he had done to me did he understand that he scared me for life.

But then it happened.

2

I found out that the same guy that had done all this to me had also impregnated me. I didn't want to tell him, I couldn't. Imagine what had happened next. He found out. I was home alone and I was still sleeping when he came into my room. I was knocked out and I didn't know what he was doing until after he was done doing it. I woke up and I felt that sharp pain in my side. I still can see the shinny knife he used. I all I saw was blood and I didn't realize until later that it was mine. He just walked away and left out the from door. I got up and I ran into the shower and just cried. I knew that something was missing and that it was the baby. Did he understand what he did, he not only killed the baby he killed me. I felt like everything in the world was gone now and that I would never get it back.

I never was the same. I was so depressed and I still am. everytime I had a boyfriend I pushes them away and refused to let them touch me.

I cover myself up in layers of clothes so one one can see my body or scares that I have.

I don't like to be touched and IM scared to get close to someone. I feel that everytime they come close to me there gonna hit me or hurt me somehow or someway. I don't have a family that I can talk to and I don't have a happy life. That's why I am the way I am. My life has been filled with obstacles that a young teen shouldn't have to deal with. I was put in situations that not even adults go through and its made me who I am today. Scared to hurt someone because I know what it feels like to be hurt. To be emotionally drained to the point of actually saying "killing myself would be for the best"

I have forgotten what it feels like to be loved and I have forgotten what it feels like to love someone back and I have yet to learn that what had happened wasn't my fault. I know that talking about it should help but for me it just feels like its causing others to worry and feel pain. I don't want anyone to be sorry for what had happened to me cause I went through it and came out alive and it was a time that caused me much pain and still hurts to this day.

Never let people put you down, never let them control you. It is you life and you decide how you want to live it don't take life for gradient. It could be gone in seconds with no notice.

What's This World Coming Too?
<3Karylin
December 1st, 2004 @ 1:56 am

oh priceless..

my friend was in the drug store yesterday and there was a little 5 year old boy walking around with a string hanging out of his mouth. Finally, he pulled it out, and it was a tampon! His mother was like "Oh he does that all the time. He likes it." Yep, and that mother definitely has issues if she lets her son do that. The girl behind the counter told my friend that the mother was in there buying makeup for the little boy last week. I swear, some people shouldn't reproduce

Thanks
SnappingTurtle
January 17th 2005 @ 3:35 am

Thanks for shooting down what i want to do with my life, or what i have planned. It hurt more than anythig to sit in the back of the car and listen to you and your mom tear apart what i said. You said you were sorry and i accept that but i still can't believe you did that to me. I hurt me so much to hear that. It wasn't bad enought that i was quiet when i got in the car but i had to try to cry quietly and i did. You didn't even know i was crying did you? Probably not and that's okay you were talking to your mom. I'm glad Dave liked your song that's awesome, because your song is great. I have tried to get through to you about how much your friendship and family mean to me but i don't think that i am getting through to you, which really hurts. I have also tried to get you to talk to me when i can tell something is bugging you. It hurts me to see you upset and i can't take it.

That is how i am feeling right now about a friendship with one of my bestest friends in the whoe wide world. It really does hurt me to be feeling this way. I don't like feeling like this but what else can i do? I want to talk to him about some htings that are bugging me but i couln't today he was really tired and we went to an Unplugged service and stuff. I ended up talking to his mom for a little bit while he was helpng tear down and then played his song for Dave. His mom was no help at all, she just sat there telling me things i already knew. Yeah, just what i needed, she also told me i am a good kid great. I am still lost on how he and his

4

dad see that i am so strong. I don't see it i see a very emotional wreck that is always crying. I know that crying is a way to release but i mean how much do i have to release. I know my life is hard but i could cry for forever if i had the chance. I have waited for so long to just let go and cry. I may get it this week on Wednesday when i spend time with him again. We will see what happens.

Punishment
Jarrett
January 11, 2005 @ 7:41 pm

Punishments suck so much, especially when there is no point to them. My parents arent going to let me go to band practices until my grades go up, which they are already high, but they have to see it on the Report Card! It is so stupid. I even tried to get it so I got my grades from my teachers each week to show I was keeping steady, but noooooo, they want the fucking report card. So unless my parents figure out that they are being total asses my band wont be able to practice fully. I hate this shit so much, it makes no sense. I'd so much give up hanging out with or something than band practice, but I can still hang out with my band, as long as we dont practice! That makes no sense at all. I guess Im stuck till next report card, so dont be suprised if my band doesnt play a show until late february, or even March.

Saturday
Kenoir
August 31, 2003 @ 4:28 pm

OMG, Saturday kicked so much ass it wasnt even funny. The day started off Ok, and I was prepped to go to the Ben Folds concert with Ben, Kellen, and John(well, a Tori Amos concert with Ben opening, which makes no sense at all!!!!). So the time comes and Ben and Kellen come to my house and we go and meet John up at Mcdonalds. WE eat dinner and we just are laughing our asses off. It was soo funny, we are just sitting there, and all of the sudden this old lady behind us just rips one LOUDLY. We cant conatin ourselves and just crack up, it was so funny. Then when the lady goes to leave she comes up to us and askes us if we have any cigarettes on us. We held it in, and when she left we laughed so much that the people working at Mcdonalds started to give us looks. So we leave and go to the concert. cough(VIP passes)cough. We got our own box, which has an awsome view of the stage. We decide to go and check out stuff cause Ben wasnt supposed to come on until 7:30. So we go to the VIP spots and see Danny and his friend(I cant remember his name), so we sit down with them and order some drinks and food. Some guy that worked for Alltel said he wanted to get a picture of kids having fun, so he chose us cause we had food and drinks and there were 6 of us. Our waitress sucked, and when we left she even asked us if we were leaving a tip.....so we left her 20 cents,lol. Then we go to our seats, and get there while Ben is in the middle of the first song. It was so awsome, Ben Folds is the reason why I have respect for Piano players. Well, Ben played one new song off his newest EP, which is soooo funny, its about everything thats annoying, this is the part I remember "Guy with Peace on his License Plate, gives me the finger and drives me out of my lane", when he sang that everyone got up and started clapping. He also played Army(oh yeah, one of the best songs) and played Rocking the suburbs, which he wrote because Korn called Ben Folds Five a pussy band that plays Cheers music(Ben didnt care, he said he liked Cheers, lol). Since they said that he decided to make a song about being a Middle class white guy and how it pissed him off.......thus comes Rocking the Suburbs. He also played Not the Same, where we got to do this three part harmony thing with him. He also played Steven's Last Night In Town which was awsome. He did a lot of piano soloing too. The concert was beyond belief awsome. Only problem was.......Tori Amos, she was good, but if Ben Folds was a 10 on a scale from 1-10(which he was) then she would be a 3(which she was). We left after she played like 3 songs. All the Tori Amos fans were wierd. I think it would have been better to have a show of JUST Ben..... that would be so awsome. Well, after the concert we came back to my house to hang out and stuff. Kellen, John, and I rocked the house out. Ben thought it was too loud and went downstairs. Then we hung out and sat around and ate popcorn and played some games. Then we went upstairs and I taught Kellen and Ben how to do code in a calculator, which is really easy. Then I did a code and it was like 7 lines, just so it would say penis. I used and If then statement, and Kellen was like how des x=5 have anything to do with Penis and Ben and I just started cracking up. Which they discovered I have a high pitched laugh which they thought sounded like a girls laugh. We went to sleep at like 5 in the morning, and when we woke up my mom made some good ass pancakes. Then John left and then Ben left. So Kellen and I just hung out and went on the internet and streamed some Ben Folds songs and looked to see if the picture that guy took of us was on the Alltel site. Then Kellen and I started playing this really old Hockey game on the Nintendo and I totally kicked Kellens ass. Then Kellen left and I have just been hanging out. I dont have anything else to write except SIGN THE GUEST BOOK, also, sorry Kaitlin that I was partially ignoring you, I didnt mean to :'(forgive me..............PEACE

Mirror, Mirror on the Wall...
babe4Jesus55
January 16, 2005 @ 10:13 pm

As some of you may know, I do not typically wear make-up, or make a huge effort to do anything fancy with my hair-normally just a morning brush out is about the extent of my hair grooming. This past week I thought I'd perform one experiment. For the first two days this week, I wore mascara. The second two I did the whole nine yards on skin tone smoothing out, then today I added rouge. Let me tell ya what I have found. Our society is filled with some of the shallowest creatures ever! (please note I only considered the reactions of strangers, not those I know best, and consequently that know me best, and have kept all other appearance factors the same-same jeans and a t-shirt, same plain hair) On the first two days with only mascara added, I did not get any more response to my physical appearance than I normally do- the stare-right-through-you look, since it is rather difficult for most to look over due to my height. 0:-) The third and fourth days I received probably 10 times as many glances of admiration as I normally do, and not just from males either. I received several comments from my fellow females. Just little things mostly... "I like your (blank)". Whatever it was they commented on, it was just stuff I normally have/wear and I never get comments on that stuff, yet I did when I made myself up. Now today, with the mascara, even skin tone, and rouge... let me tell ya. I had whistles, catcalls, and even sex offers. (Now I remember why I stopped making myself up in the first place.) most of the incidents came from a single group of freshman playing wall ball as I approached school friday morning; they are the perverted, sex-offering, perpetrators. One did the whole grab, shake, and "you want some of this?" at me. Ugh. What barbarians. 1) any civilized human being does not ask a complete and total stranger for sex, especially not at 9 a.m., 2) I'm 18, if I really wanted some, I would not indulge myself in a 14 or 15 year old freshman, I could fetch way better and 3) I highly doubt a freshman would have any of "this" to desire. the rest of this one's little friends just made retarded catcalls as I walked off; they weren't even quality catcalls...stupid freshmen. What is this society coming to? Well, an end obviously if all we care about is what other people think of ourselves, beauty that is only skin deep, and sex.

Surviving
hanginginthere
December 14, 2004 @ 10:43 pm

Ever have a day where you can't do much of anything right? That would've been today.

Everyone pray for my brother, he got admitted to a psychiatric clinic for depression and contemplation of suicide. I feel in my heart that he'll be ok, but he's medically diagnosed as depressed and he's also got his ADD to combat. He's just having a tough time in life lately. I know how he feels.

To everyone I seem to have permanently pissed off: I'm sorry. Most of the time I have no idea I've upset anyone. Today for example. I had no idea one of my firends was upset about something I had said bout her boyfriend (I said it thinking the situation was other than what existed). Well, she told her boyfriend, another of my friends, and he got upset, and he in turn to his best friend, also my best friend, and my best friend of course took the other person's side. And I thought everything was getting better. Well, to all who were involved in that I hope you understand why I said what I said and what was meant by it. NOTHING.

Damn today sucked.

Worked in the library for my NHS hours. The company was...ironic.

I'm so ungodly sick of being upset about the same thing all the time. I can't seem to get myself out of this monotonous rut. I feel like I need my life to be revamped or something. I don't even know. Everything has become so frustrating lately.

These last several posts have been extremely vague if you don't know exactly what's going on in my life. I just don't want to use names all the time to incriminate people I guess. It's bad enough I screw up everyone's life with what I say. What I type should be harmless.

I want someone I can rely on not to get me into trouble or cause me more...

"We made the same mistakes, mistakes like friends do." <<<Story of the Year

I Have Enough Sin in me to Damn a Million Souls
Trent
October 25th 2004 @ 2:23 pm

I have enough sin in me to damn a million souls.

My illustration of this is blood. We have enough toxins in our body to kill 10 people, but we don't die. Blood cleans out the toxins ... non-stop. So, if I grasp my wrist and choke off the blood ... first it tingles, then it starts to burn, and before long ... it turns black and starts to decay. Soon, without the constant flow of blood ... my hand is lifeless. The toxins will do such harm that it cannot be repaired. Right now, my blood cleanses my physical body, just like the Blood of Christ is cleansing my spiritual identity. It is ongoing. It is by the blood, and there is little that I can do to stop it, though I never asked that it begin.

Remember when Jesus washed the feet of the disciples? He just did it. Nobody asked Him to ... in fact, Peter asked Jesus to stop! What is interesting is what Jesus said to Peter when Peter asked Him to stop. "If you do not let me wash your feet, then I can have nothing to do with you." Peter then, asked Jesus to wash him all over ... head to toe. Jesus explained, "You don't need a bath again, you just need your feet washed."

Notes of interest:

*The cleansing of feet is comparable to the daily need for forgiveness. It isn't optional

*The head-to-toe bath is like the need for the initial washing of rebirth (Titus 3:5)

*We don't need it over and over, like the foot washing.

The bath was voluntary, but the foot washing was completely the initiative of Jesus over and against the objections of those He was washing. Nobody asked Jesus for it, yet nobody was allowed to avoid it. (IMPORTANT)

We need ongoing forgiveness as we sin. It is done by Jesus. We don't have to ask (in fact none of us were around when it was provided,) but we can't do without it.

In all of this, I am not taking sin lightly ... I just am giving the blood of Christ, its due credit!

I'm Quitting
x0br0ken0x
December 12th, 2004 @ 12:50 am

ROAR

i hate this crap

im quitting life at the moment..

..am i wasting my time on you..

Food Fight!
Razorbites
April 26th, 2004 7:01 am

Today was the best! All day they were planing a food fight durring lunch. At first I thought it wasn't going to happen cuz most of the time, people in that school say they'll do something and they don't. Then when it was lunch time, I knew they were ganna go through with it. This one kid baught $5 worth of cheese, or atleast thats what I heard, but then I saw him cover his sandwhich with chips and most of the cheese he bought. I don't know exactly how it started, but after the principel said we were ganna eat in our home room the rest of the year, it started.

I got hit in the head with a pear, lol, I through my nacho's and iced tea, and also got hit with alittle bit of cheese from when they through cheese at the kid sitting across from me. I saw soda hit the cam's that were up on the wall, salid cover the doors, apple sauce fly to the next table, and my friend resse through two trays of food, but I didn't see where since I was trying to get under the table so I wasn't hit. Then most of us left the caf. and came back in 2 minutes later. Eyerything was wet and sticky, it so funny, and it was so dam fun, to bad we still have to eat in our home rooms for the rest of the year. Also two lunch ladys got hurt by sliping on some stuff on the floor, people were arested, or atleast find or w/e, pluse we got our feild trip to Hursey taken away, and anything else that was planed for the few days we had left. I realy didn't care about the trips and crap, I still thought it was fun

We missed two periods, but it only took us 10 or so minutes to clean it all up. My friend steph was covered in stains from food that the girl next to her through, and my other friends katrina got he eye burnt by cheese, but no one got seriously hurt, as far as I know.

lol, that was the best, the one teacher said it was better then the any food fight they had to deal with so far, now the 7th graders are planning to do it eather tomorrow or before the end of the year, but they tryed to do it after ours, but everyone was to afraid.

Everyone smelled so bad after words. I also found out someone was crying during the fight, lol, I don't know why, but oh well.

Change
BluexDreams
July 7th, 2004 10:30 pm

A Week and two days past since last day of sick-cool, and nothing interesting is happening with my life. I keep on doing the same things i do everyday, nothing much to do. Being online, and do those braclets kind of things with threads, which cause me back-ache. Today i decided to do something, to cook. That's something that i haven't done for years, oh well, i've got to wait 1 hour so the dough to be done so i can make my first pizza. I Hope It'll be good,taste good.

In the past few days, i've been thinking about my future. My near future,after finishing high sick-cool and what i'am going to do. I for my self, i ain't sure if i want to attend university. I can't do presentations, i just can't. I can't do them infron of 4 girls that i act like a Clown infront of them, instead i just stand there,thinking of what to say and laugh. I asked and asked about if i Have to do presentations in university, sometimes i get : " For sure","Depends on what you're going to study", and " it'll be a group thing". I don't know which to beleive.

Thinking deeply about my future freaks me out. I'm the kind of shy person,but i get used to my surroundings after some time.

I've been thinking of working this summer,but the fact that i might be taking appointments just freaks me out. Which led me to think..What am i going to do when i grow up?!.

It just seems like even if i studied in university i might have not have the courage to go and apply for a job, which will all seem in the end as a waste of time and money. And then the Staying home option pops up in my head again. All the facts are mixed up in my head, i don't know how to think.

I finish from one situation, an another comes and takes it's place. I've got only 1 year ahead of me to decide weather i want to study or stay home, which i think my parents won't let me do that. God, isn't that their life job?! To prevent me from doing anything i want..all what i get is No after No...

After all those messed up thoughts that have been flying around my head, i remembered what a friend of mine told me once. You have to change,I said i don't want to, i like being like that. But it seems if i want to live, i better do change. But for once in my life i get to a point where i think i Fear the word Change. I can't just change like that..

Maybe i'm not that ready to face all those lies in my life..

Scratch Last Post
-Cat
September 02, 2004 @ 4:49 pm

i got fired. don't ask. it's utter bullshit. i'm a failure.

Feel So Empty...
idiotbubble
November 17th, 2004 @ 11:43 am

I have no idea what is going on inside me. Nothing seems to be wrong. But I just have this funny feeling. Like I feel so empty. Like a lost soul. Just sitting around, in my own world, What have I done? I don't know. When I think about it, everything is just fine. Everything is how they suppose to be. But yet, I still feel imperfect. Like there is something undone. But what is it? Miss my friends too much? Like we're too lost contact? It's just for a week, but why am I feeling like this. Just lying down on my bed, I feel so meaningless. Like my body is there, but my heart and soul is else where. What is wrong with me? Too sick of being me? Do I need a change? In character? Looks? Getting bored of myself? I have no idea.

12

Well...
YamiKaibaDude
July 28th 2004 @ 11:10 pm

Life is wierd.

Period.

After coming out, only one person bugs me about it.

I was expecting more.

Raising Mackenzie
Mackenzie
January 17, 2005 @ 1:15 pm

Yesterday I watched Raising Hellen with the girls.

Yesterday my mom left Florida (where she was with my sister) and went back to Brazil.

Yesterday my level of PMS was so high I wished I was a man.

The movie is great. Yeah its a chick flick, but its not stupid like most of the other chick flicks... The plot doesnt revolve around a cheesy horny romance, and the theorical cheesy horny romance is actually cute and godly (the guy is a pastor). And the kids are great...

Needless to say - it made me cry. but the problem is that i just couldnt stop crying. During the movie, my mom called from the airport to say goodbye, and my sister also called just to say hi. So that made me cry even more. I really miss them. Which is crazy because I have been here for 6 months and only now I am missing them.

I was so sensitive I would start crying again if people looked at me. I felt the need for comfort food but I couldnt find anything so I went to bed early. My roommate was shocked "I've never seen you go to bed this early." I just smiled, made a little joke (I wasnt necessarily sad, I was laughing, but I just couldnt stop crying), grabbed my ipod and went to bed.

This morning I woke up feeling much better. All the things going through my head all I watched the movie dont hurt as much anymore (I love kids,

I want to have kids, No I dont I wish I was never born how can i possibly want to have kids, But i really do, well, I'm not having kids cuz I am never getting married because I am gay, Well I can always adopt, No I wont do that to my children, I'll never find a partner, these girls must be wondering why i am crying so much, I am so scared of the truth I could never tell them whats going on with me, I'd hate being a mom, Stop thinking about all this Mackenzie).

Inspired by the title of this post I made a collage of me during different times of my life. Most of the pics are pretty recent because most of my pics are in Brazil but it kinda reflects the many me's...

Moving
Alvin_fan
January 17th, 2005 @ 5:22 PM

I have moved spots. I've actually been sitting here doing the same job now for over a year. However, I've recently moved cubes. For the 3rd time, I've moved. With every changeover, I've moved close and closer to the secretary's desk; the terminal point looks just an inch away from the elevator. Naturally, the phycical move makes for a rather nice change of pace. It's the neighbors you have to look out for. I'd once played around with the idea that I've actually been committed to an asylum, and the patients within these cubical walls are subjects of a sinister post-graduate program setup between HKU and U of T - a program likely sponsored by Li Ka Shing's recent Can$1.2 billion charity fund.

I was going to say, "I'm disturbed" or "a bit worried," but... Quite honestly, (rubbing my eyes), where the hell do they find these people? Two new employees - one on each side of me. Darryl and ... I don't know the other guy's name, but obviously he replaced Mr. Cheeseman from 4 months ago. We'll call him Chuck for now. Cuz he looks like a Chuck. Both are middle aged fellows, working with the conference team, apparently, but not really doing anything, that I've seen anyway. I know, cuz I'm not doing anything, so I have lots of time to observe how much nothing they do. They're both highly aggitated individuals. They can't sit still.

Daryl exhibits this nervousness in an angry, "why can't I get my work done" kind of way. He furrows his brows and presses his fist over his mouth tightly as he squints into the monitor. But I haven't actually heard him make a business related call in the 2 weeks we've moved. He's the type of guy who makes his voice sound business-like, but if you actually listen to the content, it's not business related at all. In fact, the man's been planning his vacation all morning.

He'll start the call with, "Good morning, Bob. It's Darryl here. Quick question. Can you brief me on the turnaround schedule for that flight from Seoul?" But then he'll move onto talkin' about hotel prices, whether or not there's a spa included in the price. He makes this same damn call 8 times int he morning and 8 times after lunch! He's using trick words like "Quick Question" and "brief," all spoken in a really solemn manner. Then he'll call his pregnant wife and give her a minute by minute update. "I don't' know, honey. I don't know why the price doesn't include the lunch buffet... Yes, I do care. Listen.. Why don't you pick up some movies?"

Condescending and arrogant, he likes to tell people how smart he is. He yells at pizza delivery guys and powerstrides to and from the washroom so that he leaves a "breeze of urgency" in path. People need to know he's working hard. They need to know he was a certified Broker 7 years ago, and he's come to make his name in the conference industry. Move over, my name is Daryl! He's constantly moving in broad strokes. He gets up to throw away a piece of trash with a deep breath like a professional scuba diver. When he's pensive, he likes to stomp the carpeted office floor with the flat of his foot. Poom POOM POOm. Like a marching drum. I'm thinking! Look at me think! Poompooompoom.

Chuck on the other hand, looks like a Chuck, dresses like a chuck, talks like a chuck and is about as far as a Chuck's career could probably reach given his inherent ADD or Meth addiction. He sells conferences as well, and he acts like he's constipated 18 hours a day, really really needing to go somewhere or find something, hungry for a piece of the action. He smiles with a sick desperation. I always get the impression he's sweating, even when he's not. Dressed in drab fuzzed out yellow cotton polos, he can't type for more than 8 seconds, because he'll loose his concentration and realize he doesn't remember what he wanted to type in the first place. This forces him to taptaptaptaptap on the backspace button in an exhagerated manner, almost as if he wanted the extra 5 taps in there, as if it would convince us all that he's being constructive.

Me. I have a strategy. I make long stream of taptaptaps, then I do the occasional "alt-tab" which has a definite TickTAACK sound - there's conviction to it. I'm constructive on multiple windows, buddy. Chuck, you're just an amateur. Even your customers on the phone can see what you're wearing, and quite frankly, Mark's & Spencer corderoy look ain't gonna cut it. You're like what, 36? They should ban corderoy from guys like you. I'd look cool cordory pants. Paddington style.

Chuck loves to drum his fingers on the table. He'll drum the table followed by a whistled-jingle. He does it repeatedly throughout the day, usually after a failed cold call. He'll slam the phone, rub his forehead, and do the drumdrumdrum whistle combo. Must be a form of self-motivation.

I gotta get out of here.

Corporate Whore
Petecockroach
November 13th, 2004 @ 12:03pm

I've now become a corporate whore. I'm working as a temp at the Barclaycard head office in my home town. I have my own cubicle in this huge building alongside 3000 other robots. 9-5 man! Fuk. I have a card to get me in the building. I have a card to swipe in. They know where i am. I have my own internet login. My emails and internet use are monitored. I got told off for looking at the Sub pop website for christsakes! I cannot even sneak out for a crafty cigarette or head out 10 minutes early on a friday morning. Of course i do my usual mature thing and try and rebel against this by heading out at lunch, parking my car on some sidestreet and gulp down a couple of tins of Miller lite or pop a couple of codiene tablets. Big deal! I am sure i have nothing in common with 99% of the idiots working there. Friday's casual clothes day. So i have my battered Rival Schools t-shirt on. Everybody asks me what store i got it at. Fuck off they have never heard of them. Quicksand..... Gorilla biscuits.....Rival schools....Get a grip. I am alone at work yet surrounded. You know what i mean. My first week I hit the pub with a couple of guys on my section. They are only young lads, since then i havent been invited! Don't get me wrong i'm not bothered, i don't want to talk about dance music and ecstasy tablets. My one plus point is the crazy amount of beatiful women there and the girls on my section dig me so i guess thats pretty cool. One asked me out for a drink at the weekend but i wanna go and see a band and i'm sure she would not appreciate this.

This week i blew half my pay on a load of cd's. It's been a while. I got Rogue wave who are on sub pop, fucking awesome. Kinda like the shins. They have this song called "man-revolutionary" which is so gorgeous.

I also got the Donna's new record. Suprised. They definetly get better every record. There is some really catchy bass riffs that i can't stop humming. I am afraid i let myself down but could not resist getting Papa roach's new one but i am not ashamed cos they rock, i don't care what anyone says. I also got Pj harvey, The breeders, The shaggs and a rare Daniel johnston/jad fair bootleg.

Thats it.

Current Mood: good

Current Music: Rogue wave

Wow It Has Been A While
7shootingstars
May 09, 2004 @ 6:58 am

so whats up you guys...it has been a while...

So I went to prom, without a real date. It didnt suck, even though some people need to grow the fuck up. Excuse my language, but its true. Anyways...it did make me sick seeing all these people with dates, and i didnt dance one slow dance with a guy at all. Yup I'm guy repellent. It blows.

Speaking of guys, I think i should just quit liking them, because i always like them at the wrong times. Like now for instance. I shouldnt like seniors because theyre graduating...and everybody in my grade is either my friend or just plain sucks. Except...well...this one guy...I've liked him in all honesty for 6 years...he knows but he doesnt. Ive told him, but i dont think he recognizes it. I love him more than he even realizes, and it kills me.

well night for now...

Randomness
Minou
January 25, 2005 @ 2:22 am

So its almost 2.30 am and here I am thinking about gender idenity. I have always been most attacted to people who blurred the lines. The ones where they were so androgonys you couldn't always tell. Take an ex of

17

mine. She was super femme, but put her in a pair of jeans and t-shirt she look liked a boy, a boy with big tits mind you but still a boy. It was so hot for me. Look at my husband, alot of people mistake him for a girl from behind. I still like girls who look very girly, and boys who look manly, but its the ones in between who really get to me.

I love being a woman. Anyone who knows me know that I love my breasts, my hips, my cunt. I love being a woman. Lately though I think about what it would be like to be a man, more like just look like one. I dont want a penis, I dont want to be a real guy, I just want to dress like one. Well not fully, but almost. This past weekend I experimented a bit with that. I did my hair kind of 40's style, wore a shirt that a girl or guy could wear, but opened it up so that I could show off clevage, then went with pin strip capri pants with my big boots. It was my first try at mixing up the femme and butch. Is butch even the word for it? doubtful. I looked really good. Got many compiments and such. I felt good too. Even been throwing around the idea that for Kink nite go for the pin strip suit, but just the pants and blazer. Hair back, cleaveage out.

Just one more thing for me to think about I guess.

The.Czar.of.Bombastic.
lyinghere
January, 09 2005 @ 10:22 PM

the.czar.of.bombastic...is still in the grave.. sadly my pc, belerapohon, is still not up and running.. after finally getting a loaner monitor that actually works.. it has caused me nothign but more grief.. after the nuclear scare, it turns out that *crossesfingers / knockonwood* my battery on my mother board has pfft'd.. so that will be getting fixed tomorrow I hope..

thus returning me to the wonders of posting here...

with some semblance of consistancy.. and praying to all those above me.. finding real contract work and getting company stuff done... money and living..

still living the dayjob life.. but things are well there..

crazy dumping and bad timing this week.. but fine none the less...

hmmm.. a friend of mine is starting a pagan learning circle for individual practicioneres next week.. so I'll be joining up with that.. [its similar to the pagan pub nites I'd crawl to in London.. that group actually started a legal chapter.. so thats neat...]

dunno where this is going yet.. but figure if I keep sitting on my ass, nothing will get done.. and I will slip further into my meloncoly... I'd rather be supportive with this than just sit around anyways..

hmmm.... crazy stuff.. umm.. been on WW a lot, waiting for updates on new stuff.. talking with ppl on the forum and passing on the irc info as it comes in...

ah.. this is turning into one of those rambling blogs, where no one reads past the first five lines...

new living place is AWESOME!!! I can't wait till its warmer to use our backyard!!

thinking to have a house warming around Imbolc... we shall see.. its only a few weeks away..

Minou is doing well.. after our new years day trip with EMS, nothing was terribly wrong.. she's been sick, but getting better... working two jobs now.. I'm very very proud of her, but I wish she had one stable job... be easier on her... but she is determined to do this and get her work going on track again.. I'm always here for her... and glad she is settling into what she needs to do.

hmmmm well I'm sure there is more.. but its time to get my lazy glutes moving...

cheers kiddies.. miss and love you all..

free gropes for everyone!

+laine+

Martin James McGowan
never_to_be_forgotten
February 12, 2005 @ 10:11 pm

For Martin...he is our shinning star

When we started High School, we thought our year would be filled with many good memoires and new experiences. Everyone seemed to enjoy the High School. The halls were always crowded with cliques mingling, and loud voices and laughter filled the halls of Nazareth Area High School. But on February 10th, 2005, the school took on a whole new mood. The halls were no longer filled with laugher; no more smiling faces. Instead, they were replaced with tears and pain. Our school was mourning the death of our friend and peer, Martin James McGowan.

This is a rough time for everyone in our school. Martin was one of the nicest, sweetest, and purest people ever. He had no ememies what so ever. It was either you were his friend, or you didn't know him. He talked to anyone. It didn't matter what clique you were in, if you were alone or needed a friend, he would be there. Our school reacted in a way that I would of never thought.

Now that this happened, it really puts things in perspective. He was my age, fifteen years old. He was an amazing person. It still feels like a nightmare we're all going to wakeup from, but all the pinching of yourself never seems to wake you up. And eventually you'll realize its reality. And realize the innocent life that was taken today. Seeing everyone in school with tears falling from their eyes was the saddest sight I've ever seen. This tragedy brought everyone together. Suddenly it didn't matter who hangs out with whom, and which cliques belong together, everyone just united and cried on each other's shoulders. And there was always that teacher or guidance counselor or peer who brought you the whole box of tissues when you only asked for one. And nobody cared that makeup was running from their faces and nobody felt embarrassed to cry in front of everyone else. Nothing mattered. Every tear was for Martin.

Although his death is not entirely known, doctor say that he was extremely dehydrated, suffering from influenza and possibly afflicted with compartment syndrome, which is a condition where increased pressure within a muscle compartment causes a decrease in blood supply to the affected muscles. Complaining of arm and leg pain and running a slight fever, he had entered the hospital on February 9th. It was only that night when doctors began to operate on his leg to relieve pressure when his heart "gave out."

Martins death was the turing point in many peoples lives. He showed us all that life should not be taken lightly. He had that affect on people where all you could ever do is smile when you would look at him. Martin will never be forgotten, he will forever be loved and forever be in our hearts. To all those who were close to him and to all those we didnt know him still lost apart of them the day Martin passed away. To all those who stood by his side, Martin shall never forget that...we all love him and always will..

He loved his family...he loved his friends..he loved his girlfriend..and he loved those he did not know...he loved his life..and we loved him for that..

R.I.P Martin James McGowan...

love Danielle, Amanda, Christina..and everyone close to him

In honor of you Martin...we love you..

((Share you memories about martin with the world...so he always stays with us))

god couldnt have created a person more perfect than martin

He is our angel...he is our star....

Jungle Fever
Roxgirl
January 24th, 2005 @ 4:55 pm

I've got this smile on my face this morning. I met this guy on-line over a year ago... we just never ever hooked up in real life... Until last night!

His name is Chris, and he's an IT specialist for Scotia bank. I always kinda thought he was "boring" and not active enough for me, that's why I never actively persued him. But I've been bored myself lately, and he was on-line last night so I asked him if he wanted to catch a movie with me. He was free... so we went.

Boy, he sure is cute! (I think he kinda thought I am too) He was fun to talk to... we had a good time together!

And he's a HIP-HOPPER too So I'm sure we could have some fun out dancing! We'll see. (He really wanted me to call him today ... but I don't know, something tells me to be careful of this one!!!)

Oh yeah, the reason for this subject line is that he's black. And I'm white... get it?

Silent Sufferer...
pursejunkie
December 4th, 2004 @ 7:06 am

Well... I woke up this morning in a bit of a confussion... What to believe?? I want to tell my brain to forget all about these past few weeks and move on... but my heart aches for T... I want to lie to my brain and tell it nothing has changed... but it knows... it saw that she has eliminated me from her chat life... It knows how she isn't answering my calls... and it definately knows it has no hope for any sort of future with T.... I decided fuck it... I'm not going to let this get to me today... So up I get and away to the gym we go.... The gym was average... manged to do more calories today than previous days... Musta been the burger I had last night I have managed to stay around the 122 mark on the scale... I am mucho impressed with that... especially since my drinking has gone way up!! Alcohol = empty calories.... boooo.... So.. I'm gonna try to get off the hootch... I've managed to slow down on the Diet 7-up... I am down to maybe 5 cans a week.... YA that's right I said per WEEK... 5 cans... not cases... cans! I think I've managed to kick that habit... I think I can manage to kick a few more too.... candy is almost a distant memory for me too.... I'm gonna try really hard these next few weeks to get into lean mean shape... I plan on making some of my plans reality next year... hopefully 2005 will be the year for me!!

Well... I decided to be really silly... I called T... I have her work number... I called... Voicemail... bah!! Shoulda figured.... I saw that coming... but I thought maybe I was wrong in my head... I thought maybe she would answer and tell me she had to cancel her msn account or some shit like that... but... no... she is avoiding me... I write a final... "ok I get the point... sorry.. take care of yourself and I'll always be here if you need me.. I'll fuck off now" e-mail... I hurts to feel so rejected... I really thought if anything we'd be friends... I am feeling at a loss for friends... I have NONE... ya ya.. there's you guys in C-town and Daddy... but serious... how often do we see each them?? I mean... there's no plans ever... we never really plan on doing things together when we are in the same towns and... well.. I just don't find that we ever get visited as much as we visit them.... So I just hoped I had found someone that wanted a friend to visit... a friend to chat with daily... and friend to hang with weekly... whatever... it's all gone now... and fuck it!! I don't want to cry!! I don't want to lose it again... I don't want to go down that spiral of depression and not caring... putting on weight and shutting out my world... FUCK!

Why??? I hate this.... but then again if I pulled my head out of my ass for once I would realize I am doing exactly what I don't want my single friends to do when they are single... I'm letting myself feel like shit... I making myself pine and I am doing everything I tell them not to... I am hanging on to something that isn't going to be real... ever!! So.. if I took this moment to take my own advice .. I'd realize... she's just not that into me! ha ha ha... But it's true... she's gone and I should except that.... and I'm NOT going to let myself get 'K'ized again... I'm not going to sleep in until 10 everyday and eat shit all day... I'm not going to pine away everyday and think of T every time I see a car like hers... or hear her name.... I'm not going to do that to myself again... I can't... my life is too great to get all caught up in emotion... if there is one thing T has shown me... it's good times... they come and they go... But if you are happy with you... you can roll with the punches... I wasn't happy with myself when I met 'K' online... I was trying to make someone like someone I didn't know.... When K turned out to not be who she was... I got lost... I was fucked ... mentally... emotionally.... I couldn't handle it... I'm NOT great at rejection.. BUT.. that was then.. this is now... I have enternal sunshined my brain.... I have sealed my good memories of T and I together... and the rest... well.. they're gone.. they left when T did...

I'm such a lousy liar... Daddy can read it all over my face... I've got the 'eyes'... the.. 'she's gone and my joy has left' eyes.... He asks if I wanna talk.... nah... I'd rather not cry on his shoulder and suffer inside... but I break... I cry... and cry... and cry some more... and I thought I shed all the tears when I wrote my final e-mail... but I guess not... I have come to realize that "hi this is T (blank) with (company) and you have reached my voicemail please leave a detailed message and I'll get back to you"... would be the last time I would hear her voice.... Hung over in a hotel room... wasn't how I thought I would see her last.... I'm glad I got to hold her.... and she held me.. I felt that... it was real... I'm glad I got that moment... but I've got to let go... I've got to let this out.... So I cry... until I can't cry anymore...... Ahhhhh... I think I've finally got it out!! K... so on with my day... today when we got off from work we decided to bunker in at home... We got bored after uhhhh... maybe an hour of that!! ha ha ha... So Daddy wanted to antiquing... he really wants to get his friend a gift... I see the joy in his eyes... he looks so happy that he has someone in his life to care about.. I swear the guy lives for people to care for!! He is such a caring guy... It made me miss T even more... I really wanted to have a special friend to care about... she really did light up my life for the brief moment she was in my life... I so badly hurt!! FUCK!! Shhh... ok.. silent... So we search... up and down the isles of antique world... All the old reminants of past childhoods... weird... all the My Little Ponies and Cabbage Patch Kids... ha ha ha... Wow... All the weird shit you see there... but no accoridians or harmonicas .. nothing really.. well maybe the nice armour... but.. that's it... So we then ventured home... we've had a night... we watched pay preview and ate chinese (for me) and pizza (for Daddy).... We were supposed to do something with Oli tonight.. but she is all messed up with her schedule.. she works nights... so during the day... she sleeps all day... and well.. by the time we got home... ate .. and were on our way to sleepy land... she texted me: hey!! just got up.. whatchya doin?... Yikes... she just got up?? It's 9:00, and we're planning on going to bed soon... So I texted back.. we're lazy fucks.. gonna watch a movie and go to bed.. sorry.. maybe t'morrow?.... I guess she's a busy girl.. tomorrow isn't good... and our phone chat ends with a maybe sometime later.... just like everyone... maybe later....

So.. maybe later if I feel like it I will blog... until then... take care of yourselves....

ahhh Shit
Blakist
September 1st, ,2004 7:01 am

You know, i have 6 days left and all i can think about is cutting my fucken wrist wide open... i fucked up, i really did, i lost her and now i just have my self to live for and u know what, its cool, but i dont want to..i really liked the thoughts i had, they kinda kept me going, but now its like i kinda just want to...well give up,...man this sucks

Lost Love
lostlove4ever
September 4th, 2004 @1:14 pm

okay so im back in school im in love with this guy named sherman and i wish i could tell him. he had the best times ever this summer and i dont want it to end :sad: i love everything that is going on in my life but i have to move and that really sucks cause i just started to meet some good friends especailly sherman, talaban and those who shall not be mesioned well g2g love always angela

Thank you all
Stt1m
July 21st, 2004 @ 4:19 pm

Thank you for ruining everything.

Those who claim to love me and are protecting me, yes you who I haven't spoken too for fucking months.

Now fuck off and die, even that is too good for you.

Belly Space Competition
islandArtist
January 25th, 2005 @ 3:16 pm

Last night I had the most horrible sleep. I was completely exhausted, I didn't have my usual nap synchronized with my daughter so there was no excuse. I was in a heck of alot of general abdominal discomfort and the baby WOULD NOT stop squirming, kicking and hiccuping well into the evening. I was on the verge of having a hissy fit because I was so tired. Finally, I got up and took some advil and while waiting for it to kick in, realized that I needed to have a bathroom break (if you know what Im saying). After I relieved myself I crawled back into bed and fell asleep immediately. So did the little nipper in my belly, not a squirm or wiggle.

I guess *someone* wasn't comfortable with a lumpy bed and wasn't too shy about letting me know.

Pregnancy is not a graceful thing- and don't let anyone tell you different.

We're off to the doctor this afternoon, we are getting the results from all of our latest tests. Fingers crossed that the Doc has nothing interesting to tell me.

I'll be sure to keep you updated

Sex in School Restrooms = Unhygienic
samantha
February 17, 2004 @ 8:40 pm

Before I even start, CATHERINE HAS OFFICIALLY EARNED THE TITLE OF DUMBASS. We were gonna go to the swim meet tonight at 5:30, so I could get a good lane to time, and she was going to drive. 5:30 rolls around, then 5:40, then finally 5:50, so my mom drives me up there. I'm expecting her to be up there, maybe she had forgotten to pick me up, no such luck. Then I realize there are no lanes left, so I'm completely useless. So I'm standing around, talking to people for an hour, then it's 7:00 and the meet is practically over. Guess who decides to grace us with her presence, you guessed it, Catherine. It was pretty funny actually, she was practically yelling at herself, I was merely a spectator. Now that that's out of the way, not much happened first and second hour, but then in Skankman's class, I realized he was wearing the skank-pants AGAIN, he wore the whole outfit yesterday. Fourth hour was especially boring today, but now I want to be in the CIA. Lunch was special, there weren't many quotes to speak of, but Cat, Lia and I were standing in the commons, close to our lockers and I said something like "I just saw a guy running out of the girls bathroom!" then I saw a few security guards around, but I thought nothing of it. It turns out that there was a guy and a girl fornicating (sex for all of you lucky enough not to be in Skankman's class) in there, with another guy taping it. Good times. I guess sometimes you just gotta have sex in the unsanitary school bathrooms, they must of used the handicap stall. Not much else happened today, but there are two very important words I must share with all of you, wanker and flog, now onto the quotes:

1. Sam! — me — Michelle yelled my name, then Steph looked back, so I yelled it to her, don't ask why.

2. He's obsessed with staring at you while he's going to the bathroom. — Cat

3. He did sex in the court. — me — We were discussing the Scarlet Letter test, and the word fornication and someone said that they put "Giles did fornication in the court" so I translated it into layman's terms.

4. He doesn't want you pasting things he said to me. — Cat

5. You're a stupid head. — me — Cat said something stupid, so I called her on it with a no fail comeback.

Laters! (Sorry, I couldn't resist. If you haven't seen Bend It Like Beckham, disregard the last comment and replace it with bubbye.)

Changing Myself
pussicat
June 8th, 2004 @ 10:47 am

Have you ever looked into the mirror and just felt like you didn't recognize the person staring back at you??

Its just I so have this image, this ideal of who I should be, who I want to be. And I don't fit into it at all.

I am trying to find myself. But how? Where is the first step in all this chaos?? Should I start with small meak humble little steps forward or just close my eyes, and jump head first into it all? even then what am I jumping into really?

I see myself as a free spirit. Embracing my differences, being unique and loving it! Not caring what others think of me, just going with the flow and being open to all possabilities. I want to be healthy, maybe I should be a vegetarian? I always wanted to be and even tried kindof off and on but never really. I want to drink herbal tea and do yoga. Meditate as the sun rises out in my yard without worrying if the neighbors will think I am strange or not. I want to show how much I care for the earth and the enviroment. I do care but I am not showing it. Not be wasteful as much, ya know.

I think it really all comes down to fear. I am so afraid of people judging me. I want everyone to love me. Or atleast not confront me and think I am weird. Oh Goddess I have issues ;(Even with my boyfriend who I love so much, I just like can't be me completely around him without feeling weird. I don't know whats wrong with me.

I am so lost....

The More You Ignore Me, The Closer I Get
plainfame
September 5th, 2004 @ 6:58 am

Time for all the little t-blog poodles out there to get thier next injection of well us. So i would ask what have you all been up to lately and how you are but i most probably wouldnt care so lets get to the point. Now all around the world things movies are being made songs are being sung and pictures are being painted, drawn, taken and whatever. And through out all these things one factor annoys me no end and it is how you say 'censorship'. Yes censorship, because we in this new world are supposed to have a bigger freedom but even still a lot of what we do has a little black square super-imposed on it with Censorship written across it in white writing. They say they cesor it so that it doesnt affect people and make them become violent or whatever they call it. But you dont see the censor people running around waving machetes or trying to dominate the world using a series of mirrors and a pen torch. So obviously it cant be that bad. And stopping violence in movies where it is fake is kinda funny because you can watch the news and see and hear about more violence that is real. Ugh ive had enough i shall pass this over to my partner in crime Mr Fame.

Oh and stay tuned for the gold cow may come questioning soon (oooooh mystery)

censorship is a bit of a double edged sword. we have the freedoms to say and do most of whatever we want, as long as it doesn't really hurt anybody. now, let me explain how censorship should work. howard stern needs to be censored. mainly cuz he's a big moron with stupid hair. he does no good and gives no information or knowledge to the world about anything important. i'm glad they pulled the plug on him. but why can i still hear him whining? oh cuz he's capable of doing nothing else. that's an example of good censorship. i'll give you a bad one. the radio. don't bleep out the words. c'mon. we've all heard em. if you don't wanna hear it, turn off yer radio. who listens to the radio anyway? next, movies. there's a problem in my state with people refusing to watch rated R movies. i can understand wanting to avoid nudity cuz c'mon, it's just uncomfortable. but violence and language = entertainment. just see the movie, it's not gonna hurt you. most of the best movies are rated R anyway.

here's the bottom line. people are gonna say and do whatever they want. get used to it. you can't hide under yer little security blanket and it'll all go away. it's all still gonna be out there whether you like it or not. and hey, if they stop making movies and music, you'll always have this blog to come home to.

Mistake
hillary
January 5th,2005 @ 9:17 pm

alright- at some point things have got to get grounded- Im just wainting for this to happen. PLEASE GOD! MAKE SOME PART OF MY LIFE STABLE. Or I should learn to do this on my own. I have decided to make sure I go on the right path- towards something I want. I have the ability, I just don't do it. I choose the wrong way everytime. I am not going to do it any more.I WILL NOT DO IT ANY MORE!!!!

This LIfe don't last forever-

Voices in Their Heads
carcinogen
May 3rd, 2004 @ 7:11 pm

Why is it that God never made an appearance. Not even to his most faithful followers?

It could be as is said, that we could not survive being in his presence. Our human bodies, to fragile and unpure to withstand the awesomness of his being.

Or maybe its actually something else. God said that we are made in his image. Well, wouldn't that mean that he looks like a man then?

People wouldn't be as willing to follow a man...or someone who looked like a man. Hell, we killed Jesus, even though he performed miracles and said he was the son of God.

It seems to me that sometimes people hold more credibility as a voice. Radio DJ's sometimes seem more knowledgeable or credible because they are just a voice. When you see them sometimes it reduces them to what they are. Just a person.

Or what if the god they were speaking to wasn't a god. What if they had reason to hide their identity.

Either way, hearing a disembodied voice can have much more of an impact than seeing a body accompany it.

It leaves the imagination to create its own source. So by only presenting himself as a voice, God was able to create a more convincing argument that he was a God.

And what about the burning bush? Well, that still didn't reveal God's form, but it gave a physical presence to show Moses that it wasn't in his head.

Something to think about?

Me Insecure?
CrazyBeautiful
January 1st, 2005 @ 8:21 pm

Nothing is worse then old habits and insecurities begin to surface again.

I'm at home having a Dawson's Creek DVD Marathon and combating with a nasty stomach bug. I have fallen asleep and awaken a few times. I had my usual talk with CM this afternoon, same time every day. I realized I hadn't heard from him this evening, so decided to give him a call. A few rings voicemail, ok, I'll leave a message then he'll call back. So I call again, becuase sometimes he picks up, thats just him. I call back again and straight to voicemail. I'm starting to buckle and have awful thoughts that haunt me fom past relationships. And all of the insecurities are come aface.

I just had a thought while writing this, it could be his way of getting back at me for not answering my phone last night but that is not like him.

I need to think of something or hope he calls me back, becuase I have the worst thoughts running through my head right now.

Smokin Cigs...or not?!?!?!

cmaze

November 15th, 2004 @ 11:44 pm

i just got done going through boxes and bags and under my bed. i was trying to find rolling papers. i was trying to find rolling papers to roll the dried up tobacco left in the refries in the ashtray. the refries aren't big enough to smoke by themselves and i'm not myself. i'm not myself when i'm craving this hard. i can't believe i've been turned into this. i've been turned into the person i laugh at on tv when they talk about quitting cigarettes and how they are a slave to the habit. i laugh at them. i laugh and then go out for a cigarette. i go out for that cigarette and think about quitting...then i realize that i don't want to quit. then after i've realized i don't want to quit, i realize i don't have any more cigarettes and all the stores around are closed and my pockets are empty. then i start pacing back and forth...back and forth wondering how i can fix this terrible feeling i have. the feeling that i need something i shouldn't. the feeling that i can't control it and the fixation on NEEDING it. then i sit down and try to sit there...just sit there...waiting for this terrible excited rage to pass. this nervous internal twitch is growing and i'm waiting for it to stop. then i look at the tv and see that guy whos talking about how he went through his garbage to find a cigarette and how thats why he quit. because he wasn't himself. then i think to myself how i should do that. not quit, but go through the garbage to find a cigarette. then i look at my hands and see them shaking. then i think about that movie train spotting and what they went through with heroin. and i realize that its not that different. its a drug. its a mind twister. a disaster. i fucked up reality. a moment suspended in time that used to be called life, but has been given up for just a drag. thats all i want...just a drag. and i laugh. i laugh because at that point i'm thinking about how sorry i feel for the guy in ghost when he busts open the cig machine and realizes hes a ghost and can't smoke a cig. "just a drag, man." god, what a drag, man. and then i get pissed at the people everyone calls big tobacco. what bastards. smart bastards. smart pathetic fucked up careless rich ass motherfucking bastards. the whole lot of them. and then i sit for a second and wonder if i can quit. yes, of course i can. wait, what are you talking about...you can't! shut up, yes i can. nuh-uh. yes-huh! nope. yup! fuck off. and now i've gone crazy, but not forever. just for now. and tomorrow i'll wake up just fine. then i'll go back to craving and trying to hold it in...hold it down...hold it until it fades. which it won't. not for awhile at least. but, hey, i did it to myself. 3 packs a day...you're on your way to hell, but you don't get a nice handbasket with a nice bow-tie...you get shit...you'll die oh yeah...die die die and you know why...its cuz you gave yourself away. but i can still quit. i know i can. i should. its only right.

but damn...i still want one. i want one so much. fucking bastards. nicotine is the enemy. the enemy. enemy. but it feels so good. jesus, i can't believe this shit. the only way that i can for sure stop wanting is writing. maybe thats not such a bad thing, but i feel like a loon...and sound like one too.

puff puff puff puff.

its never enough.

i'm quittin.

Hate Filled Heart
Euphoria
December 20th, 2004 @ 3:19 am

I dont know why but my mind tells me that I hate everything. I dont want to be around people, I dont want to deal with the bullshit of everyday life, I dont want to pretend like nothing is wrong. I dont want to be a part of this family, I dont want to get married this summer, I dont want to be a nobody for the rest of my fucking life. I am tired of always living for other people. For how long must I continue to do these things. I am so sick of hearing everyone tell me that I am young and that everything is going to be okay. I dont know how I am suppose to feel. Why cant I be one of those happy people. I dont understand why I always feel down and unwanted. I dont feel like I will ever amount to anything. And I probably wont so I guess its good that I dont get too excited about anything huh? Well, maybe I'm just one of those unlucky people. I dont want to get married just because that is the next step on the list. I want to know that I can do something for myself. I want to know that I can be somebody special in this world. I want to be able to be proud of myself. My fear is that I never will!

Strange feeling
Ekayanie
May 7th, 2004 @ 6:55 am

As I was leaving work last night, I had a very weird feeling all of a sudden. My heart was beating very fast. I felt very very VERY uneasy. Somehow, my heart felt very heavy and I felt that something bad was about to happen either to me or my loved ones.

So I quickly called all my close friends and freaked 'em out by saying that this could be my last goodbye.

When I got home, I called up my mother in Indonesia to check whether she was ok. Then I made the love of my life SWEAR to me that he would watch where he was going when he went home after work and TO CALL ME ONCE he got home. YEss dear, I love u and I'm worried.

My mother didn't pick up the phone. Luckily, my bf called to reassure me of his safety..hehe:P Am I paranoid u might ask? hell yeah !!

So i didn't get to sleep til like 3am in the morning from all the worrying. And guess what, my mother called me back at 6am. It turns out that she had been ill and was asleep when I called. BUT MOM! why call at 6 friggin a.m in the MORNING!?!

So after this very long story, my message is.. IF you've got a strange feeling about something..AND I MEAN A STRANGE FEELING THAT"S VERY STRONG ...Don't ignore it even if pple call u crazy ok? Listen to your gut feelings..who knows..u could be right...

Til next time

And She Killed Herself
Hex
January 28, 2005 @ 9:31 pm

Today was the day that my friend tried to kill herself. For the second time.

(these are my personal thoughts so air -because your the only one who reads this shit- do not judge me)

You know i do not even know how i feel about this whole situation. I am upset for her, i really am but do not want to be sucked into the trap of being too caring and worrying myself so much that i become depressed again. She had her reasons for doing it but to me it is just a huge cry for help. I do not think me or any of us in the group are qualified to give her the help she needs. She needs to go to a therapist who will help her sort her head out. Oh yeah she already does. God i really do not know how to feel. Cry for attention yes, but should we give it to her? She already cuts herself and has slashed her wrists before this whole incident so maybe she will just be like a little unstable her whole life. But do i want to be dragged down with her? I want to be a good friend to her but on the other hand i am genuinely scared that the depression will come back. This time, i know it will be worse and i do not know how much of it i can take before i crack and start self harming again. NO. That will never happen. No matter how bad the situation it really does not fucking help. *Sigh.* I really do not want to desert her but she does not realise how much she is hurting us as friends. Someone else would have fucked off by now but for some reason or another we are still here trying to help her.

When this happened before there was another girl, A, who was close with pb (i feel really guily for calling her that but what else should i call her?) she was really badly affeected by what happened the first time and decided enough is enough im not taking this shit anymore. A is still friends with pb but they are not as close as they used to be and i do think ever will be. Maybe that is what will happen in this situation? Who knows. All i know is that i am not crossing the line where i put my sanity at risk. I will go that far but then i will stop, no matter what happens. I myself need the number of a decent therapist to discuss my issues with! Know any?

I have organised with the group to meet up and go to visit her in hospital tomorrow. I do not know what will happen. But hopfully we will be there to support her ... I could phone her now...im sure she has her phone on... any idea's the invisible person i am writing this too?

Y is blaming herself for what happened. It is not her fucking fault. She thinks it is because she was the trigger factor, her not talking to pb, she thinks this may have upset her to the point where it pushed her over the edge.

I care but i do not feel any remorse in my actions, pb apologised to me and i accepted it, i do not think i have anything to feel remorse about. *sigh* i really need to write so much stuff down but i do not have enough time.

Sex!
dyingangel
May 7th, 2004 @ 6:50 pm

nice title eh? its friday night and its typical date night..ally,nick, fox, sarah, jeff and lauren are going on a group date so that should be interesting. so here i am sitting here, all fucking horny and no one to do anything with...this blows! my friend brian wants me to go over but that will only end up with sex..and not something i really want right now

i know i just contradicted myself, but i dont want it with him if it will ruin our friendship..

plus i have no way of getting there...shit!

xxx

The Last Time
sleepingbeauty
May 31st, 2004 2 2:03 pm

This time is going to be the last time, the last time again. I do not want to be redundant anymore. Skipping like a broken record you can play again. But I will do it all again. Put it behind me, then you rewind me. This time is going to be the last time, the last time again. Once again, I have been trying to wash away the sin. Because I wake up on the bathroom floor. I will not do this anymore...starting tomorrow. This is going to be the last time, the last time again.

Question Yourself!
Acidlolliepop
May 3rd 2004 @ 5:52 pm

I've thought a lot about my last entry. Life isn't that bad. In my mind it represents purgatory, but it's livable, and i truely apreciate the opportunity given to me. But again i have begun to analyze. I like where i am now, only because i actualy dread the things to come. In the "after life" it would be eternal happiness. eternal would not be very motivating for me. there would be nothing to look forward to, to keep my twisted little gourd inspired. But thats ok, it just make me apreciate all things

35

even more. But that is just to clarify a little. Im not as sad and lonely as i may seem, i just question this too much; maybe i should stop taking things for granted.

Needing A Life
Courtney
August 16th ,2004 @11:34 am

God....once again i spent last night crying myself to sleep. part of it is cause i was home sick but the other well thats a littole more personal. see theres this guy that i met at a dance 5 years ago. i've had a crush on him since we met, anyways i moved out here to malaysia and we tried a long distance thing but it didnt work. i realized afterwards that i well...... loved him. my problem is im not sure if her feels the same way. he says the words to me but i just dont know if he means them. and it hurts so much. cause if he means them then its great and im on cloud 9 but if he doesnt.......it'll break my heart. i care for him soooo much and i dont wanna looses him. but im scared to open up fully to him. im terrified that if i tell him how i really feel he'll take off and leave me alone almost as if he were....abandoning me. Christ here i go again with my sentimental drivel.

i gotta go now and clean up my face so it doesnt look i've been crying.

L8tr days

Life Sucks
rabbitofthemoon
November 21st, 2003 @ 9:47 pm

all i am doing this weekend is homework. it should be wonderful.

i love how im failing at school and at life.

life sucks. i feel like every1 ive ever loved has betrayed me, and left me behind in the dust. i hate this world-every1 is full of shit, an asshole, and never think about ne1 else- and im one of them too... i hate it. i hate it. i hate it. I HATE IT!!!!!!!!!!!!!!!!!!!! everything's a sick joke. im so sad and everything is horrible and im so alone in this world and no one is there to support me, to be on my side, and tell me things will be better...they're all out screwing me over or playing pool while my heart is torn out and all i wanna do is cry and cry and cry and never stop. nothin 2 do and no one to talk 2 because i am alone and no one gives a damn .

nothing will ever change and my life will continue to suck. the only satisfaction i can get is that if u fuck with me, i sure as hell will try to make u pay, in any way possible.

i hate my life, and i hate the person i have become. i hate being sad and bitchy and annoying and depressed and lazy and shy and submissive and aggresive and spaszmatic and pyscho. i hate it i hate it i fucking hate i am now.

Yes
Gideon
June 17th, 2004 @ 12:10 am

Once again this would just be a post about work, but I figured I'd go for a happier post. So I was sitting in my living room after work (I mean) and I hear this large thing coming down the street. now the only reason this is so unusual is because it was at 11:30 at night. So it turns out it was an ambulance. Great. So the pulled up almost right across the street from me to an elderly couples house (89+) and I figure, "alright, maybe they just fell, they do that alot" so I watch and then they pull out that stretcher thingamajig "shit" goes gideons mind. so they took one of em away, and while the ambulance was there the other was just staning in the doorway...watching. I felt so bad for em, I donno, just kinda sad watching your loved one getting loaded and taken away in an ambulance.

Right, hows that for a happy post?

G

Sex as Golf?
Sirsch
Febuary 6th 2003 @ 11:11 pm

"Hi, my name is Sam, and I'm 16. I think you could compare 'friends with benefits' to the driving range. You just go there, and you're not committed to playing a whole round of golf. You just go, find out what shots are working for you, so when you go and play for real, you know what clubs are working for you and what's not."

Not a direct quote, but pretty darn close :)

37

Perfection
Kines
August 3rd 2004 @ 10:05 pm

I got a perfect score on my math test, but was quickly reminded that this test means nothing and I shouldn't feel to good about it, because half of it was just stuff from earlier calculus classes. Which might be true, but at least give me the pleasure of enjoying my perfection for one class period.

Stupid Things That People Say
Abby
November 22, 2004 @ 11:12 am

I thought I would post this just to prove to everyone that people who go to my school aren't all super intelligent. There are a lot of people who are pretty clever but a LOT of girls have been brought up in bubbles. And they have all said some fascinating things.

'I mean, as we go to a girl's school, there is no point in knowing boys at all! They are all violent.'

'Reading the newspaper is a nerdy thing to do.'

'Porn? Isn't that a meat substitute?'

'Boys are all on drugs these days'

'No-one cares about punctuation any more'

'Spelling doesn't matter'

'State schools are so 1998'

'Facist? Isn't that someone who is fashionable?'

'We're the upper class'

'Wires are chewy'

'What does PC stand for?'

'I'm not stupid.'

These are all as true as I am typing this. Quite amazing really. Maybe they should have a general knowledge section in the entrance exam. Agreed?

Porn
Lynne
January 13th 2005 @ 3:12 pm

I was reading an especially interesting post over on Alas, a blog about Catherine MacKinnen, the contriversial U of M law professor, and Deep Throat. It has me thinking a bit about porn and sexuality and my own very mixed feelings on the subject. Let me just start by saying that I don't think there is anything wrong with sex between consenting adults, no matter what they choose to do, although I will admit that there are a lot of things I personally find "icky" Like when some friends of mine were giggling at the idea of the street in Ann Arbor named "Felch" and I asked what "Felch" was and then decided that there probably are just some things I am better off not knowing.

Ok, here is the thing though. While I do not have a problem with sexuality or nudity and such...I *do* have a problem with a lot of porn that is out in the world. So much of it seems to be made with a total attitude of misogyny or a view of women as just bodies. I know that women's bodies are sort of the point of porn and all. But some of the fantasies I have seen in porn movies have been very disturbing to me. Of course, I havent seen many porn movies but the ones I have seen have made me wonder about just what it is that men really find attractive. An example would be the whole body shaving that seems to go on sometimes. Are men really that hung up about body hair on women? And if so, why is that. I mean, *women* often have body hair. They naturally have pubic hair and hair under their arms and on their legs. *Children* don't have body hair. And ok, I am not really being critical about women who choose to shave their legs or their pits since that has really become a cultural norm. But what is up with the full vagina wax? Do men have some desire for women who look like children?

I have also yet to see a porn movie with a man really showing respect for the woman he happens to be fucking. I mean, most of the movies I have seen seem to involve sex between strangers. Is that really what men want? I don't think any of the men I know would want that. They all seem to be into meaningful relationships just like I am. It seems weird to me that porn movies never seem to reflect that. Maybe that is why I find them so boring. On the other hand, there seems to be a much bigger market for anonymous sex for men. I mean, I cant recall ever seeing a male hooker who was out streetwalking for women "johns" (Would they be called "Janes"?) *shrug*

And then I wonder. Do they even make straight porn for women and if they did, in what ways would it be different? Would it be just as sexist in it's own way? When I think about it though, there must be a niche for straight porn for women. I mean, women are sexual too. Look at all the "bodice rippers" women read. ah well. that is just what I am thinking about today. And before anyone gets on my case about first amendment stuff, I dont think porn should be banned as long as it is produced in a legal manner (I.e. no one is coerced into it).

You Know You're in 2005 When…
Eatroach
December 20th 2004 @ 3:32 pm

1. You accidentally enter your password on the microwave.

2. You haven't played solitaire with real cards in years.

3. You have a list of 15 phone numbers to reach your family of 3.

4. You e-mail the person who works at the desk next to you.

5. Your reason for not staying in touch with friends and family is that they don't have e-mail addresses.

6. You go home after long days at work you still answer the phone in a business manner.

7. You make phone calls from home, you accidentally dial "9? to get an outside line.

8. You've sat at the same desk for four years and worked for three different companies.

10. You learn about your redundancy on the 11 o'clock news.

11. Your boss doesn't have the ability to do your job.

12. You pull up in your own driveway and use your cell phone to see if anyone is home.

I Blog, Therefore I Am

13. Every commercial on television has a website at the bottom of the screen.

14. Leaving the house without your cell phone, which you didn't have the first 20 or 30 (or 60)years of your life, is now a cause for panic and you turn around to go and get it.

15. You get up in the morning and go online before getting your coffee.

16. You start tilting your head sideways to smile.

17. You're reading this and nodding and laughing.

18. Even worse, you know exactly to whom you are going to forward this message.

19. You are too busy to notice there was no #9 on this list.

20. You actually scrolled back up to check that there wasn't a #9 on this list.

Letter to Young Man
Kitten
January 26, 2005 @11:08 pm

Dear Young Man,

Young Man you are on the verge of experiencing life. However, in your eagerness to explore don't let things get in the way of what you truly want out of life. If I could give you anything it would be this advice. Don't let your pride keep you from being vulnerable & don't let your anger hide your smile. Remember that you are loved because of who you are, not what you can acomplish. The roads that life may take you down always have a destination, be careful which ones those are.

Above all, remember that you are the young man that God called you to be, and he will never forsake you.

From the heart of,

Young Woman

November 22, 2004

I Heart You Brendan
Sweetdreams
November 6th 2004 @ 8:51 pm

wow so life has been going up and down.. lets see this week has been overlly stressful on me..

i close friend... lied to me... and i was really dissapointed about that.. i thought i could trust him and i know he made a mistake and everything and i know we are still going to stay good friends i just hope hes gonna change and not lie to me anymore... watever...

went to towson friday with a whole shit load of people.. and it was absolutely amazing... im happy to say i now have a boyfriend <3 i love you brendan... and omg i saw josh.. havent seen him in like 4 months.. i was so incredibly happy... then i spent the night at sam's house.. with tina and that was awesme.. i love hanging out wtih them.. then had a huge as breakfast then i went to drive timee and parallell parked yay.. lisence in 20 days.. then came home and crawled up in bed... watched chasing liberty.. it made me cry... then pat called... (random) said thers a field party tommorow so which should be interesting but whatever... then my parents start flippngout that like 50 ppl are going to be outside tommorow night drinking and omg i wish they would gimme freedom to just do whatever i want to do.. i swear to god they are so fucking overprotective.. i cant live life like i want.. i cant have fun they have to know everything and everyone im with im not allowed to go to parties.. not allowed to drive with anyone and it fucking sucks.. they fucking control my life then they think that they can just mess around with my life too... asking me to move to north carolina.. like what the fuck.. im not leaving this state.. whether they like it ornot.. im not moving ... they cant make me i will seriously run away and rebel and like threaten them... im so fucking pissed off i hate this fucking house i just want to leave and run away and just get outta this fucking hell whole.. i need my lisence... for god sakes i cant walk outta my house to my neighbors and go to a party.. like what the fuck.

but other than being at this house.. my life is good..

i love you brendan thanks for making last night so amazing... i miss you

Angry..
xoceanxavenuexx
April 24th 2004 @ 5:58 pm

I am really really mad. but first off, today i was in the car with my daddio and my sis drivin to school, and wen we got close we noticed people were being directed out of the school, n a bunch of kids were standing outside of the school. SCHOOL WAS OUT. no power!!! whooooooooot woo!!!! hahaa. um, but then i went back online for like..hours. nothin else to do.

i went downstairs to get lunch, and i heard my mom and dad fighting in my dads office. they always fight. my dad always says 'she is going to divorce me soon because of you and your sister' & stuff. well, i heard my mom say 'GO AHEAD AND CALL THE ATTORNEY! WE DON'T AGREE ON ANYTHING ABOUT RAISING OUR KIDS..' blah blah blah. i'm thinking this is the time.my 'rents are gettin divorced. of course, they could change their minds. i'll keep you updated on that. but if they do, & one of my parents gets custody [n u know..the kid normally gets to pick if they are old enough], i am SOOOO staying with my dad. if we switch off and on, i'm still being with my dad mostly. hes much easier to get along with, nicer,etc. my sister will be able to drive soon, so like durin the summer when i need to get somewhere, or durin the year wen my dad is on business trips, my sister can drive us to school n stuff. n we can both cook, so we don't need him for dinner. there is no way im staying with my mom NO WAY.

THEN.. i remember about sum stupid little diary/journal thing my mom always writes in when shes mad @ us. so my parents and sister had gone to go get my sis's new car (i said somethin 2 her when she came downstairs about them getting divorced n shes like 'i think they are too'..), and so i went and found her hiding place and scanned a couple entries. one of them really stook out. she said somethin about her watching dr.phil or something, and how they were talking about cheating. and they gave ways to spot if ur husband is cheating on u. she wrote a couple (one being 'lack of sex'.. didnt really need to see that one.. TMI), and she said how the ones she wrote were stuff my dad does. like.. dress better, have his own phone line (MY DAD NEEDS HIS OWN PL FOR WORK!), not telling the hotel or # that he's staying in when hes gone, etc. she thinks my dad is cheating on her! im gonna kick her ass!!! god i hate herrrrrr!!! !!!! ahhhhhh life sucks. ill find out more lata.. so ill keep ya updated. xoxo.

43

Publicity Stunt
Shanyn
April 28th 2004 @10:31pm

123: so

123: did you cut again

Xxx: yes

123: omg dude you gota sto[p

Xxx: NO@

Xxx: !

Xxx: dont tell me what to do!

Xxx: ill stop when i want to!

Xxx: and i dont want to!!!

123: no dude you have to i am not jocking

123: jokeing

Xxx: theyre not bad!!!

Xxx: god

123: no you have to stop

Xxx: why?

123: cuz dude people care about you and no one wants to see you doing this to your self

Xxx: how would you know who cares about me?

123: i do —-yeh. sure.

heres to the girl whose most ::*B-E-A-U-T-I-F-U-L*:: with mascara tears streaming down her face ((CHEERS))

yeh i cut. i smoked. i wrote "hi. loser" on my wall. with blood. it was sick, twisted, but oh so perfect all in one.

amanda gets me! i know i cut for 'attention' but not like you would think. i dont realize it but i do. i want people to know im not happy. so i cut. but i dont want to cut anymore. its just like i need it. its like my own little 'high' how amanda puts it. when someone realized im 'hurt' or crying or something. theyre all like 'are you okay?' and dont even tell me your not touched when that happens! i want to know people actually care about me. because most of the time it seems like they dont. 'sept amanda. i know she cares..but now im kind of questioning it. but shes talking to me. shes such a sweetie. i LOVE HER!!! gina quit on her! god how could she? i told but i dont want to ditch her! i wouldnt do that! it hurts to-o much! its happend to me before!!

Sexy Saturday
Roseatheart7
June 19th 2004 @ 3:38pm

Today is saturday.the day to look sexy.lol.

lets see here.....today,im just going tolet go of everything,and go to my friend,maria's party. Yeah,i dont know what's gunna happen,but im prepared. sometimes doing things that you dont know the outcome of,can sorta be good.Well....right now,im off to being a cerial maniac!!!!!!!!

love yas

byexoxo

The Forever Wakefulness of the Week
Lauren
January 30, 2005 @ 4:27 am

Sleep has deserted me- permanently, I fear.

Every night this week has been a struggle. I can't get comfortable, can't keep my eyes closed long enough, can't relax, can't stop thinking, can't stop worrying...

It has worn down on me so much... Three hours of sleep a night is just not enough. I'm learning to survive on less and less rest, and it seems that every day I'm feeling more like I'm walking through a thick fog. I can't think or speak properly, and my concentration is nonexistent.

This needs to stop.

I feel dizzy a lot of the time, my hands shake uncontrollably. I can't shut my mind off... I'm constantly thinking and worrying and wondering what the hell to do about it.

So much changes so fast... There's just never any rest. Everything I try to do or say seems to go wrong, and no matter how I try to fix it, it just changes again.

I need a vacation.

I need time, away from all this chaos. Time to let myself be me, without the pain and the confusion. I need an escape.

Suicide
HappyHardcore
June 14th 2004 @ 9:12 pm

One of my best friends paul is really scaring me talking about suicide

He first started out msging me saying...

: im slittling my wrist and blowing my house upo

: tongiht!

This isn't something uncommon for him to say but he seems a lot more serious this time. He began to list reasons why he is going to do it like not being able to get girls, his family life, and not getting anywhere in life. I had to tell the girl he really likes(angel) to try and fix things. Hopefully this will work!

It seemed like it was working but then he tells me it is the end and goes away with this away message:

"I find it kinda funny, I find it kinda sad, the dreams in which I'm dying are the best I've ever had..."

Well hopefully he doesn't do anything stupid, but I don't know and I am really scared for him .

I hate suicide

Good Eye Sniper
likeabadstar
October 17th 2004 @ 6:05 pm

i got in a car crash with my mom yesterday 4 hours from home. we totaled the car. it was SO fun! then we went to the police station and took a taxi ride until we got a bus station and ran in for tickets. we got home 5 hours later, without car.

im still deaf in my right ear, and moms arm is still beat up.

i hate this game.

Mood
WithEveryKiss
Friday, January 14, 2005 @ 10:02 pm

Right now I'm in one of those moods where I hate myself. I'm so tired of people giving me shit about things I just can't seem to help. Yeah, I know I'm spaced out and I procrastinate and forget to do stuff... but I can't concentrate long enough to take care of anything. I feel like I'm going crazy, like the world is spinning out from under me. Nothing I do or say is right anymore, and I'm not good enough ever.

I wish I could just give up... that's all I want to do right now, just throw my hands up and surrender. I'm so tired; I'd give anything to just disappear for a while and straighten my head out.

Here Is A Story For You
luluthebrit
January 7th 2005 @ 5:04 pm

Kelly was my absolute BEST FRIEND last year and the beginning of this year. Last year we were fortunate in having many classes together. This year we arent so lucky. We have no classes together..not even lunch. We never see eachother,but of course we arent going to let that stop us from being friends. We saw eachother on weekends and hung out at every possible time in school..basically walking together.

I dont know why things started to go wrong.I think it was the fact that we were both making new friends,friends that we saw often.It was also the fact that I started dating.

We became aquantences.Then she started talking about me behind me back.Bad things..obviously. I confronted her.That was our first fight ever. We did eventually make up.Things went back to the way they were,when we were best friends.But that faded.

The situation now is strange.We talk online sometimes and when we do its like we're best friends.I see her in school and i do the best friend thing...Kelly on the other hand ignores me.completely.

WHAT THE FUCK?

Strokes
Cutter
October 8th 2004 @4:46 pm

I suppose that there's plenty I could write about, but lately I'm finding it difficult to blog. I suppose that it's about spending the last 5 and a half years online... writing and writing and writing... I suppose that I'm pretty over it. Every now and again you get someone who gets something out of what you write, but generally speaking, no... at most, you can pat yourself on the back for being a good drumming chimp. It's just entertainment... drama, for other people.

Do I really care? Maybe a little. I'm sure that deep down inside of me I want people to care about what I have to say, but I can't care too much. I did that for a few years, and it did nothing other than make me want to hunt people down and shoot them. When you care, you put your heart on the line. Not a good thing to do with the Internet. My conclusion, after 5 and a half years? As quickly as possible, take it offline.

It's not real.

I argued that point, once. I used to want it to be real... to be typing back and forth with other real people... to believe the "I love you!s" and "You're family!s"... It's not real though. The words were, generaly speaking, empty. News Flash: If only one person thinks it's real, it's called a delusion.

So, why do I continue writing online? I don't know. I think that right now it's just about killing time... and getting the occasional ego boost. There's nothing quite like hearing "you're right!" to give me a stiffy. Doesn't take all that much to make me happy, I guess.

In a while, I'll drift offline. I'll go back to pen and paper, and Word docs. The thought is a pleasant one. I don't even recognize my own handwriting anymore. My writer's callous is gone. It's sort of sad.

Instant gratification. That's what it's all about, I suppose. It used to be that I didn't care if anyone ever read what I wrote. In fact, I preferred that no one ever did. My writing was for me. It was an outlet. Then I wrote online and people ooh!ed and ahh!ed... and the rest is history. More! More! More! Feed me! Feed me! Feed me! Stroke my ego! Harder! Harder! Harder!!!

I used to be able to get myself off just fine.

Sad indeed.

Tears In Dreams and Life
fallensnow
January 16th 2005 @ 3:03 am

This afternoon, woke up from a bad dream. It wasn't the first time I find myself crying in dreams, but it was the first time I woke up crying from a bad dream. I only cry to sleep, I don't wake up crying.

It was another quarrel with my mum, and I was sitting in this very chair I'm writing in at this moment. She was on the safa about a meter away. I don't remember what it was about, but she hit me, and kicked me in my shin, from where she was. I'd say again, she isn't a violent person. But she did it again and again, and I couldn't run away. I wasn't tied to the seat, but felt like I was. I just couldn't leave. I cried, and told her she was hurting me. She didn't listen at first, but after awhile, she seemed to really realise what she was doing. She stopped. And said 'Sorry'.

And I awoke at that word. Yet I was still in the dream. And tears just flowed down my face the moment I opened my eyes. Realising that I was alone in my room, and not tied by an invisible force on the chair, did not help. In my mind, I could feel the sharp pain in my shin, and the 'sorry' was ringing in my ears. I wasn't thinking straight. And I just continued to cry, till I fell asleep again.

Why? I wonder. Why did she hurt me, why couldn't I run away, why, did she still apologise, why did I cry, even after she apologised. Why?

In real life, she hasn't hurt me physically before, except the one time when she threw a hanger at me. But the pain had been there all along. The emotional scars she unintentionally puts upon me. By unintentionally, it's different from when friends hurt me indirectly. When it's indirect, it's due to my own extreme sensitivity. But the things she does and says, hurt me very much directly, and painfully, even if she doesn't do it purposely to hurt me. The words she says especially. Words can cut. Very deeply.

But I can never escape from all these, can I? I'm stuck. I'm tied to this unseen force. I can't run. Just because she's my mother.

Yet, sometimes she feels sorry for what she says. After some time, she tries to appease me and make me feel better by putting on a disgustingly friendly and cheerful mood. She tries to buy me food she thinks I like.

But as I once said, you can hurt one unintentionally, and try to heal the scars again, once, twice. But when it goes on repeatedly, when she lashes out again before the original scars have had the chance to heal, she only opens up the fresh wound again and again. It never heals. Never would again.

What's the use of an apology, if it would only lead to sorrowful tears once again.

Live Dreams.. Dont Dream Them
sorcha66
December 12th 2004 @ 12:38 am

im not sure what i'm going to write about in this post. my parents are just two seperate beings who happen to live together. i'm so annoyed with it. they work so hard to avoid each other. it's weird. im so lost when it comes to guys. there are about 6 who are definitly interested in me. i was interested in one, greg, but i'm not sure. the one i think i really could like, alex, i also think i'll never get. alex.. i'm fascinated by him. he's so "tough" i guess, but when he talks, i mean really talks to me, i can tell that he's really a very caring guy. it's so incredible to watch him with his little neice. everything about him i like. but yet, i just have this feeling that there's no way. grr. life's been.. different. i'm so happy.. but not. i mean, i guess for an outsider just watching me out in the world, i'd seem perfectly happy. but, i don't know. school's going great, dance couldnt be better. it just seems like i should be happy. i have friends now. ha. but i'm just not. i don't know. it seems like i should be living my dream, not just dreaming. but i don't even know what my dreams are. i guess this whole christmas season thing makes me think. it's aweful, thinking. i highly suggest that you don't do it. makes me all sullen at a time when i should be happy. i wish i wasn't the youngest. i want brothers and sisters here. with me. not the far away kind that never call and never care. although i love my siblings with all my heart. i just wish i could re-live my childhood and spend more time with them before they left. life can really weigh me down. whatever.

Drastic Mood Change
ChloroformxKisses
January 26, 2005 @ 11:00 pm

I feel like throwing up.

Feel like crying.

Feel like screaming.

Suddenly realization dawned on me.

Graduation seems so close but so far away.

Something new is starting. It scares the hell out of me. I'm not sure what to expect. I'm too afraid to hope...

Tension... And Release
jbassman1325
January 19, 2005 @ 10:19 PM

It's not just Tae Bo anymore.

Anyway... I just read my last entry (the one from earlier today) and I read TAG as "tog", as in the German word for "day." I think Finals have eaten my brain.

Aside from that... we both saw it coming. That doesn't mean it's not a bit of a bummer.

A lyric I can't get out of my head, although I've no idea why:

"She's all alone again Wiping the tears from her eyes Some days

she feels like dying She gets so sick of crying"

Well, since there's no school the rest of the week, I think I'm gonna go play video games til one in the morning (Ben, it's your game I'm playing... and the legendary birds are indeed in it, you fool!)

People on my list for today: Ashley (for being so understanding... as usual), Tish (for being my support group and waiting for Ashley with me... three or four nights running), Ben (for the game), everyone at school (HALF A YEAR TO GO.... YIPPEEKIYAY, BITCHES!), Dah (for being so gracious about her victory- not), Miss Murdy (for lending her noir expertise to everything), and everyone else who made today not only worth living, but worth caring about.

Peace, love, and understanding. To all of you. But just for tonight.

2004
blueangel566
December 31, 2003 @ 7:00 pm

Why does 2004 REALLY have to come? Cant I just freeze time and enjoy what I have, instead of being thrown into the mix of a brand-new year, where I dont know WHAT the hell is going to happen?? People have had to go through this, well, since the beginning of time.. or at least since calendars were invented. But 2003 was the best year I've had in a LONG time... 2002 was awful.. my life spiraled out of control and I wish I could take it all back.. 2001, well.. not many people in America can say they enjoyed THAT year.. and in 2000 my grandma and great-grandma both died, and they were my best friends. 1999, of course, was the best year of my life.. heh.. that reminds me of today..

I walked down the street to get the mail, and it really felt like a summer day. It made me think about before I started liking baseball.. and how I spent my entire summers at my grandpa and grandma's house... and there was a group of us girls in the neighbourhood that would play together ALL the time... and the adults in the neighborhood used to call us the "girls of summer", ya know, like the song "boys of summer". Yep.. just me, Abby, Maghen, and Latresa. After my grandma died in the spring of 2000, nothing would ever be the same again, and I stopped going over to my grandpa's house. The 4 of us eventually went separate ways.. where are we today? Well you all know me.. Abby is a stuckup snob who never even looks at me in the halls... Latresa hangs out with white 'wannabe-black' girls who use her... and Maghen? Poor Maghen.. she's been in juvenile hall twice, and works part-time as some kind of underage hooker deal..

Well.. enough about the past.. *sigh*.. This year has been TOTALLY AMAZING!! I got more into baseball then EVER, concentrating more on the other teams outside of the Tigers. I met a whole BUNCH of wonderful people, right here on Xanga! *wink wink* You know who you are!! Lets see... jeez, I am doing SO much better then I was a year ago.. lets just say a year ago, I was not quite stable with myself LoL. Things are just so much better then they ever could be, considering the pathetic filth Im forced to say Im friends with. LoL that sounds so mean. Oh well.

As for New Year's Resolutions, I have 2:

1) Stop having such a potty mouth

2) Start standing up for what I believe in, whether it be my idiot so-called 'friends' or a guy I wanna ask out.. Im sick of making myself suffer!! Peace out, see ya'll next year.

Shopping
ThisIsMyNewName
January 07, 2005 @ 1:17 am

Yet another great part of going back-to-school is going shopping for back-to-school clothes. I dunno why I didn't remember to do all this "back-to-school protocol" before I actually started school! Anyways, tonight I hit up Forever 21 which just so happens to be my newest fave store.

I tell ya, listening to dressing room conversations really crack me up. As I'm praying to be able to squeeze into the ever-so-cute skirt I had picked out (which also just so happened to be the largest size available ~ I tell you, most of those clothes are made for midgets!), the girl in the room next to me complains to her friend, "Ah, man- the small is too big on me." (*"Oh, boohoo" I think to myself*) Miss Anorexic continues, "Hey Lindsey, would you go get me an XS?" (Meanwhile, I'm all proud I can close all the buttons on my L skirt!)

The chica on the other side of me was conferring with her friend whether or not she should buy the skirt she was trying on. They were determining whether or not it was appropriate for the occassion and then also figuring out if they'd have other time to find something else in the case they opted not for this one. She ultimately decided to borrow something from his fashion-savvy sister. I found listening to their conversations totally enthralling as I was changing wardrobes because I couldn't see any of their faces and was only able to imagine what they looked like in the outfit they were fretting over. Actually, it wasn't the clothes I was interested in hearing about- it was their whole thought process involved. (Ah, I see my psych class is already having an effect on me.) Or...maybe it's just that I enjoy eavesdropping.

So half a paycheck later, I'm attempting to leave the store when all of a sudden, yet another super-duper cute skirt is staring me straight in the face, impeding my ability to make it to the exit. Grr. "I hope it's not my size," I think to myself as I see the exit in the horizon. But noo, dangnabbit, it WAS my size. As much as I enjoyed the whole dressing-room-conversation scene the first time 'round, I just paid for the skirt & skedaddled my way out the door; this time without getting further distracted!

Ok, so now I have the school supplies, the school clothes, all my textbooks, and - most importantly - the eagerness and motivational drive associated with going back to school! I honestly and truly love all my classes... In not a ONE do I sit there and stare at the clock and count down how much longer til our 5-minute break. I'm totally intrigued by each subject, each professor, each activity. I'm so happy! And I'm on a 3-day break right now but at work tonight I was totally thinking, "Man, I wish I had class again tomorrow!" Love, love, love it!

What's Going On With Me?
chadbradfordfanclub
January 26, 2005 @ 2:35 am

Something happened to me today. I was reading some old entries and I started to wonder, "WTF is this shit?" Reading the shit I've written has had something of a negative effect on me, if you can tell. It's all gone, forever. I'm reading these entries and I know what I'm talking about, I know the full story, but its crap. It's worse than teenage poetry. All that I can think of is what the fuck I am writing about and what the fuck was in my mind at the time.

Well, that's all gone, pretty much. It's not DELETED, just hidden from the public eye. The next question at hand is what to do with this xanga. There are several options I have at hand.

1. I keep posting on this blog and make a true effort to write and make not shitty entries

2. Keep posting here, but limit it to sports or something of that nature and keep personal entries on my Friend's blog.

3. Drop this blog all together, goodbye forever. If this does become the case, I will most likely return to my older blog account, in that event.

There we have it, 3 options to choose from and it is my decision and mine alone.

Laughing Like No Tomorrow
emogirl210
January 24, 2005 @ 9:38 pm

colorme: i always leave your house feeling a little less like me

colorme: and a little more like us

Best friends are indeed a good thing. Tonight was spent eating chocolates, making messes, giggling, editing photos, talking like losers, untuning guitars only to have it tuned back, and becoming just like everyone says we do.

It's so funny how you can be so different from someone, and yet you can become so similar when you play off of eachother.

conclusion:

Good Friends = Good

Chocolate = Good

Laughing like there's no tomorrow = hecka tight.

live like no tomorrow.

<3

Dad
GrUmPiTa
Sunday, August 29, 2004 @ 9:08 am

I've been up since 8 or before, for... who knows why..

I talked to my Dad yest.. He has been in Peru for a wk.. when I'm just sitting here I keep wanting to call him -=(even. tho our convos go like this 'What are you doing?- What are you watching?- What did you do today?- Are the kids there?- What are you doing tomorrow?- Ok, call me later.. bye)=- then I realize he's not even in the country..

Perfect World
LiLcRaZiEgUrL506
January 29, 2005 @ 3:10 am

It's saturday morning.....3:13 am on my clock, and i cannot fall asleep. i am like wide awake, with my eyes REALLY big! i could like go to work right now! too bad no one would be there. but yes i cant sleep....too much junk on my mind. stupid me, i think wayyy too much. *sigh*

It's so hard to pretend like everything is ok, when i know that it's not. it still hurts so much to this day, and i don't know how much longer will i be feeling the pain. i wish i could just put everything behind me and just continue on with my life before......but i can't. everynight when i can't sleep that's all i think about. and when i think about it, i start crying. knowing that i shouldnt cry i try to stop, but i can't get my mind to stop thinking about it. it makes me sad and that's like all i think about...there are so many things i regret and so many things i wish i could have said. there were so many things i SHOULD have said. but i didn't. i think that's why it hurts so much...to let my feelings be unknown....that's always the reason. i feel so unmotivated ever since....and i try to act like everything's ok, but it's not. i've been trying to get things back to normal...but it's gonna take some time. i just really hope that time will ease my pain.

i wish i could just take the time to tell everyone individually how they have touched my life and how much i appreciate them for everything they've done for me, and all the love and care i receive from them.

Take care, love your friends and family.

Rapist
lildiva
June 17, 2004 @ 4:21 pm

35: hey

11: on oprah this woman went to prison for shooting her rapist and she went to jail for 25 years to life sentence

11: i looked at my mom and i was like...well how long did the rapist get

35: i kno right

11: no i mean...she went to prison for shooting him....

35: she killed him?

11: yeah

35: ohhhh

11: and i asked how long he went to jail for

35: did he even go to jail

11: no...hes dead!

35: oh hahahahaha

35: i get it now

35: sry

35: the blond

11: its ok

35: i get it!!!!

35: HAHA

11: it took me a while too

The Real Deal
Jixavius
May 21, 2004 @ 2:01 pm

What is the Real Deal?`...

What is the Deal to begin with? Well, every time you thought you were saying something, buying, selling, asking, replying, thinking, just speaking... or running, facing, going, coming, getting, giving, and down from every little thing like looking thoughtless without one any idea where you are/what you're doing, up to the biggest blobbiest things as throwing speeches to anonymous people screaming your name mistakenly spell by their ignorant minds, ears and tongues to feed their lusty brains... each and every one of these actions can be derived from what can be viewed as some "deal", no matter the importance you attach to it.

So what is the `Real Deal`? ... Thus, the real deal becomes each and every thing/action you undertake in your so-called real-life, believing that what you are doing and the way you are doing it is genuine... Well is it?

I will try to discuss the mere ideas and thoughts that might stand out from the other train of cogitations, when it comes to "genuine" behavior and "serious" talk... For most of the time it is so little 'serious', and 'genuine'?... we wish!!

Let us look for the Real Deal, the untampered, pure and simple truth... let us filtrate the heart from the body and see what happens.

Why are you thinking? Stop right there!

Is that thought of yours the `real deal`?.......

Insomnia
Nenerz
December 31, 2004 @ 9:18 pm

Insomnia once again holds me in its hands.

I know not what exactly is making me cry. It is hard to distinguish what the source of these tears are...be they tears of joy, or tears of sorrow, yet they are tears nonetheless. As I come to realize the closing of 2003, there has been a series of rising and falling action within the plot of my life. It has caused me to realize what mistakes I have made, only to hope that I do not repeat them once again. I have also reflected upon the people whom I have met, which to no avail have aided me in my search to find myself. I have once again begun to write more clearly, with more passion than I ever have before...and to make certain that I will not fail those who trust me with their hopes and dreams. What potential they hold for me, the effort which they believe I put forth...is not nearly enough to fufill their wishes...I will NOT be a failure. I WILL overcome my fears, and I WILL push myself to the limit. I will not let my future and my ambitions intimidate me. And I will not allow any one single person to stop me. In the pursuit of success, I will push aside love to become what I dream of doing...being successful.

As much as I hate to admit, the choices I have made in the past are not quite what I would now consider appealing. I have disgraced myself, and associated my name with negative thoughts and feelings. thus far, my actions have become a nuisance in the harbor of my life, which I senselessly have taken for granted. And as I cry these unknown tears, I think to myself...my life is just beginning.

Bring it on 2005 !!

Finals
-wes-
January 20, 2005 @ 12:10

1. THE FINAL WAS SO STUPID. it was a lot of questions that were so in depth that none of us knew it. I can't even describe how.. indepth it was. argh.

anybody wanna help?

So finals are stressful. today i was crazy. like.. i was tired and dying.

umm other that.. hi. nothing much else

America
Mr_Bungle
January 24, 2005 @ 5:10 pm

I think that in no country in the civilized world is less attention paid to philosophy than in the United States. The Americans have no philosophical school of their own, and they care but little for all the schools into which Europe is divided, the very names of which are scarcely known to them.

Alexis de Tocqueville

—Democracy in America, Vol II

So true, 'tis a sad world.

Why Do I Blog?
theseeker
Friday 01.28.05 @ 2:10 am

Why I write this blog

This blog was actually inspired by my father's death last year. You see my dad left us with many happy memories. He also left us some published writings that give some insights about him. But one thing that I wish that he had was a journal. I would love to read more of his thoughts about things that mattered to him. And those are the same kind of thoughts that I try to document in this blog. My primary goal is to have something for my daughter to read when she grows up. Through this journal, I'm hoping that she would have a better idea what I was like during my younger years. What my thoughts were about the important issues and events during those years. Most of all, through this journal, I would like her to know how much I love her and her mom.

Why I write in general

Writing keeps me focused. Focused on the important things in this life. It forces me to seek the truth on relevant issues and to filter the irrelevant ones. It helps me distill my thoughts and harness my emotions. It rejuvenates me when I share my dreams and aspirations. It exposes my humanity when I share my fears and my failures. It helps me reach out to the people I care about. It gives me the opportunity to serve God and glorify Him. It allows me to talk to myself and to hear myself. It allows me to know myself and in the process, it helps me grow.

What Are We Here For?
AcidRainbow
January 3rd 2005 @ 4:06 pm

I was watching this show yesterday...and it got me thinking.

What is the point of life anyways?

if we all die at some point,why do we even live...its pointless

why went we all made immotal or something,then we would never die.

maybe some ppl live because they think there is someone watching over them that would one day bring them to heaven and it would all be good.

Well thats a bunch of shit....fuck it

and some people believe that we come back as something different[a second life] i wouldnt even listen to those people...their probablt a bunch of fucking hippies. if there was life after death why are alot of people so afraid to die?

to me life is pointless and there is no life after death,its just a bunch of shit.

I Miss Her...
TNT25
December 8th 2004 @ 12:33 am

i've got alot to figure out, i've got alot to think about, i've got alot to forget about, i've got alot to live without, so many things to miss about her...

i didn't write that i found it but i dont know where.

everybody probably already knows this but in case you dont, she dumped me for another guy. they arent together anymore but that doesnt matter because we arent either. i said some things in an email that i regret and i want to apologize. liz, im sorry i wasnt being a very good boyfriend but it was kind of hard because the only way i get to talk to you is on the internet and it was taken away. i have it back now. i got it back last night. i wish i could take back all of the things that i said. after i wrote that i felt really bad and there was nothing i could do to get that message back. i didnt mean what i said and i hope there is still a chance for us.

Ugh
foreveralone
January 27th 2005 @ 5:14 pm

Idk how today is gonna go... I remember why I didnt remember.... and I realize what my dream ment... I feel like such an ass for forgetting... then coming home and seeing my mom cry.. me asking whats wrong... Im an idiot!! I try to forget it... Try to think it never happened... I still feel guilty for it... I can't help it... I'm going to think its my fault for a really long time... its been 3 years and I still think its my fault.... I think its my fault for both of them... *curses at self* fuck.... I can't even cry... I dont even FEEL like crying... and it makes me feel even worse.... acting like it never happend isn't going to help at all... thinking that its my fault sure as hell aint gonna help at all... but I want to feel *something* over it... not nothing.... grr....

..me..

Feeling Human!
surrogate
January 22nd 2005 @ 6:25

Good Evening Boys and Girls!

Surrogate reporting here, and... dare I say it, a surrogate, I think - I pray, slowly returning to full and complete health.

Just in case, mind you, I'm going to hold back from jumping into the interview with Jesus for a couple of days, just cuz I feel so badly about how I've already chopped the thing thing up due to this silly illness. So, for a day or two, some observations from my warmly tucked perspective on all things bothersome about what it's sounding might be our next Battle cry and Echo...

Try this: Holler!

I R A Q Q Q Q...

there... now hear the echo?

I R A N N N N!

That is amazing!

These Bush Planners are always a step ahead!

....

Then I'd like to paraphrase the Senator Barbara Boxer - Condeleeza Rice exchange for any of you who missed the verbatim repartee':

Boxer: "Quote, quote, quote."

Boxer: "Quote. Quote, quote."

Boxer: "Quote. Quote, quote, quote." Am I quoting you correctly. Ms. Rice?

Rice: "I resent you using my own words to impugn my integrity"

Boxer: *I'm QUOTING YOU YOU STUPID TOOL!* (unspoken)

....

In the the spirit to which this blog is dedicated, which is simply to love everyone, even our enemies, I want it known that I do love our newly refinished and resurfaced president (600 grit, water sponge) and his staff. And I wish them not only better judgment and clearer thoughts on all of our behalf for the next four years, but also - and far more importantly, I wish for them a newly found, or at least a rediscovered sense of self criticism and critical analyses - perhaps healthily attached to just enough of a sense of shame and doubt to keep them from carrying out any extraordinarily silly actions before they properly think things through.

Also, may the term "a complete moral certainty of one's convictions" be given an automatic four year hiatus as a reason given for any political and/or military decisions made on behalf of this country. This Moratorium may be lifted also when someone is in office who understands the absurdity of the term itself.

Be good to Everyone!

Last Few Days at NorCal
sexitslow
September 12, 2004 @ 11:22 am

I gotta to say.... shit happens all the time. Just when you think you're through with some dilemma, there's another one lurking, ready to give your life a turn. Three years ago... haha.. THREE years ago, i got into a car accident just not being careful and being a newbie drive i was .. i got into an accident on the highway with this girl. Shes now sueing me for over 25000 dollars...for the medical bills shes had to pay. Yea..i feel bad..about gettin her in the car accident with her in the car.. but if she hasnt felt like shit.... or even mentioned anything really in the last 3 years and all the sudden just decides to sue me.... err.. i think there something pretty fishy. God.. i have to go finish community service and now i'll have to handle this civil case after i get done with that. I swear i never have my way with the law. haha.. ALWAYS something.

I have a few days left in norcal (sept 29) and remembering all the good times i had up here it makes it hard to leave. At the same time.. i think i need the break and just to really do something on my own. Yeah... i think ill be back up here in a year because there are many things that socal wont have for me. Having those things in mind.. i just hope they will always be here when i come back.

Hug
semui
January 13, 2005 @ 4:10 am

What a depressing flight back. Back! not home. I hardly consider this place home. Is it jetlag? Is it the salty inflight pretzel snacks still on my breath? Perhaps it's the thought of me being inbound again so shortly. That in 24 hours I'll departure on yet another plane reporting for duty at my gaining unit. What ever it may be, I can't help but to feel down the pooper.

It's 4am, and dead silent. The only light in the room is coming from my laptop screen, radiantly shining back upon my face like a rude awakening. For the split seconds I allow my eyes to blink, I can still envision my friend's merry smiles. My ears are still filled with joyous laughter and giggles. Is there such a thing as enjoying yourself too much?

The memories I gained within the last four weeks will not be traded for anything in the world. It is those memories that will acompany me while I'm roasting under a blazing sun in the middle east. But right now, reminiscing of those times just reminds me of the places I have been and loved. And I realize it is of no comparison to the places I remain and will soon be going.

Yes, I acknowledge the fact that I brought it all upon myself. As a soldier, these are the sacrifices I chose to make when signing my name on the dotted line. And there is nothing I can do but to stick by my decisions. I am still 100% capable, and am prepared to engage upon what ever may lay ahead of me. I do not see myself forcefully coming over my dismal emotions. But I can however, set it aside.

I think I need a hug.

Momz
AzNCoWCoMpAcToR
January 31, 2005 @ 2:01 pm

It's terrible. In all those teen movies, in probably mostly everyone i know, they all hate their parents. Usually its like a "Omg i hate my mom" or a "my mom is such a fucking bitch" or "my mom is a inconsiderate whore" kind of hate.

Often times it's because your mom does questionable things. Alot of girls are uber sensitive about this like... (as quoted by jkim a thousand years ago):

"omg my mom didnt let me go to the mall today. i hate her so much im gonna write a poem"

or a "my mom walked into my room today and started cleaning things.. what a bitch!"

Your parents are the ones who for one: MADE YOU. they made you, they raised you until you were able to be "concious" and make your own decisions. they give you the money you spend (For the most part), they give you food and bedding and most importantly: a house to live in.

We all should respect our parents and love them because they're our parents.

As much as i hate it, i would say that i "hate" my mom too however. For probably the same questionable reasons other people hate their moms. Barging in my room, irritable and high pitched (typical chinese voice. egh our family get togethers are so loud...). She wanders around my room, goes "WHATS THIS DOING HERE?!" "WHATS THAT DOING HERE?!" "PICK THAT UP" for like probably 30 mins. then if i talk back, get a lecture.

I have begun to dread when my mom is home. or car rides alone with her (Deathtrap... and not the good kind). Or really, talking to her about anything. Shes a great mom, shes very talkative, very outgoing but she doesn't listen. that is what bothers me the most. i bet she doesn't remember why i have a bag of cords on the ground, or really, doesn't care why. Even if i'm using it, it apparently is supposed to be stored away even though i need to use it at that moment.

Regardless, i really shouldn't hate or dislike my mom. But that is the natural order of things. we should all respect our mothers.

but god help me. elaine, je.. please. haha

-wes-

ps. "your mom" jokes are dumb. very dumb

Understanding
BiteSizeThis
October 09, 2004 @ 4:31 am

They say that the older you get the closer you become to your mother, because you start to understand and respect them as a woman. I always thought that was a load of crap, until recently. I've been away from home, days on end and at first the absence of my mother didnt affect me at all. I was having a great time being away from lectures and my homelife. I would talk to my mother every so once in a while when she needed to let off some steam or give me a short run down of what she thinks would be the best plan for the next 10 years of my life. I was even convinced that my mother was doing fine without me, until she would start calling me for no reason at all, just to say hi or ask what I was doing and ending the call in "I love you." You would have to understand my mother to comprehend what was going through my head. My crazy Japanese mother is the most independant, stubborn woman I have ever come in contact with. She believes strongly in tough love and not showing your emotions. "I love you" is a phrase that is rare in this mother daughter relationship. This is a woman who has given me only about 30 hugs in my entire life. And now she's calling me out of the blue just to see how I'm doing.... In a sweet, childlike voice? Something is wrong here... Can my mother actually be capable of loneliness?

To be honest, I was starting to miss her a lot. The lectures I didnt so miss so much, but her stories whether they were one of her pathalogical lies I truely enjoy learning from them. What makes me laugh the most is how I have taken so many personality traits from my mother. Im extremly stubborn, so I was quite amused that she admitted that she missed me first. I wouldnt have a problem admitting how much I missed someone but my mother I just dont think I would know how she would react to that sort of a emotional comment. I believe strongly in tough love and I'm not very good with sympathy. I need to work on that... side note. So I have to admit that I respect my mother so much more than I did a month ago. Because she's aging into this incredible human being. She seems to have so many more emotions and she doesnt have a problem opening up to people like she did before. I think when you start to understand your mother or father for that matter, and respect them for the person that they are and the faults that they've made and learned from you really start to understand and respect yourself. Maybe thats just me, but it feels like everytime I learn something new about my mother I learn something new about myself.

"All women become like their mothers. That is their tragedy. No man does. That's his." ~Oscar Wilde, The Importance of Being Earnest, 1895

P.S. Kingdom Hearts <3 Rox

Feeling Weird
wTf_iTz_sOdA
Monday, July 07, 2003 @ 11:10 PM

for some weird reason i'm just feeling empty... i really don't know the reason why... i just wake up sometimes and feel like there's nothing i can do to make it better... i just hope it goes away soon... i'm starting to feel worthless... it just seems like everything is not going the way i would like... everything is just bad timing... =\

Skoo
pHuOnGiE83
May 16, 2004 @ 5:05 pm

OMG!!!! i feel like shit right now...! ahhhhhhhhhhhhh!!! i cant stand it.. i
really cant take the feeling of failing out of school... theres so much shit i
have to take into consideration, im basically failing out of school.. heres
the situation, at the end of this semester i have to get a gpa of better
than 1.50... but i might not be able to do that.. if i dont, i get kicked out,
but if i get better than that.. which i think i might be able to get a 1.70...
but that doesnt take me off academic probation.. so i would take one
class in the summer, and if i get a C or better my gpa will be a 2.00.. and
when i go bak to fall semester ill be off probation, but the thing is.. that
summer class is like 600...!! =(it would be great if i knew i would get
the best of things, but theres always that negative thinking that brings
me down to 0... even if i decide to go to a community college, it will
be hard for me to go bak to a cal state... cuz of the fact that i would be
leaving with a gpa of under a 2.00.. and if i did decide to come back, i
would have to enroll into a special program, which basically eats up a
crap load of money, because i would have to raise my gpa with those
classes, and those classes are 600 each... thats like half of a normal
semester of tuition.. =*(not to mention theres only 1 week of school left,
and then finals week... theres not much of a chance for me to raise my
grades... ahhhhhhhhhhhhhh im going crazy thinking about it.. lately i've
been going out to get away from things, when im out i dont think of this
problem, but once im home alone in my room in the dark... it all comes
back.. its like taking drugs, it goes away for that time, but once its over,
life is back to the way it was before u took the drugs... i know i cant
blame anyone for whats going on with me, its my own fault for being
lazy and not taking school that serious... now im paying for it, and what
a way to learn my lesson... i wish i had a chance to do it all over again...
"if only" ... i just hope to god my gpa is a 1.70 and i get that chance to
take a summer class and raise my gpa.. then ill be on track again... sad
thing is, my parents know NOTHING about my problem, and i dont want
to tell them.. no matter what, i have to hide it.. sighs, this is the point in
my life that i regret the most... i've always been like.. blah i dont care.. i
can fix it.. or it isnt really relavent in my life.. so i never cared much for
anything.. but this is IT.. the thing that can either make or break me... well
yea... thats it.. i dont have to go back to a cal state, but it would be better
for ME... so many ways i can go.. which way is the best.. hell, i dont even

know... and im out of time... schools over, summer is here.. sighs...!! talk about depression... my friends are behind me, want me to do my best, but they cant fix my problem.. all they can do is stand behind me and try to boast me up from being down, take me out, try to have a good time with me.. but they always have their own problems to deal with, and i do feel like im all alone.. not the best feeling in the world.. but i guess its part of life, its what is shaping me as a person... i guess.... =/ who the fuck knows... i dont really care either, wait.. im talking out of anger now.. ok blah.. i gotta get ready and go to church..... bye world....

Pics of My Ass
iTs_MoLiCa_fOoL
January 22, 2005 @ 11:02 pm

karl: so u got ur dress for winter formal yet?

me: yea..but i think im gonna do my own hair and nails

karl: o. so u guys renting a limo?

me: no. prolly just ride in andy's car

karl: oooh

me: i want candy.come with me

walk to vending machine

me: OMG look at my ass.its so hugeeeee

karl: *looks* uh huh..

me: look at it! its liek bigger than _____'s ass. but at least my ass is nicer

karl: hahahah. sureee...

after 5 seconds

karl: u need to take pictures and give me them

me: o.O WTF. im not taking a pic of my ass u perv!

karl: whaaaa??? nononono..i didnt mean u ass..i mean like winter formal me: liar. perv #$%#$%#$%!!!!!!!

hahahahahahahaha!!!! oh karl.. ur such a perv... and an assman.. but its okay.. i still love you.. and i miss you... DORK!!! ur neverrrrrrrrr HERE anymorrrrreeeeeeeee!!1 *sniffle* its funny how u go to my school but i NEVER see you... booo!!! stay longer afterschool.. lol.. its alright... when i get my license.. i'll take you home... NOT!!!! hahaha WALK BITCH!!!! >=)

im so nice <3

You Died at 3:00 p.m.
NewLife
January 31st 2005 @ 11:12 pm

I once heard this..

"not having a father is very unhealthy for someone"

So am I suddenly unhealthy,mentaly,physically?

nah. i highly doubt it. but it still crosses my mind.

Well i ate too much mcdonalds and pizza in one day,ha? unhealthy enough for ya,shrinks and psyhcologists who are part psycho themselves and trying to analyze people,thinking they know everything,like me.

i over analyze thinking i know,too. but i admit,id ont. but id like to think ido,but i am not gunna be like this forever.

Dad,you died at 3:00 p.m. in the ambulance. but id bet you already knew that. I wasnt prepared to hear it. At your funeral, I kept saying "wake up,Wakeup!" "comon lets go now" I was so in shock,i made myself believe you were sleeping all this time.

No one woke ME up,Nor you.

No one bothered to tell me the truth,and i couldnt even tell the truth to myself.

looking back, i was only trying to protect myself,from hurting,and crying.

SOmetimes i am not as strong as people think i am. im sick of being strong,you know how it is dad,when your so close of putting down your shields,and you do. and its like..wow.'

goodnight dad,i think tomorrow is gunna be a good day!

Two Years of Delusion
glenn87
January 29th 2005 @ 11:12 am

For the unforgettable character. What I always wish for was his .... Waiting for messages from him even knowing that he will never initiate. Until when will i stop fabricating. Everytime, when I was waiting for him to answer my call, I will start to tremble with excitements and fear but there was no reason for those. But when he picked up the call, I always lost of topics to talk about, or had call during the wrong time. The same thing happened again, without confessing myself. Maybe even i tell him... He will never love me. I already knew it. Always knowing it. All are just my fabrications and unrequitted love. He cause my delusion, causing my stupidity... Love? If that is what love is, I will never believed in love ever.

How Can You Live Like That...?
Davidmasaki
January 28th 2005 @ 6:45 pm

I have recently come to a bit of a revelation about the limitations of my own mind that may interest some of you...

We all have flaws in our minds regardless of whoever we may be. I find that despite what i say and do that i do not at all times exhibit these traits in my mind, if i may explain. Supposedly someone in the halls drops their books. I walking by see this and decide to stop and help the unlucky individual. Afterwards i am thanked and the person is on their way. I recieve a warm feeling of satisfaction from aiding another and feel good about myself. Such an action would lead one to believe that i am a good person and try to help others, and for the most part this is true. However, then i find myself laughing at jokes and stories of my friends about people suffering and dying such as dead baby jokes, ex; How can you tell if a baby is dead, anwser, the dog plays with it more. Is this not an incredibly abnormal behavior for one we have classified as a good

71

person to find this a laudable joke? How is it that the suffering of another is able to make me feel light hearted when helping another gave me a feeling of satisfaction? One could argue that both situations are similar in that both involve someone who was adversely affected in some manner by the world around them. The dead baby jokes are about a child getting harmed somehow, that is obvious. The situation where i assisted an individual in the halls is a event where someone had a set back, and i aided them. Without them being screwed over somehow though i would not have been able to help them, so one can argue there i am taking pleasure from the misfourtune of another...however, there are those that say that i am actually taking pleasure it helping another and seeing them suceed to an extent. So the situations could be quite different depending on ones view point.

However i am losing the original intent of my entry and going on a tangent, if i lost you or am losing your interest i am sorry.

i feel that so many values of our society are so vague, so contradictory, so worthless once broken down, all those who feel they live life to a standard that is not their own are in some way hypocritical. There is no way once can adhere to a code to such an extent as to not contradict some value unless the code in itself permitts contradiction, and then in which case, what the hell?! that's stupid as all hell! ahh...

yeah, my rants....gotta love em

we can only live life well to our own standards, with so many changes in life, so many conflicts, it is rather difficult to live with a stern set of ideals, and in which case is that really living? Do humans not desire freedom above all else? Do they not claim life is worthless without it? When living by these codes, you are restraining yourself, hindering your freedom, hence how can you truly live? By living by your own set of ideals that arn't handed to you by some other person, you can really apply to your life. You can really decide when something matters and when it doesn't rather than jsut have blanket statements as most creeds do...I feel as though this entry is becoming an attack on religion in some fashion.... Huz zah! well yeah, i'l stop now since i feel as though i'm losing ppl.

Btw, if you liked this rambling, let me know, i'll write more often

Turn Around Life
dazedandpuffy
January 5th 2005 @ 8:42 pm

Have any of you ever had a compleat relization in life?I moment where you look back on everything you've done wrong.Well I had one of thouse moments.I couldnt get myself up for school this morning.I had no energy or will to see daylight.My mom had to unscrew my door knob just to see if I was still alive.

I had to do Somthing about all this sadness.First of all,No more zoloft. Second,Tell everything to my therypst,Nomore secreats.I cant spend my life thinking things will get better on there own.Sure somtimes they might,But this time I had to do somthing about it on my own.Somtimes you just have to sink to the bottom befor you can swim back to the top.

Cause you know im real.

Stray Thoughts
goethe
January 4th 2005 @ 12:55

Everything is falling apart at one o'clock in the afternoon. I am having a bad headache. I left some important things at Habagat and i hope its still there when i get back later after work. I like the place and the people there.[[[Drunk and noisy last night.]]] Life is slow now. I know i must resurrect my poetry again. its been a long time since i've written its almost a stranger to me now. Smoked half a stick of cigarette today but who knows later when night comes. Where am i?

Restless
mulder
January 3rd 2005 @ 5:42 pm

Do you know how it is? When you just can't sit, or lie still?

Even when you're dog tired, even when you've had a whole day of work, and your body do wants a rest, you can get restless.

It's the brain's fault really. Thoughts run after each other, colliding into one another, never resting, never stopping.

Have you ever really tried to clear your mind? I mean really clear it, from thought, color, image, sound, everything. If you do, you'll find it next to impossible. Even meditation uses a focus object in order to occur.

It may be a sound, breathing, a color, or an image, but you have to anchor your brain to something.

Ever wondered what would happen if you could really empty your mind? I read somewhere that when you could reach that goal, you'll reach a new level of existence, a new sphere of consciousness.

Have you ever felt enlightened? what do you make of that concept - enlightenment?

In accordance with the prophecy!

Let Me Tell You About My Day...
Brutal SyF
August 14th 2004 @ 4:20 pm

Shitty.

Let Me Be Loved
awake
Decemeber 31st 2004 @ 10:44 pm

PARTY TIME TONIGHT!

Id sacrifice all money and materials for love.

And my new years goals

-to not have goals for the next new year

- let more things out

- Learn People And Myself

- Not to be quick to assuming.

-TRY.

thats pretty much it. i go tot let myself have the ability to do things out of my control,life gets a little bit too tense unless you get a little bit crazy,and laugh at the corniest jokes,and spend money without a cause and not worrying whats in the bank. So today..im going to spend money.. and not worry why i did or how,im just going to. im going to laugh at the stupidest things,because sometimes its so dumb it's funny.

seriousness= a no no.

Life is an Experience
jazzyhaze
January 6th 2005 @ 9:04 am

Life is an experience, juz like an interaction between an author and the reader. You noe, like reading a book, you get to see and feel wat the author is trying to tell you? It's the same with life. : Reading is an experience, life too...

Juz that life is more complicated, with more interactions with thousands of different people. Whether it turns out fine or fantastic or bad depends on the situation and the people involved.

Looking back the past year, it had been tough. Coming to terms with loving a guy who may or may not (I dun haf the courage to ask and the feeling he gives me differs all the time. Sometimes I feel loved, sometimes, I feel that he is trying too hard) love me. Trying to catch up with school work. Planning for graduation. Making new friends. Keeping old ones. Breaking away from family, being independent.

It hasnt been easy but who says life is? : No one at all. Im playing the lead role here. I can change the way it is. But Im not.

For the time being I dunno how to. Maybe inside me, I dun wana change anything. Or maybe there are juz too many things to change and I dunno where to start. I cannot run away from my responsibilities. I haf to face it. But now, juz lemme indulge——wallowing in my own pitifulness....

To see?? To Notice??? The Same Thing??
mitchdolittle
January 6th 2005 @ 11:49 am

To see???To notice??? The same thing?

It is funny how some event that seems insignificant and mundane on the surface can start a train of thought that can't be stopped until it is thought thru until the end. Yesterday I was entering the Mall near where I live, the same entrance that I have been taking for years but this time something happen that made me pause. Like I already said what made me pause was unimportant on the surface but had an affect on my inner life. I simply noticed the ceiling over the food court when I entered the door, a ceiling I am sure I have "seen" many times before but never really "noticed". I guess the difference had to do with the light as it came thru one of the sky lights, the light grabbed me, I looked up and thought the sky light beautiful and from there noticed the rest of the ceiling. I suppose in the past I must have looked, seen and then forgot; did not notice anything to grab my attention and then open myself up to what the ceiling had to show me.

This led me to consider how I "see" and "notice" the "others" in my life. I suppose I get comfortable with seeing some of my friends and acquaintances in a "certain way", sort of figured out and boxed in so to speak. Not necessarily in a negative or a bad way but just "seeing" and experiencing but not really taking "notice" of them.

I have found that self-knowledge; the deeper it is, leads to a greater understanding of others. Self- knowledge leads to a deepening ability to have empathy for others since I have the same problems; or could easily have them if I allowed myself to take a certain path. In other words the problems, that others get them selves into is not something strange to me. However this can only go so far since we all have inner depths, needs and assumptions that can only be made known by communicating. I have had friends that I have know for thirty years who one day will make a simple statement that will force me to revaluate my understanding of who they are, this leads to a deeper appreciation of them most of the time, but not always of course.

Speaking up is one way for "another" in my life to shine a light in my eye so that I will notice the one doing the shining, in a more intense way instead of them being a sort of predictable backdrop in my life. To see someone in a different light can be uncomfortable until a readjustment is made but it is well worth the effort. When I speak up in a new way to my friends they are also forced to see me in a new light, they may get angry about it, or wish that I never said anything.....none the less they have to rearrange their ideas about me. Of course if they don't want to do that it can cause the relationship to end. No friendship comes with a guarantee that it will survive.

A friendship can only deepen as we face one crisis after another and work through it. We are not static "beings" but constantly growing and evolving, at least in our inner selves. It takes courage to allow what we are becoming out for others to see. Nothing can be gained without courage. Something that I don't always have......like I said before I am after all talking to myself and bringing my readers along for the ride so to speak.

Even in little things it can be important to speak up. I don't think people for instance want to take advantage of others. It is just that those who feel that they are being "used" won't let it be known. How can someone change how they treat you unless you let them know how they are being experienced? I have been brought to task by friends who let me know that certain actions cause them anger or hurt. Most of the time these statements are fair and a good dialogue can lead to some sort of understanding on both sides, along with both sides understanding each other on a deeper level. I don't understand how people can think relationships can thrive if no real communication is present.

I am happy go lucky clown on the outside, I can easily make people laugh and give them the attention that they need. I love people but am cautious who I show my deeper inner self to. I find women easier to talk to in this regard, with men a little harder; the language does not flow as easy with men as it does with women. Carl Jung stated that women show a man his soul, so perhaps talking with women is really getting in touch with my soul. Perhaps men do the same thing for women. I do know that if I find it easy to talk with intelligent women on a deep level and they (or at least some) find it easy to talk with me that way also.

Peace

Mitch

Tim's
thisisnotablog
Febuary 1st 2005 @ 8:35 pm

wow, the random title for today just reminded me of this kid i knew from one of my MANY old schools... this was one of the three middle schools i've gone to... his name was tim, and he was in band as i was. now one day after lunch (when band was) he came in late, and hit excuse was "I fell and slid into a wall and got a concusion.... it hurt..." *limps over to chair* *plops down* "HI JUSTIN!" THE END.... that was useless...

so...

the layout and happenings of my day...

homeroom... fuck you miss hoover.

band... *hits head on table* LOOK, MY HEAD AND INSTRUMENT! sorry.....

history... i wrote a note to gail that had like four sheets of paper and only the one in the middle had anything on it... it said "hi gail" in very little letters! it's funny to see erika trying to dodge Sebatians smell by leaning towards ben...

language arts... damn substitute... "everyone, this is a group activity!" *slids away from group*

science... "fossils"

lunch... iowejreioghnauiobguievsn

math... fuck you miss hoover

spanish... "hola, you habla un poquito espanol.. no hay perfecto...

OH OH OH! sometime during the day, me and alek who made our own world desided him and i are god! and adam the person who joined after is jesus! and in our world me and alek have beards! WOOT!

i've got crazy friends....

Gold Medals and Monkey Slippers
billlyryan
January 16th 2005 @ 12:25 am

It's icy out. Its cold and icy and windy. I'm out of Dr Pepper or soda of any kind. I'm on my last roll of toilet paper and yesterday evening I started my regime of 8 glasses of water a day.

I'm reading a surprisingly good book right now. I went to breakfast at the Cadillac this morning and skated my way home and took a nap. I woke up about an hour ago after four hours. I had a dream that I was asked what I wanted to drink and I said "all the Seven-Up in the world."

I'm leaving for Australia in March and I think I'm more excited about this band-aid on my finger. Yesterday I went to Powells Books to sell half of my books and coming down the stairs from the parking lot, I scraped my finger on the handrail so bad that it bled for half an hour. I got a band-aid from the book buyer and 71 dollars. Today I put a fresh one on and didn't realise until later that it's on my finger absolutely perfectly. I managed to line up each side perfectly so that my knuckle bends and the fabric stretches. It fits like a sleeve.

I found this gold medal I won when I was eleven for throwing a base ball 129 feet, today. I've been wearing it around and thanking "all the people who've made this dream possible." I have a pair of monkey slippers that wiggle when I walk, and a pair of old linen pants with paint from some pieces I've worked on, an old Harvard T-shirt and a pink hat.

Next to my gold medal I found an old journal I kept when I came across country. I was coming through New Mexico and we were stopped at a restraurant. I don't know who I was writing to but this one sentence was in bold and written so hard I could see the impression on the next page: "There is a place in New Mexico where the river runs red from the clay and the grass is so green, that if it were the sea, its depths would match your eyes."

I'm still wearing the gold medal right now. And it's beginning to rain outside my window.

Falling From Grace
FinalyFree
January 24th 2005 @ 5:25 am

I had a great weekend in the Mountains with the kids! I had fears it would turn into a 3-ring circus, but I'm happy to report it went off without incident. For this I am both thankful and relieved. On Saturday evening we were making our way back to the hotel from a rushed shopping trip when it began to snow! The beautiful big icy flakes excited us all but for me it triggered many fears. I am perhaps on of the least coordinated creatures able to walk upright on the face of the Earth. I trip over thin air! I began to imagine all sorts of horrid falls as we made our way around the narrow, winding road. These fears are well founded as I have had many a good fall in my 39 years...

One of the most memorable was about 11 years ago. It was winter time and I had made a late night trip to the grocery for among other things a gallon of milk. Our house had no back entrance, you had to park on the street in front then walk up two series of steps. The second set were connected to the house. They were wooden and open underneath. Just as I reached for the front door the gallon of milk slipped out of my hand bursting open. After a few choice words I got some hot water in my mop bucket and half-asssed washed it off the porch and steps. I went to sleep shortly thereafter not thinking of the milk. The next morning my routine went as usual, after getting my daughter dressed for school and trying to force feed her breakfast I went out to start the car. The icy wind startled me as I opened the front door. My bedroom was right off the porch and my ex husband was still asleep after working overtime the night before. I never gave a thought to the water/milk mixture from the night before until my left foot hit that first step. The next thing I saw was the sky above me and the ice covered steps below. I fell for what seemed like an hour. It happened so fast I don't think I even screamed. That was probably a good thing since the shear impact of my body on those old steps made enough noise. I landed on all fours hard against the concrete pad at the bottom. As I gathered my thoughts and my dignity a city worker stopped in front of my house to see if I was ok. Apparently he'd seen the whole thing as he was driving by. Fantastic, the horror of me bouncing down those steps braless in an old ratty pair of sweatpants was now emblazoned in the mind of a man named Bart. Just then my front door flew open and my ex was standing there in his underwear and he said "What the hell are you trying to do? Wake up the whole *&!$%^! neighborhood?" Thank God he did that, me standing there explaining to Bart I was ok wasn't humiliating enough, luckily the 'Boy Wonder' swoops in and adds insult to injury! I wish I could say that was the end of the story...

I took my daughter to school, kissed her goodbye and promised her I'd see her in a couple of hours to eat lunch with her. It was Parents Day and my attendance was mandatory. I went back home and realized I hadn't broken anything in the fall but the soreness had already began to sit in. My son was still asleep so I figured I might as well nap for a bit until he got up. About an hour later I heard him in his crib, as I slowly opened my eyes I knew I just didn't feel 'right'. I didn't realize how not right I felt until I tried to get up. My back, legs and arms were so sore I could barely move them. I went to the bathroom, pulled up my shirt and was frightened by what I saw. My entire back, butt and thighs were already turning a yellowish, greenish, purple color. I was one solid bruise. I wasn't sure I didn't have broken bones but at the moment I didn't have time to attend to them. I had to be at the school in an hour and a half and before I could do that I had to dress and feed the baby and make myself presentable.

When I got to the school it took forever to unload the stroller and make my way into the school. I was very involved as a room mother and PTA officer so there were people to 'meet and great' the minute I walked in. Every breath I drew made me cringe. I'd never even thought about having to 'sit' down to eat with Jade! How in the heck was I going to do that? At that moment I had a horrible flashback to the previous school year when an elderly woman attending 'Grandparents Day' had slipped while trying to get up from the small picnic-table type accomodations. I'm sure alot of you have seen these death traps for adults? The little round seats are attached to the tables by a series of metal bars. This poor woman had lost her footing while trying to get up, slipped and became lodged under the table. The rescue squad had to come and use the 'jaws of life' to free her from the lunchroom labyrinth! I was mortified for her as I was now mortified for myself. I debated about not even attempting to crouch down to eat, but Jade came up to me beaming, grabbed my hand and at that point I knew I had no other choice. I was lucky enough to get an end seat because I had a sibling in a stroller. To this day I have no idea what we had for lunch nor what any of the table discussion was about, what I do remember is the gut-wrenching pain I was in! But even moreso was my mounting fear of becoming yet another victim pinned under that table. I still remember the looks of bewilderment in the children's faces as the poor woman laid helplessly on the floor. I was picturing the number of therapist visits I'd have to attend to relieve my daughters anxiety of eating in the lunchroom after the table ate her Mother! Finally I pulled myself together just in time for the bell, I kissed Jade goodbye while still sitting firmly in my seat. All of the children had left and the sweet cafeteria workers were starting to clean the tables for the next group. The head cafeteria lady knew me pretty well and came over to ask if I was ok. After telling her of the morning's events she slipped her hand under my arm and helped me ease myself up. What a precious woman, I think maybe she'd fallen from grace before too. I hobbled my way home, put Jacob down for his nap, grabbed the heating pad and headed for the sofa.

It took several weeks to work all the soreness out. The bruises went from bad to worse. I looked like I'd been in a terrible car wreck. I showed my backside to more people than I ever had before in an effort to expose my clumsiness, and well, honestly to get their opinion of should I seek medical attention or not. I choose not to. I would monitor the color changes every day and finally decided that while I did look like a punching bag I wasn't seriously injured. To this day I freak out at the thought of walking on icy surfaces, hence my high anxiety this weekend in the potentially bad weather!

I come from a long line of 'fallers' and have passed the gene onto my kids. My son was playing with a balloon in his Dad's living room, just tossing it back and forth with a friend. He dove for the balloon and smashed his hand into the bottom of the sofa. Ya it swelled up, ya he complained alot, but it didn't even bruise. The next day when he was still complaining I took him to the Peditrician, she was a little worried and sent us over for x-rays, it turned out he'd broken a bone in his hand! The torch has been passed.

While I was excited to see the snowy stuff this weekend I too saw the potential for bruising! I've often joked I wouldn't be able to survive in a region that saw alot of snow and ice! Do any of you readers have the 'faller gene'? If so I wanna hear about it! And Bart if you're reading this you could give the other readers a little insight on what wittnessing a spectacle like me falling was! Or if any of you have seen other 'fallers' in action...share with us :-)

Whatta Bitch
PhishePi
Febuary 1st 2005 @ 6:23 pm

Thanks for the encouraging comments. I got two whole ones, whoppee! No seriously thanks. I just get frustrated with them cuase this happens all the time.

I think the people at school think I'm a bitch. I heard someone today saying 'Ain't she a bitch' (we live in kentucky, so you hear the ain't word alot). I'm not really a bitch, I just can't stand some types of people,

1. People who act like morons

2. People who don't act their age

3. Fakers

Can't stand them, and this person was all three. So maybe I was a little rude to her, so sue me.

I can't wait until highschool is over.

-The Bitchy Phishe Pi

This School SUCKS!!!
Brit4387
January 31st 2005 @ 12:13 pm

Are school is fucking gay, every website most students go to they block. They blocked xanga from us so we couldn't use that and all it was was something just like this that's what i don't understand. They are only allowing us to pretty much just do school work on here. But, what sucks is that i have so many blow off classes cause it's my senior year so now half the time i have nothing to do, cause like the teachers are playing cards or not really doing much! But whatever, i only have 3 months, and 2 weeks left of this fuckin high school and all the drama bullshit that's a waste of time if you ask me! I hate when people walk around and pretend that there not a drama queen when you know they are, or they sit there and say i'm done being a drama queen when you know there not. Are school is really bad about that i mean you can be walking down the hall and you hear someone telling someone about somebody else, or even who's pregnant and who's not or who did who. WHO CARES, it's there business i mean i can understand if it directly affects you but if it doesn't then stay the fuck out of it. What also bugs me is that when people think there so much better than you, and they ALWAYS get voted for homecoming queen or prom queen cause it's pretty much a popularity vote. I hate how students get favored i mean they want us to be treated equal and to learn to respect and help one another but then again some students get away with alot more then others. Every teacher has their favorite and he may say OH NO i don't favor my students but you know they do. One last thing is that people need to stop talking behind eachother back and if you have a problem with someone then take it up with them don't be a pussy and hide it and never say anything to them. Sorry that this is so long i just had to get some things out i mean there is still alot more but too much to type right now! Sorry if this was so boring to read. ~Brittany~

The Phone Call
Jos1221
January 17th 2005 @ 9:42 pm

As a young teen in the Virgin Islands, there was not much to do for fun. I was kept in a very short and tight leash by my grandmother. At the time,

I was also a member of a cult church which pretty much controlled my every move. Yes, I was BORED!

For fun, I entered my name and address in a popular magazine for penpals. Within a matter of weeks, I was receiving tons of mail. Desperate for friends and a taste for other people's lifestyles, I answered each and every one of them.

That is how I met Iris. Iris was a young girl who was also bored and looking for friends. We immediately hit it off and we wrote to each other for about five years straight. She lived in Puerto Rico. So close, yet so far away as I had no means of meeting her in person.

Life happened. We both moved away from our homes and eventually got married and had kids. We lost touch for about two years until I received a letter from her at my current address. Elated, I responded and we are still penpals. This may sound odd to some as email has replaced the personal touch of a hand-written letter.

We had each other's telephone numbers, but oddly enough, we never called one another. We would just write. Imagine my surprise when I received a phone call on my cell from a number I did not recognize. I answered the phone and gasp! it was Iris. To hear her voice on the other end was exhilirating. My friend, my pen friend, for over ten years!

There was so much I wanted to say. . .

unfortunately, we got cut off because I entered an elevator!

Religion Has Become a Coverup
snoopy007
January 17th 2005 @ 8:01 am

Ive been reading religious blogs and now I want to make my own...I used to be a christian.. I read the bible and tried to not cus and all that jazz.. The bible says that it is harder to get into heaven then it is to fit a horse through the head of a needle.. (dont think they actually say horse but something along those lines) We are supposed to try and be good so we can get into heaven,, It doesnt seem worth it to me to give up " the fun sins of life" when no matter how hard u try ur probably going to hell.. When I was a christian I didnt feel all rejoiced and good and wonderful, I felt like it was hard..Yea everything worth having is worth working for..but what if this doesnt even exsist? What if its just a big scam and we just die and thats it.. A lot of christians arent even real christians ne way ..People use religion to blame for their sins and misfortunes.. religion merely gives people something to believe in and something to justify what goes on in the world.. Youre not going to ever justify the world, shit happens and you move on.. It gives people a way to make themselves feel better for doing shitty things..theyll do crap and then ask for forgiveness and everything is ok..umn.. no its not.. and God tells you to put him first to put him above everything, your own life, ur parents.. Why would you love him more than yourself or your parents..why cant you love them equally? Why does he have to be above everything.?.yea hes god but is he just on a power trip?? and hes so great and nice but look at the shit he did to his son when it obviously doesnt work..its still hard as everything to get into heaven but yet the point of his son going through all of that was supposed to be to forgive us of our sins so we can get into heaven or at least have a good chance..Why does god sit back and let things like wars happen.? Then someone would respond god gave us free will..god didnt give us free will we just rebelled ... but if hes so great and wants everything to be so great then y doesnt he stop crap like that? then maybe people would believe in him..But then there is the argument that he wants us to choose him..well if u ask me god is being kind of picky..and what if you dont even believe in that ? what if ur jewish is he going to send all the native americans all the buddhists all the jews to hell?? I dont know.. im kind of confused on some issues..im still trying to figure things out..but for right now i think the closest thing i am is agnostic..ne way have fun reading this...Oh I thought of something else, youre supposed to be happier when u believe in god and all that jazz..Well i know devil worshipers who are very happy..you create ur own happieness..I dont feel ne different or think life is ne different now then it was when i was a christian...And if god did ever make peoples life crappy to those who dont believe in him then thats actually pretty evil and sacreligious and not very godlike .. just a thought..and thats the last one.. so have a great day people

I Dunno
encrptyer
January 31, 2005 @ 11:06 pm

i dunno.......damn

i feel so empty again, i don't know why, but i just do, it's like something's been ripped out of me. for a while i felt really normal, then i lost it again.

i don't know, it might be because i haven't talked to grace or something, or maybe the emptiness has been there, only i've ignored it with the talent show stuff. i honestly don't know, i just feel like i'm empty inside and that i'm alone. like i'm by myself and it will stay that way. i hate being alone, honestly, i can't stand it, even though i do alot of activities that are individual, or i do plenty of them that concern other people, i still feel really alone. god i hate this feeling........

Office Dilemma
gfak40
January 17th 2005 @ 8:42 pm

Last Monday I slipped while walking into work from the parking lot. It was icy, but not too bad. It really caught me by surprise. Falling is so comical at times. One minute you're strutting along in your Dockers and la-ti-da shoes with the traction sole. Next thing you know you're sliding down a flight of stairs, body parts and office supplies flailing and flying everywhere.

In this case these were cement stairs…seven of the suckers…all with a little bit of ice right on the lip. In itself that wasn't so bad because there's a hand rail, and as soon as I began to slip I instinctively reached out for it.

Now, you gotta admit that there are times when you just *know* God is a practical joker. Either that or He simply enjoys humbling a few of us once in a while. Like this time, because the handrail was covered in more ice than the stairs. I'm not talking a small patch here and there. I'm talking a perfectly smooth, perfectly formed layer of the stuff that covered the entire rail…even the underside.

Grabbing the rail simply added a little more velocity to my impending fate. I slid from stair to stair as my hand glided effortlessly along the rail. About the third step or so, ass met concrete. And on steps four through seven as well, getting more and more acquainted with each other as I went.

My gluteus maximus slid off the last step and ground to a halt on the walkway. I sat there for a moment, reflecting upon the joy I feel ending my well-deserved weekend by driving to work, and falling on my ass. I'm amazed sometimes I don't get up and go straight back home. Or to a bar.

I got up and assessed the damage. No broken bones. No head injuries. My back was OK. "Damn…no LAWSUIT!" I carefully went to the entrance, found the bag of salt, and walked a few cupfuls back to the Stairs From Hell. At least people after me would have a better chance. I also notified building maintenance, but as it turns out they were told about it ten minutes ago. So much for our big-ass Safety initiative.

Speaking of which, I have to laugh at our Safety thing here at work. They make such a big deal out of it, even for us office schleps. Makes me wonder how many people go home on disability for paper cuts. I wonder if I can claim "work related stress" because they don't stock my favorite tea?

The thing is they make such a big deal out of it, and yet the focus seems to be on *workplace* injuries. The lasting impression we all get is this – it's OK if you get maimed or killed *GETTING* to work, as long as it doesn't happen on company property! And if you do get hurt on the grounds, do your best to drag your wounded body onto public land. Don't worry – we'll clean up the blood evidence.

Anyway, I walked to my desk, sat down, and immediately felt moisture. Shit. Not only that but I wore black pants that day. I figured black pants and white snow debris probably didn't make a good combination. Thing is, I myself couldn't see the damage. You ever try and look at your own ass? Granted, I knew this guy once who *could* look at his own ass, but that's a story for another day.

I didn't mind if my ass was wet, but I had to know if it had visible marks on it. I went into the men's room. I tried to look in the mirror, but it was too high. Next I tried jumping up and down while I twisted my ass towards the mirror. That's when Greg walked in.

Greg knows me, which is a good thing in this case. I'm not sure how I'd explain to anyone I didn't know why I was jumping up and down in the can. I quickly gave him the rundown of my situation. Then there was an awkward moment of silence as we both realized a potential solution…I simply needed Greg to check out my ass.

I pondered the possibility for a moment. The first problem was this – what do we do if someone else walks in while I've got my back turned to Greg, slightly bent over, jutting my ass out to him? Think about it. There's really no graceful way to exit that situation.

What would be worse is if Greg was in the middle of telling me, "You're ass looks fine to me."

And then me saying "You sure? It feels wet. Is there any white stuff on it?"

And then Greg – "Nope, I think you wiped it all off. No one will ever know."

Me – "Oh good. Man, my ass really took a pounding."

Yeah…it would be pretty damn hard indeed to explain *that* particular conversation.

STOP IN THE NAME OF LOVE
skotmaudlin
Febuary 2nd 2005 @ 8:15 am

Well another year has went by and I have already failed at my new years resolution. Quit smoking! How could I have pick such a difficult challenge in all the possible choices out there? It is said that attempting to kick the cigarette habit is akin to a user trying to drop the heroin habit. I could believe this to be the truth. It takes strong determination as as a constantly reminded plan or strategy. Something that can ultimately be enforced not just by one's self but by those around you. The truth of the matter is that it is just down right impossible to accomplish without the assistance of another. I may have fallen off the wagon once or twice but now that I have someone in my life things will become much easier in my quest to snuff out the cigarette once and for all. Even then it will still be a tough call to heed. Never smoke again? I think not. Chances are, even if I do quit, I will on occasion have that cigarette or two every once and awhile, and I don't think of that as a failure. In case it was missed earlier, I am now with someone. I am so excited, it is like a whole new life is beginning for me. The world has seemingly changed for me and see no problems in me succeeding to change me in this personal way now. It is true what they say about the power of love.

MAKE A MOMENT
Rand
Febuary 1st 2005 @ 6:55 pm

Pick one of the many moments that make up this day, and set it aside for something truly special. Take that one moment, and make it the best you can imagine.

In your one special moment today, let go of every last bit of anger, fear, resentment and sorrow. Fill your moment with hope, love, beauty and joy.

Spend that moment appreciating how truly precious life is. Experience, for a moment, complete, profound and unrestrained joy.

Understand, in that moment, that all you could ever need or want is already available to you. Resolve, in that moment, to fulfill the highest and best of your possibilities.

In one special moment, live a life that is exactly the way you know it should be. For one special moment, be fully and without reservation the person you truly are.

Make yourself a moment filled to the brim with the best of life.

January
stony
January 30th 2005 @ 3:27 pm

Uggh. January. What an all-around crappy month.

Blech.

Hope or Pain
glenn87
January 29th 2005 @ 12:57 pm

What am I expecting? Every time the phone receiver. I'm grasping trembles My heart leaps, But soon I'm let down with a sigh. How many times will I continue to do this? How long am I going to believe the words, "some other day "When it will never come? It's better to forget. Thinking that I just dreamed for a little while, Though I know very well. A miracle

89

will never happen,Though I know very well. I'm sorry I told you abruptly that day

That everything became suddenly unclear. The last time that I saw your tears. Is still clinging to my memory.Why couldn't I believe in you. Right in front of me? You see? It must have been good enough. Only to love what I was loving, Almost clumsily. I wonder if I could leave. Something for you. When time passes by. What will be left for me?

My heart going on wishing for a miracle? Or just a scar?

Poetry...Written By Me of Course
Marijane24
Febuary 1st 2005 7:30 pm

something spoke to me,
it embraced me..
made me feel at home.

I fell asleep for so long,
I woke up just a little late..
but in time to change,
then I left....I went to vent
went to that favorite place I have,
atop the rocks,
a solid fall.

I made it to the top,
opened my eyes just a bit
to let the sun in..
I saw the ocean, waves and all..
mist upon my skin.

Uniforms?! What the Fuck?!
BroKenDreaMs
Friday 01.28.05 [1:09 am]

I'm NOT wearing stupid UNIFORMS! They made our parents do this stupid whore of a survey on rather our school should have uniforms or not. My mom said no, but all the kids that aren't going to our school next year said Yes just because they want to to torchure us people below them. My teacher said that for everyone 1 parent that says no, there's 3 parents saying yes. And for the people coming next year, for every 1 parent saying no, that's 5 saying yes! What the fuck is this?! You can't make us wear this shit! You've already got enough school rules to lay on us! FUCK YOU TOO SCHOOL BOARDS! Comment what you think.. pweez.. Oh! And vote for me at featured blogs, it's right above the tblurt thing. Click that, and then hit vote by my name!

$_$

-Liz

The Real Me (Poem)
Julie666
June 24th 2004 @ 10:39 am

Ok here is a poem i have been writting so let me know what you think.

I dont think that anyone will see what im all about
That anyone ever will,i really doubt
But i dont want them to see the different sides of me
It is hard enough showing them what they already see
You know, keeping up the exterior
While im neglecting the interior
My life is gradually falling apart
I dont want to rebuild it, i wouldnt know where to start
The cuts on my arms is nothing to my fucked up brain
I mentally abuse myself even though it brings me pain
Its just that this has always been my way
I cant change that easily no matter what you say
I keep thinking once fucked up always fucked up right?!?
Because whatever i do i can never win this fight
So now you know that the girl you see,
Is not even close to the real me!!!

Hope you liked it!!

Fear
SoakedByGrace
Febuary 2nd 2005 @ 9:18 pm

Fear is not of God † Those who love God are not supposed to be afraid. So why am I so terrified now? I don't even care who is reading this. This thing in my neck could be something really serious. I'm so so scared, and I feel so alone. I know that I have God, but he's not a human being that you can feel, ya know? I can't physically feel God's arms wrapped around me. I want all of this to just go away. The last month and a half can just go away. I want my parents to stop yelling at me about all this. I want people to stop looking at me like I have the plague. I want more than anything in this world for Iz to call me. His voice alone was comfort for my soul. My biggest fears? That this thing is really serious. That I'm going to get really sick. That I'm just going to wither away and noone is going to notice. Because I wasn't the best daughter. Because I was a sorry girlfriend. Because I wasn't respectful enough to my parents. Because I wasn't affectionate enough. Because noone could seem to accept me with my faults. I'm so afraid. Please, someone notice. Please.

In the; We Are
dreamreality
January 23rd 2005 @ 3:00 am

In the mouth of madness, we are lost;

In the sands of time, we are sinking;

In the land of lust, we are fucked....

Top 10 Scariest Thing
XtreemKos
January 9th 2005 @ 6:49 pm

Im listing the top 10 scaryest things of all times. If you are weak minded,Easly sick,or pregnat, Do not continue.

Scaryest thing #10:

Cheerleaders/preps/jocks- These creatures are hidious and evil! They suck the life out of Punks/goths/and regular people BUT.....they suck up to Teachers and old people making them seem harmless. Nicknamed: The Human Parisites. Beware of them. Stay clear of them. And hate there 'living' guts!

Scaryest thing #9:

Teachers of anysort!- These Creatures also suck the life out of you! They make you do evil things. Like homework and stay for detention (see scaryest thing #. They do this on purpose to make sure you can't go out some where and have fun. They pile it on you like theres no tommorow(thats what some of us think to). Need I go on?

Scaryest thing #8:

Detention-This is the worst place to be. Just thinking about this makes some kids Queasy. I don't know about you guys but at my old school it was worst than being in Prison (not that i'd know how that feels *shifts nervously*actually suprisingly I don't). They set you in a small room. closet size. With a camera (no lie). Theres one chair. You sit there and look at the blank white wall. Its been plastered up. Like someones hit it repeatdly(good idea).*Shivers* Shall we move on?

Scarest thing #7:

Chinese Arithmatic-This is so confusing your head will spin. Literaly.(I should know) Try it some time. Give it to you teacher and watch them explode trying to explain it (........... *evil grin* that a good idea actually *sees her future list* We moved everything up 1 because tachers are now extinced.) Hehehehehe..........*Coughs* Ehhm Sorry about that. Next!

Scaryest thing #6:

Childcare Parents- Half of you are probaly like WTF? But if your like me these should be # 1. They think they own you. They make you stay close to them. They feel like everytime you go somewhere your going to kill someone. ....Nothing more.

Scaryest thing #5:

Brittany Spears/Ashley Simpson/and Boy Bands (Anything relating to these also)- This is the worst. Not only will your ears be sore but you could possibly go deaf. This IS a health Hasard. It has Hypnotiz the

Adults of America and made them tonedeaf. They are like banshees. you can die from there voice.STAND UP AND FIGHT THESE HORRIBLE THINGS! (Don't forget your ear plugs!!!)

Scaryest thing #4:

Losing you skateboard- This has made kids all over the world go insane. If this has happened to you contact 1-800-WhereTheHellIsIt.They can help.

Scaryest thing #3:

Barbies- These plastic machines of tourture have corupted the young girls of the world. They stare at you as you sleep. They are perfect. They can do everything. So why are they evil?........because.....because......*thinks*......Because I said so and this is my blog!

Scaryest thing #2:

Clowns: The mear thought of these makes me want to pull the sheets over my head and hope the bed is waterproof.

Scaryest thing #1:

BEWARE!WARNING!ATTENTION! This is harmfull to your health. If you feel faint or if you have a weak heart DO NOT continue. *Deep Breath and shivers*

Micheal Jackson

AHHHHHHHHHHHHHHHHHHHHHHHH! *Has heart attack and dies.*

Ouch
viciouswhisper
November 30th 2004 @ 9:29 pm

UM. Heather just called me from the hospital. She broke her collarbone falling off an upside down ladder thing in the rain. 10 foot fall. She may be coming home. Not sure yet. This was 2 weeks into training.

Also I guess I should mention she's at one of the top 3 hardest bases, and its the hardest coed base. However, she loves it and is having fun. Except now all she can really do is march.

She isn't able to graduate on time now because of this, so she's at high risk for getting a new different shitty job like a truck driver. No one goes into the army to be a truck driver. I really hope she doesn't get effed over for her job. I really hope so.

sigh
XSatanicAngelX
March 2nd 2004 @ 10:20 pm

Where the hell did I go wrong in life..Everyone got pissed at me....What the fucking hell..I hate my life..It's gay..Why not just die..I'm all alone... Today seriously sucked.....

Girls and a House Warming Party
CrazzzyDucK
January 24th 2005 @ 12:26 am

School's starting in less than a week. It should be fun but it probably wont after all it is school. It's tipping more on the scale of not fun due to a certain factor, the women. There all bunch of manipulitive bitches well not all of them, but none the less i still have to avoid them. I have to aviod them to lower the pain. For every female friend i seem to make at the school they seem to 'want' me or try to fuck up my relationship with Burga. Im not sure if it's her or if its them but my heart belongs to her so i'll believe her over them. I've gone through having a reasonable collection of female friends to none what so ever! I've recently lost Jennifer, it's a big deal but its not. Im so confused, i know i miss her company but i also feel as though i shouldn't feel anything for her. What i do know in my mind is that im hoping she's not too mad at me for getting rid of her as she was a good FRIEND to me.

Speaking of women i'm once again unsure of the status of Pippa and I. By the sounds of things she wants to be friends again and i thought it was all done and finished. I wont take her apologies anymore and i also think that Burga has had a word with her for me to try and get rid of her.

Enough of the boring stuff. We've got new neighbours and i thought we were the new ones to the street. Anyway they had a house warming party and i was invited thinking that the neighbours never come. But i surprissed em and actually went to there party. It was a bunch of 20+ year olds drinking there keg of 45% Whiskey and playing PS2 and other

95

various activities. Overall i had fun and found that it was my sort of party. Pissed one guy off though, but i had the people who are renting the place back me up so it was all good. It was harding breaking into the crowd as such but there was this bunch of 'taken' chicks who accepted me in to there group so i was chillin with them for the first few minutes i dont really know how long it's a party what sort of details you want from me! I was doing the drifting thing after that prob about an hour. Cut my hand in this hour trying to open the bloody VB my mum gave to bring to the party. Twist top my arse! I asked this large dude he tried and then got out his bottle opener. I need to get myself one of those. We were talking for a little while about Uni. A Bachelor of Arts useless degree it's a total bludge i might try it . Or get a mate too just so i can laugh at him. Jokez. Drifted a bit more after that, nearly about to leave out of boredom also out of anger and embaressment over the flaming VB cuts, when them chicks caught me on the way out. They said something like you weren't thinking of leaving were you, i made up some crap that i was just wondering around. They invited me to sit with em i was like eh got nothing better to do. So me being the fool sat down. What a shame i probably wont see em again they were quite nice people to talk too. They ended up gettin up like 10 minutes after i sat down probably didn't expect me to sit down and i followed them in there wonder to see who else was at the party unfortunatly they split up so i lost em found a couple of em and started talking. We were actually talking about me not fitting what a great conversation hey. In the middle of the conversation Alex, and Tom two of the people who live at the place where the party was on at, yeah they came up and took me away from the women i dont know who was happier to end the conversation me or them! Yeah took me and started talking to me about me being the neighbour and neighbours. Supposed there's a hot chick named Anna or anya in one place and another chick in another close to em. Im just like i've only recently moved in here myself and i tried to get em to go knock on her door but they were too chicken!

Yeah im babbeling shit again, well the rest of the party Tom and i got on well as mates, the other Alex well he was more interested in the ladies and whiskey man did he make em strong i ended up watering down the last one he gave me. By watering it down i mean i put more coke in the glass. Yeah im welcome over there place anytime they told me even if they aren't home! They've got a sega set up out the back yard!

Well catch you all later!!!

Sad Story
Taylor
May 15th 2004 @ 8:11 am

....this is a sad story....to me neways....ok i promised myself i would never love again no matter what...i promised..to hell...geuss what...i did.... its shit i think....i love this person so much but i cant have her....o well imm not ment to lov neone neway i hurt them...o well the person who im in love with nows i love them...so that person dont tell...well i g2g bye

GET A JOB
Naale
July 10th 2004 @ 9:03 am

I'm am so sick of being asked for changed by healthy young kids who are just can't be bothered to get a job. Every single street punk out there god damn it. I had a squeegee kid ask me for change, when I said I had none, she said she could hear it... It was my fucking keys she heard... I had a penny change from the solitairy bun I bought myself at the Superstore with my last 30 cents. Just cuz I don't look like I'm in the streets, doesnt' mean that I"m not poor enough to be in the streets... chances are, I have far less money than any of you guys do.. actually, I guarantee that I have less money than you.. even when I have money, it isn't mine I owe so much.

I'm all about giving money and/or food to people that really need it, even though I myself don't have any, but these guys don't need it, they are just avoiding the real world... which is fine... except that really, begging for change? That's just being lazy, if you want to take yourself off of the grid, buy some seeds, an axe and a saw and go take off into the woods, start your own commune or something, but don't ask people for money and then get obnoxious when they don't give you any. I'm quickly at the point where I'm going to tell one of you off because I'm sick of how irate you get... if you need something, fucking work for it, you are all able-bodied kids. The old folks in wheel chairs are a slightly different story... unless they are only faking being in the chair of course, but I"m not passing that kind of judgement.

I was once hanging around with some punks with my friend Ben, and this friend of theirs comes up and was like, "man, I made $30 panhandling for change today." WTF? The guy had a part time job and was begging people for change on the side!

When I lived in Victoria, I saw a couple of girls begging for change... and applying fucking makeup at the same time!!

Grrrrrrrr that makes me so mad.

GET A JOB

In Other News: I did inventory of my cupboards and fridge... this is what I have left:

1 Pkgs Angel Hair Pasta

3 Pkgs Mr. Noodles

2 Sacs of Lipton Cup of Soups

1 Can of Tuna

1 Cups worth of Rice

Sugar

Some Various Teas

Jar of honey that my friend John gave me.. it is half empty

Fridge:

Standard condiments.. Ketchup, Mustard, some Teriyaki

maybe two sandwiches worth of PB

A Week's worth of Coffee

2 Days worth of milk for my coffee

A 2/3 full tub of margarine

And that ladies and gentlemen, is what I have to survive off of.

Near Death Experience
fatalerror
August 7th 2004 @ 1:11 am

today was my day of just finding out the not so great stuff and being in the wrong place at the the wrong time. it started out at my doctors this morning when i found out that they were going to have to take out my toenail on one of my toes because of all the breaking, stubbing, etc. that i have done to it. all good, except for this 'digital blocking' which numbs the toe with electrodes that are stabbed into your foot for the entire procedure. and i have to watch it, wide-awake!

next was my near death experience in a mexican road block gone wrong. driving along with a few of my friends tonight we decided to mexican road block with this one guy. well he just glares at us and starts to speed up and i keep speed with him to keep the block. well he decides to take off and i kept right with him. however there is the problem with the road that we are on, it goes from two lane to one and the speed limit drops from 50 to 30 usual with a cop right at that point. going 80, i entered the area where it drops to one lane and lose sight of the guy i was racing. expecting that he is along side me in his black suv i continue driving straight, into oncomming traffic. well lucky before the next car can reach me, i see the guy, completley on his brake in my rear-view mirror. quickly switching into the other lane i slam on my brakes, lucky to see that their is no cop there to write me a wreckless driving ticket. well this guy just does not want to give up, and ends up tailgating me for like another 3 miles, what an ass. anyway, that was my near death experience for today. nothing else really exciting happened. i was hoping to talk to leelee tonight, because she seems like she needs somebody to talk to, but she was away ::tear:: well, i need to get some sleep to get rid of this accident thoughts, well maybe i will work on my book instead. whatever the case, everyone have fun and i'll ttyal.

as always,

fish ^_^

Cause I Said I Dont Need You Anymore
NewLife
Febuary 2nd 2005 @ 4:50 pm

"Cause i said i dont need you anymore,but then again..I have said some stupid things before."

i have really done alot of thinking. and ive cried alot of tears,but i'm here.

My BestFriend: We've been best friends since little girls. and now were all older. And we still laugh like we were little. ANd it's just one of those friendships you always want to last,and always will.

Ive been thinking alot lately..since ill be leaving in march. I wont be that far from her..ill only be like 15-20 mins away from her. but see,i know we wont keep in touch that much,and i really wouldnt want to anyway. cause im ready to let go,and we both know it. you cant hold onto something so long

i really believe that when I leave..We wont be close as we were. but you know what the weirdest feeling is? is that..Im accepting to it. IM OPENLY ACCEPTING to the fact that,i can find new best friends. i feel guilty for having that feeling,i feel like im trying to get rid of her,but im not! i can look at myself in different persepectives. I just dont get me.

and i feel like..i can really move on...without her...

and that i really..dont need her anymore.

i feel really guilty for saying that. cause we had more good times then bad times. but part of me wants to move on and meet new people.

I dont need her anymore... And..i think it's time for me to move on. and im so wiling to move on. usualy,the case is that you never want to move on with your best friend and you always want to remain like best friends. but honestly..i want to have a clean slate. and start expericing new people,and not the same old crap.

i dont need her anymore,HAH! ifeel so....good when i say that.

HookUp With Guy At Work
poohbeaw
Febuary 3ʳᵈ 2005 @ 6:40 am

soo..

Remember how I extremly liked this guy at my work..

WE HOOKED UP LAST NIGHT!!!!..it was just..a spur of the moment kinda thing. he is amazing though..won't lie about that!!!!!!

This morning..he made me breakfast it was the most sweetest thing everrr!! i felt like i was married to him,and he was my loveeellyy devoted husband! and then later,we went out for chinese! hehe..

i feel so loveeed:) I want to make this something serious and real..and he said he wants to,too! he seemz like hed be a good dad!

Feel So Blue
juliadewi
September 6ᵗʰ 2004 @ 4:09 am

Is it better to be a bad gal than to be a good gal, like me? Everything I do is 'right', I mean, I don't smoke, don't drink alcohol or drugs, never absent without telling the office, etc. But why my life is so damned boring right now? I'm just a pawn of my family. Working everyday. Nobody understands how tired I am. If I stop or rest for a moment, they call me LAZY. Oh, you can imagine my crying heart .

cause I said i dont need you anymore

Night of Disaster
typicalGirlx2
July 25ᵗʰ 2004 @ 2:47 am

Went to the skate park at 6. Lisa, Jamie, and me all waited there for an hour for the crew to show up. We were watching really hot guys BMX, skateboard, and rollerblade. haha. Then we got a call from Mike saying the plans got screwed up so to meet them at the park. Lisa's dad was supposed to pick us up at 10 at the skate park, and there was no way we could wait there for 4 hours. We couldn't call Lisa's mom or dad because they were out to eat. So I called my home twice, and my moms cell twice. No one picked up. So, I called Dad's cell. He wasn't there. Finally, we called Jeremy(sisters x) for Andrew's cell #. He gave it to us. As he gave us the # Lisa, Jamie, and me each had to remember 3 digits of number. Lucky me, I had the last three and forgot them as I dialed. We didn't wanna call back because we didn't wanna be annoying. So I called my mom one last time and she picked up. I told her to pick us up and she did. On the way home, entering the park we saw Mike, Mike, Shaq, and Alex. We all got out of the car and chilled. Mike seemed upset because I wouldn't khim or go by him. When he and Alex went to go get drinks at the store, and Lisa and Jamie went to go find Jeremy and Erick, Shaq and I stayed at the bench. Shaq told me that Mike was telling everyone I liked him and that he was pissed because his friends were flirting with me. At the end we all gave hugs good bye and as me and Mike hugged he asked me if I still liked him and if my answer to his question was a no. I said no, not exactly and he asked if I had talked to Lisa yet, I said no. he said he'd call me tomorrow and we'd hang then, but I have my new born cousins crisining tomorrow and won't be back until 4:30. I really like him, but how will I tell Lisa?

QUOTE OF THE MONTH
JenGen82
January 14, 2005 @ 1:09 am

+ - QUOTE OF THE MONTH - +

Setting: Hiatt, Jimmy and Jen are working out at 24 hr fitness. A girl's chest exposed with the bra covering it.

"Oh! Breasts!" says Hiatt, "I haven't seen those in awhile!"

Jimmy, and Jen started cracking up being unable to finish their current reps.

Awesome night with Jimmy, and Hiatt. We had a great workout and ate some Pho right after. Mmm... Then grab a lot of snackie-poos and rented Harold and Kumar go to White Castle. Balys joined our munchies festivites as well and it ended up a good night. Now, I'm fuckin sleepy, and I'm gonna sleep well for the next 5 hours. Werd.

Pregnant Lactating Nuns and Worse Deviances
madprocess
January 30th 2005 @ 5:48 am

Tonight I went bar hopping with a few of the people I work with. Okay, so it was two bars and it was just my team leader, that I have a crush on. Big whoop.

Anyhow, this is the first (and hopefully last) time I've ever driven when I probably shouldn't have. But that's not the point.

The point is perception.

I like her. It's probably more in a lustful way, because I don't know too much about her, but from what I know ain't terribly pretty. The rational part of my brain says to leave her alone (hell, the rational part of my brain says to stop fucking around on the Internet and get some sleep) while the lonely desparate side of my brain fantasizes and hungers. The fantasies are never sexual. They're always where we're happy and living life to the fullest.

I know this will (should) never be.

I don't know what I want or what I value. Until I know that, there is no way for me to have a healthy relationship with anyone.

Until then I guess it's tBlog and Jim Beam for life.

Which at this rate may be cut short (if I had the balls. But if I had the balls then it wouldn't matter, because I'd have the balls to live my life the way it should be.)

FUCK

High On Life
DONTkickDUCKEES
January 31, 2005 @ 10:20 pm

I'm having such a great day. *shock* I know.. I don't head many entries with that declaration =P but I seriously am in a faaabulous mood. I took a 3 hour nap today since my eyes were desert-dry, and must've been pretty tired, because I sunk into a strange but wonderful dream about a Nazi soldier taking care of Amelie (from the French film).

It was so strange.. and there was this one character who was reading the story from the outside and continually saying that it doesn't matter— Nazis are evil. Naples says I should make it into a story or some Amelie fanfic. I think history class is seriously taking its toll on me..

+

But holy crap, when I'm in a good mood, I babble so much more than I'm not. So this entry is going to be long as hell. Bear with me—it's going to be slightly cheesy, but for me it's a bit soul-rocking, almost like I'm coming to terms with something.

I had a little period of disillusionment a week ago.. and it lasted a week, or maybe a few days, although it felt like a battering eternity. I still don't know what triggered it, but my idealism just crumpled, or maybe it wasn't idealism, but unrealistically high expectations of myself and others, and finally the strain of people unknowingly subverting those expectations just crashed me. I blamed others for not being enough.

So I really plummeted, even skipped a school day to hide in bed, but in retrospect it was worth it. I'm not sure what it was about *this* plummet, but it kinda took the blinder off on a lot of things, and I think I needed that reality dip in some way so that when I came back for air, I'd appreciate what I was breathing so much more.

Watch. This is where it gets warningly cheesy. And as if I've cribbed heavily from Buddhism and self-help books. And they aren't decrees or anything. I don't want to sound preachy. It's just some things that I've privately realized on my own and want to share.

+

Lessons:

a. the grass is not greener on the other side. You're a gardener. Tend to your lawn rather than longingly looking over at others and pestering about where they bought those seeds and what a nice hoe, because god knows you have the ability to make the lawn flower.

b.When you stop expecting things from people, you'll find they're much more receptive because you become more receptive, less judgmental, less critical, less likely to match them up against your unreachable ideals. Change yourself and almost subtly other people will pick up on it.

c. Let go. Engage. Live now so you don't fear the next moment. Your body instinctively knows what to do, what to say. If you fear others' expectations, let go of that too. Nobody's watching. You can do anything.

d. I know incredible people. I can't think of one person in my life who isn't incredible in some way or another, and I find myself really frickin lucky that somehow we managed to be on the same path at the same time. I have incredible friends who I admire and adore and think the world of, and too busy in my self absorption 1/2 the time, I've never ever realized it and have taken so little opportunity to tell them so. I have incredible, incredible family and I am so unbelievably lucky to have the family that I have, the cousins that I have.

e. Whatever you go through now will be worth it in the future. You think they're annoying pests, but they're not—your insecurities, your angst, your little daily trials, they all build you up, build up your self-awareness, your awareness of what it means to be human, your awareness of other people and our now on this planet. So don't regret anything.

Now I feel like this is where I'm supposed to throw up my hands and shout Hallelujah but seriously. Unless it involves collective nekkidness... Il'l refrain.

+

I'm curently on an euphoric high, getting off a phone call with Elissa aka Napoleon. We just had a really interesting conversation. I find really personal conversations awesome cuz I get all intense and into it and, sorry if this is a cliche... it's kinda staggering finding out how many things you never knew. It's funny how much we think is set in stone about the people we're closest (errm this word looks wrong for some reason) to .. and the conclusions we arrive at... but the fact is, everyone is too fluid to ever be just their image or what you think of them or what they want you to see.

And then most of the time people just get pissed when they realized how others don't remain inside their box instead of thinking about how human it all is.

If only more people took the time...

so we were talking about the sort of people who sincerely/genuinely take the time to know someone else. Which is pretty rare. The truth is not many people want to know who other people and if they do outside of ego-stroking or something for their own means no matter how well-intentioned, and it's always in a rather superficial skimming way, where you only get the top bits.

Well.. I have more to say on this but I'm TIRED and I need to sleep.. I want to babble on about my theory about how vulnerability=power :. humanity but I'm probably gonna forget come tomorrow..

+

Elissa's really cool btw. Everyone should bathe and loofah her with compliments till she drowns in the suds. =P Talking to her is so relaxing and easy and unpretentious and she never says shit just to please... not to mention her expertise in bed. WOOT. Honestly.. I'm really frickin lucky to have her as a friend, because god knows how hard it is to find someone to genuinely relate to in high school.... and plus she is so deliciously silly.

your assignment: MENTION ELISSA IN YOUR BLOG ENTRY. Bonus points if you say something nice about her (or evil, it's all the same to me).

and ps. don't feel left out if I don't mention you, there'll be dedications in future entries.

Teacher Edicit
deformedfrogs
January 31, 2005 @ 5:57 PM

hehe...its coming back =P...i know cause a very funny incident told me so...story time!

so, i went to langley today to help out w/ the science teachers, something for fairfax county, and i just talked to some people in the beginning, moved stuff around. Then lunch comes around, i didnt do much, but then, we were just standing around a table, half sitting, the other half standing, and puhlick came by and started talking to us. So, she randomly started talking about growing ears and noses on random parts of your body and then cutting and pasting them into the right place. So we got to the topic of hearing and we were talking about how she has really good hearing. So, puhlick said something along the lines of "well, i can hear guy's voices better from a distance, like, judahs and jeffs voice is easy to distinguish." and so, i just had to say something so i said, "well, its probably because my voice is so sexy."...everyone cracks up, puhlick laughs/*"doh!" expression* and turns around for a sec, then turns back around all serious and stuff...the we started talking about something else and i made some more remarks...not as funny or inappropriate, but yea...

So, the moral of the story is don't say something inappropriate to a married teacher unless you know for sure that she's not gonna kill you... lol...but i think i can joke around w/ most of my teachers...actually, only broad, puhlick, and brocketti...hmm.....oh yea, and dont try to steal ur apchem teacher's keys...i did like 5 times, and i think it pissed her off in the end...lol.....

<X>

Blow Up This Mother Fucker
smokeycat
Febuary 1st 2005 @ 7:26 pm

So I caused a raucus, stirred up shit. I encountered a "recovered" pedophile on the net. Now I am too sensitive some days, but this man has been running rape and trauma survival sites for a few years now. When he told me he sexually abused his step daughter I was shocked. I was confused I shared details down to the sexual names my boyfriend and I gave each other. I feel used and scared and think his real intentions are to feed his ego. To tend to the needy; to tend to the guilt of having made his step daughter so needy. I am not so fucking needy and feeling needy and vunerable in front of such a hypocrit fuck, makes me angry angry angry. I shared how I was sexually abused by a man at age 15; he was 30. I shared how he threatened me with rape and intimidated me into having sex with him. I recounted the shame and guilt but always felt he wasn't really believing or listening. Or maybe it was me who needed to believe myself; or maybe I was accustomed to not thinking I'll be believed or it was always my fault.

I am angry angry angry. I don't care, if you don't believe it hurt. I don't care if you don't feel the pains I have felt because it is the only damn thing that says it's real, it happened. I don't care if you think I am a liar I don't care if you think I am just a whore. This man should not be dispensing advice to anyone. He told me the way he could manipulate a teenager would make me cry.

I challenge every hacker, every good person, every strong person to blow this website off the map. Get rid of this mother fucker.

Here is a poem the guy wrote about molesting his step daughter. [link]

He told me he is just a "softie" like me. Except he's got my bitch out in full effect, and softies don't have sex with children.

So you think I am crazy.
You think I'm a liar.
You think I am an activist.
What a lonely existence to be an activist.
If you only knew what I have seen,
if you only knew what I have felt
then you would understand.
And yes it is lonely.
Let's blow this mother fucker off the map.

Are you in?

M.A...
Godsmack
Febuary 3rd 2005 @ 12:35 am

you intrigue me
with your dark hair
your dark eyes
your dark mind

you fascinate me
with your mind
with your words
with your world

i long for you
lust for you
crave you

i want you to teach me
touch me
discipline me

you make me think...

What a Strange Life.....
darknessfalls99
August 16th 2004 @ 6:10

Why does it seem when things that you want to happen, happen at such awkward times. And for the wrong reasons. Can anyone say they've really experienced "too much of a good thing" and have it turn out wrong?_? Where has the time gone. Time moving fast with me moving slow. For the first time in a long while I've wanted nothing more than peace and quiet. Should I pursue happiness at my expense or others? Should I say what I feel and end up getting hurt or say nothing and slowly die? Where does one turn when all roads lead to a fork?

Hope u like

Death is quite welcome
It's an escape from the pain

But where do I flee
Passion burning deep
Only for the one I loved
Doused by all others
You told me where I'm supposed to stand
But how is it that you can understand
All my pain when my life is a lie
How I always fall no matter how hard I try
That you see the good inside of me, no matter the mask I wear
How is it you make me feel like someone truly cares?
Is it true love I feel for you, or are you playing a simple game
I've been hurt to many times before; no longer will I be without aim
I hope you know that I'll be there to catch you if you should fall
If you need to talk to me, just pick up the phone and call
I hope I live up to all the hype, the fame, the fantasy
I just hope you look into my eyes and see the real side of me
Don't have somebody come between and run some interference
Because the truth is the reality behind the appearance
A friend in trouble, one who's seen so much pain
A brave front, but inside, a pet left in the rain
Trying to act nice, but being torn up inside
The hurt coming to the surface, nowhere to hide
Trouble with family and so called friends

Yet she insists its okay, tries to pretend
I can see how much is gone, having been hurt myself
What can I do, I really want to help
But I'll never know unless you give me a clue
On how to stop the pain, please, tell me what I can do
It's killing me to know that I can't be so near
That I'm so far away and you're so full of fear
My shoulder is light, but my heart so heavy
With my shoulder so dry, I feel so empty
I'd like to do more than I possibly can
I truly want to help, please don't misunderstand
I'll always be here, so long as we're talking
And I'll always try to help, so long as I'm walking
This may not be the worst, but I know it's not the best
Try to cheer up, because being so depressed
Can lead to a road you may not get off of
You're standing on a bridge, you don't need pushed or shoved
So let me help you down, help to make you smile
Make your sadness go away, laugh once in awhile
I know the path is rough, and there are many forks in the road
But please, if you'll let me, I'll help to show you where to go

WTF
chikii
March 27th 2004 @ 11:20 am

I have been so busy lately which is not entirely a bad thing but it is not so much a good thing either. got two jobs and i have an appointment with the school on wednesday

HAVE BEEN SOBER FOR 3 MONTHS yay me i am so proud

i had the biggest craving to go out and party today though but i am doing so good i won't want to fuck all that up

My daughter is teething so bad and my son is getting his two year molars sometimes its like they plan to do things that will drive me to the looney bin at the same time especially shit i have never seen a bunch of kids shit so much in my life...speaking of

I had a nervous brakedown at work on friday because some old man took a dump on the washroom floor and i was the one schedualed to clean it no fucking way i will not i was puking just the sight of it...

thats about all for now oh and umm 1 other thing

i think that is pretty sad so many people use this girls pics lmao atleast use not so popular ones

that is all ciao

It's 1st Time in Blog
bono
March 21st 2004 @ 5:05 pm

hi all. so glad to meet u.
because my country's languge isnt an english,i cant speak english well so u're hard to understand my words.
i wish i learn english more using my blog.
would u mind help me?
i wanna be acquainted with u.

Butterflies To A Child
Discredit
December 3rd 2004 @ 10:44 am

An ambitious child ... full of innocent dreams ... playing in the field with the butterflies a float ... But times have changed ... and dreams have shattered ... once an ambitious child ... now a tortured soul ...

... Where once dreams were ... now rests an emptyness ... full of hatred ... and fear at the same time ... an innocent smile turned into a cold gaze ... lifeless as if death took over ...

... Now the child ... not so innocent no more ... walks the streets ... looking for meaning ... a purpose in life ... that the abuse it receieved ... from a father full of anger took away on that day ...

... When butterflies where a float in the field ...

111

Keep on Trucking
saintmase
March 3rd 2004 @ 12:54 am

fuck me
fuck you
I dont care
oh wait
I'm still breathing
fuck you
fuck me
happy face
socialize
pretend
fuck you
fuck me
fave coke?
fuck pepsi
great conversation
fuck you
fuck me
fuck 'em
still breathing
fuck you, you fucking fuck
keep on trucking

... A Second Spent In Fear ...
addicted2u
Febuary 2nd 2005 @ 10:51 am

I've walked a million miles with you... But nothing felt so real... As holding on to your strong hand and wondering what you feel... I've tried to read your emotions thru with smiles, tears and time ... I've even tried to show you me thru my fucked up little rhymes... But in the time i've spent with you... i realize how you work... and every time i look in your eyes ... there's a second spent in fear...

I don't know how you'll react when i wanna say a word... when i want to share life time experience but your scared i'll flirt or cheat... so i've done my time of waiting... i'll just do it all your way ... cuz i hate the feeling that i get in the second spent in fear...

My Fault
Rawk
January 7th 2005 @ 11:48 am

Back in highschool we all made fun of you ... pushed you around like you were nothing ... we didn't care about you ... nor did we like you ... but looking back at that now ... i sit and wonder ... was it my fault ...

... We teased you every chance we had ... we embarassed you when we could ... you didn't deserve it .. but we didn't care ... you were the school geek ...but now that i'm older .. i look back at it all and wonder if its my fault ...

... You tryed to be our friend .. yet we pushed you around .. used you and took advantage of you ... we treated you like you weren't even real ... but now all i can do is wonder .. was it my fault ...

... Its to late to find out now .. as you took your own life ... but i sit here staring at the wall ... cuz i'm sure it was my fault ...

Some Strange Feelings
bloodmoney
May 13th 2004 @ 1:10 am

I've been really hormonal lately, but that's typical for people my age.

But recently I've also felt, well, unfulfilled.

It's really hard to explain, but although my mind says that I should be concentrating on doing well and getting out of here, my heart says otherwise. At times, my body aches for, well, I really don't know. But deep inside I feel this longing for something, and I really can't explain it.

I don't know if it's physical, emotional or a a mixture of both, but I feel like a puzzle missing a piece. I'll never be complete until I find out what's missing, and I'm no good to anyone in such a condition.

I pray to God every single night that He will give me the strength and guidance to find my place, but I'm not getting anything from it. Sometimes I even feel like praying is pointless. And that really bothers me. I know that some of His greatest gifts are unanswered prayers, but I need to know.

I promised myself and God that I would never contemplate my life in a negative fashion, and although I try with all that is humanly possible, I can feel this part of me that's still connected to the depression I was submitting to at this time last year. I've confessed my sins and been forgiven for thinking about taking my own life, but I feel so isolated and useless.

It rips my heart out to think that my own children will have to grow up in this world that seems to have forgotten how to love. Life is not easy, but no one should have to be subjected to this. No one deserves this kind of pain.

I wish that I couldn't feel at all.

I keep asking God what I'm for,

And he tells me "Gee, I'm not sure..."

Amongst Us
atea
Febuary 12ᵗʰ 2004 @ 3:16 am

liers are amongst us all, we just dont know who they are. even if we think that everything is perfect, there are still lies. if someone told you your bestfriend is lying to you, you dont know if they are lying, or if the person is telling the truth and you best friend is actually lying. either way you dont want to believe it. no matter how true it seems, or how untrue.

haha! enough of that shit. sry, my brain just went loca on me. anyhow ....

How can Something so Abused be so Purrrfect?
pinkfallenangel
January 29ᵗʰ 2005 @ 6:52 am

The reason i'm so happy is that my cat was at the vet for like 5 days and she's like my baby. I love that cat. She's only like a year old so she's still like a kitten. Anyways, she was sick for 2 days straight and we didn't know why she was puking all the time (sorry for saying that) so we took her to the vet and the vet kept her there till today. We were so happy to see her. It was like the the longest 5 days of my freaking life I swear. I missed her soooo much. I don't know what I would do without her.

I actually stole her from someone I knew. They used to treat her like shit. They would throw her against the wall, put her on the ceiling fan and turn it on so she would go flying, blow an airhorn right in her ears, put her head in their mouth when their mouth was full of smoke from a joint, they put her in the fridge, and they were talking about putting her in the microwave or the oven and turning it on so one day I went over and it was just the one guy and the kitten came and fell asleep on my lap and I called my mom to pick me up and I had her in my coat and I showed my mom and told her what they did to her and we brought her home. See I don't know how people could treat an animal like that. I swear she was probably only 3 months old and they were doing this. It makes me cry thinking about it because she is the sweestest animal ever and for someone to do this is unbelievable. I mean what could make people do something like this? Obviously they are fucking selfish and weak because treating animals like shit means that you can't fight a person your size or bigger or smaller so you have to fight something that is smaller then you and that can't fight back. For those people out there that abuse animals *FUCK YOU, YOU PEOPLE DESERVE TO GET TREATED THE WAY YOU TREAT ANIMALS* It hurts me inside to know that there are animals out there getting abused right this second and I can't do anything to stop it. Just think about those poor hopeless creatures getting thrown around because of something they did and their owner not liking it. Like I mean what I say and if I seen someone beating their pet I would knock their teeth out. I'm not an abusive person when I don't have to be but when I have to be then you're fucked. Sorry for swearing but it's the only way to put it. And for people who wear fur *FUCK YOU TO. IF IT WEREN'T FOR YOU THEN SOME OF THE POPULATION OF ANIMALS WOULD STILL EXIST TODAY* How would you people who wear fur like it if I shaved your head and just killed you for the fuck of it just to wear your hair? Obviously you wouldn't like it to much!!!! Some people deserve to be alone in a dark, cold room just to starve to death. Animals don't do anything wrong and some of you seem to think they don't deserve to live but just to let you know, YOU DON'T DESERVE TO LIVE!!!! They were here before us now let them be here longer then us to. I'm not no person for the WWF or anything but I love animals and it hurts me to think people treat them like this. So anyways, on a happier subject I;m hopefully getting a job and moving out on my own. Me and my sister will be moving out pretty soon so that would be fun. I know I can survive on my own but if I get fired or something and have no source of income and have to move back in with my parents then I won't want my family saying that they told me I wasn't able to make it on my own cause I am but jobs are hard to find now. If you don't have an education then you are screwed. So about this guy I like. I don't think he likes me. But how would I know for sure? I can't ask him and i'm sorta scared to find out what he says. I'm gonna meet him and what if he thinks i'm fat or ugly or something? I'm sorta scared and I never get scared over guys. Well we will see what happens. Well I gotta go. Bye.

~*Pink Fallen Angel*~

Ugh
StrawberryFields
Febuary 24th 2004 @ 10:50 pm

My Mom..won't shut up..ugh..

Some stupid, retarded, ignorant little 14 yr. old moron not too far from where I live decided she was gunna run off to NY with this guy she met online. So they issued the Amber Alert and shut down EVERYWHERE, news trucks, police EVERYWHERE. Everyone thought she had run away. Thankfully, they found the little idiot in NY with her cyber boyfriend. At least thats the news right now.

Anyway, as soon as I walked through the door, my mom started grilling me about what I do online, where I go, who I talk to, if I give information out, do I talk to strangers..Etc..And I was honest with her, I told her I DO talk to some people, and go to message boards and crap. Now she is saying she is gunna get someone from my Internet serice to come here and trace all of my internet activities online.

UGH. I'm worried, bc I HAVE been to sites that are dirty, and I HAVE had convos with people I don't know, and I talk about private things, etc. Why do they do this to me?

I'm 19 friggan yrs. old, and they treat me like a baby STILL. They say its bc they love me and they don't want me to get kidnapped, but seriously, why do they do this?

I don't ask about their private things, or track their sex life (ew by the way.)

I have a right to privacy, I think I should be able to make my own choices, decide right from wrong, and experience life.

Don't get me wrong, I have some awesome, cool parents, but I guess theres always things that vex us about each other.

116

Problems Never Stop
woozy
March 6th 2004 @ 12:35 am

Yeh so i called up the modeling people i was put on hold bleh w/e......

me and my sepdad had another hiuge fight

this time for sure he was nt gonna hit me but he did .... hahhha that was unexpected he threw me my shoo wat a hoe it was late night and i had my pajama so i got really pissed and put on a tshirt and pants and i was about to walk out but he didint fuckign let me he was pushing me back and we argues and then he eventually said no the one who has to leave here is me and he starte dpacking up his shit and said he was leavving today and hahaha since hes a fag and hes a shit talker in the morning he tels my mom" i was thinking about this and i want u to put my things back when u get home from work". wat a fuckign pussy! anyways i dont want to stay here i hhonestly dont my mom doesnt understand that tho she just brushes me off when i say i dont want to be here call mya unt no wat does she do she ignores me w/e........ some day she'll learn that i dont wanna be here that day will be......... when i leave from here and sadly enough for her that will be soon....

hmm....... good-day....

Sex in New Orleans
adpierin11
Febuary 4th 2005 @ 1:40 am

Well I found out some more juicy shit. Wow... I really can't believe her.

This past week my two roommates, S and E, and some friends R and K all went to New Orleans to celebrate E turning 21, and to visit some family. E just returned yesterday and tonight we went to go get something to eat. And this is what she told me:

While up in New Orleans, S and R, had sex every night. Hmmm.... this got me thinking.... doesn't S have a boyfriend??? Why yes, yes she does, it's the guy I wanted to date but she went behind my back and they started dating. So once again she cheated on him (we'll call him M). This is so aggravating to me. I'm just waiting for M to find out.

Why would you throw away such a good thing like S and M have for R???? Oh before I forget K and R were suppose to be dating, wow S really thinks about herself now doesn't she? It just really irks me because if I ever went behind someone's back to start dating someone they liked a lot, I would make sure I didn't cheat on him ever. She could have ruined our relationship (lucky for her I am forgiving and understanding), and now I hear K can't even look at S or R. And what I am really wondering is how is R picking up these girls???? God, he's not even cute and he's quite an ass.(There is a pic of him with three other girls down a post or two)

You guys were right maybe I should have said something to M, but it's not my business. Shit, I wish I was never told this crap. Drama always has a way of finding E and then she comes and tells me.....

Well on Sunday we are all heading over to R's house for a Super Bowl party, and R,S,M,K,E and many others will be there drunk. So I'm basically saying that this shit will probably hit the fan on Sunday. But I'm not going to be consoling anyone I am going to be the one drinking and laughing my ass off because I'm not the one who does stupid shit like this....

Yay to me for not being a stupid slut

You Wanna Fight a Pork Chop?
muzak9
January 31st 2005 @ 7:21 pm

Friday night brought my buddy Mark and I an interesting encounter with a very aggressive yet entertaining Portuguese individual. He walked up to us and asked us if we'd like to buy some 'crack'. So Mark's 'tongue in cheek' reply was "No thanks, I heard crack stunts your growth". Seeing that the 'crack dude' wasn't much taller than 5 feet, he took offense to it. He replied "Are you calling me short? You wanna fight a pork chop?" He put up his dukes up and started jumping around like a boxer from the 70's. Then he put his arms around the 2 girls he was with and said "I got hot girls. Look at these girls, I got hot girls! You calling me short?" After laughing in his face as he danced around like a little pansy, he tried to take a couple swings at Mark. His girls were trying to drag him away, but he kept coming back. We got bored of his little dance after a while and jumped in a cab to leave, because he clearly wasn't lucid. I remember driving away in the cab and looking out the window only to see the self proclaimed 'Pork Chop' fighting some other guys on the sidewalk.

The moral to the story, don't do crack.

Bad Trisha...
RiotGirl
January 14th 2005 @ 10:56 am

I'm totally skipping class right now. I just took my math midterm and I'm braindead. Anyway, this has been a bad/good week. Monday sucked because I found out that Justin has a new girlfriend. Of course, I found out from Ashley because Justin's too much of a wimpy prick. As far as he's concerned, he can seriously go to hell. Words can even begin to describe how much I hate him right now...but anyway, it's time to move on with my life. That's where the rest of the week comes in. Me and the girls went to Bob Evan's, and who was our waiter? The cool guy from aerobics! He was really nice, and we left our usual note with our e-mail adresses on it so he could e-mail us. He sounds pretty cool, so...we'll see.

Ok, the Zach situation...I think he's backing off. YAY! I told him that there wasn't any chance of an "us", and I really I hope I didn't hurt his feelings, but he said he was ok with it. Other than that, I found out that there's ANOTHER guy that likes me. Why can't we go back to the days when everything was simple? When boys still had cooties, and the only guy in your life was your dad? I dunno...but anyway, I hope things start to look up soon.

Wow! Go figure!
PyroRaven62888
January 27 2004 @ 7:34 pm

i have so much trouble with men its rediculous! first i find this boy i wanna be with....i loved him, well i found out hes moving this friday! i was crying! well then i found out i liked this boy Austin, i really like him, and i went out with him....then i lost entrest...then i broke up with him and now i want him back......whats whit me?! : maybe one of you know whats up with me.......well i hope!

Raven!

Whats a Dickfor?
Frylock
April 11th 2004 @ 9:45 pm

I remember when someone told me, "There's a dickfor on your head." And I said, "What's a dickfor?" And then everyone laughed. That's when I got my gun.

Who's Tired of Being the Good Guy?
shithouse18
December 23rd 2003 @ 7:28 am

The night was hot, and in the distance was the sun beating down on the gentle city, the City of Angels. Although there were no angels in this dark. and desolate location.

She was young, around 23 and full of life. Her name was Lenne, and she was returning home from the market with a loaf or bread and a small pallet of sugar.

The Devil in the cornor was licking his lips as he passed her at the corner store. He was broad and muscled, and when he walked he left his presence in the mind of all malicious killers. Not even the most evil of souls would try and stop him. He was silent and crude, spitting as he walked.

Her on the other hand was the exact opposite, smiling as she turned the dark corner. With her items curled in her arms as gentle as if it was her only child. She had a suffle, warm, and athletic body. Wondering eyes squinted to see the light from her pert presence. She often hopped and skipped like a nervous girl at weddings.

But the Devil was not amused, he began to smirk and laugh as she passed. She began to pick up speed as the darkness enveloped her into a blistering panic, in which he only grinned.

He began to rip and shred her clothes in the silent ally. She attempted to scream but to no avail, she could not be heard. As the Devil reached into his pocket, he removed the only thing in which to cease her angry screams. The green apple was not just a food but a mamming tool, and he used it to his best delights.

As the screaming subsided he began to think all was well but nothing could prepare him for the large brick she carried in her purse.

As the brick collided with the Devils head he fell uncouncious laying on topside of her aggitated body. She then pushed him off so she could breath easier, and just about that time the police had arrived and took the malicious mastermind in. One policeman turned to the lady and handed her his jacket, "Are you ok, miss?" she then turned around and slammed the brick into his head leaving him motionless on the ground. She smiled and dropped the brick upon the ground, "That was a new dress!"

Darn Economics Teacher
FriedChickenAndBeer
March 14th 2004 @ 1:47 am

I overslept. I slept at 12 midnight and woke up at 5 pm...

I went to my school to get my report card. My grades are high except for one subject, Economics. Pretty shameful huh? Yeah, I wanna kill my teacher... He was beside my adviser while I'm claiming my report card. He's not looking at me so I didn't greet him... I'm angry at him anyway even before I saw my report card. My adviser already told me that I got a line of seven in his subject before the issuance of card. I told my mom about it and she told my godmother, who is my Economics teacher's cousin, about it too. My mom told me that my godmother talked to him about the grade he gave me. She told him that he is the only reason why I wasn't able to go to University of the Philippines (It is one of the most popular and respected school in our country which is said that all the students who are studying there are really smart). He gave me a 77 grade in his subject this last quarter and the university doesn't want to accept me. My teacher asked for my name and then he said that there was no problem about me as a student. I should have asked him to add some points to my grade so that I could enter the university. My godmother told him that the grades have already been submitted and finished so there's nothing he can do. And now, his conscience is killing him! Ahahaha! When I saw him in school at the issuance of card, he's not looking at me! Ahahaha! Oh how I love my godmother! But anyways, I didn't really passed the entrance exam in UP because of my Reading Comprehension. I got high grades in Math, Science and English in my entrance exam in UP. My sister, who is a graduate in UP, said that maybe

I answered the exam hurriedly. *shrugs* I don't know, time is limited. Maybe I'm just too nervous when I took the exam.

After getting my report card I went to University of Santo Tomas to submit the requirements. Yeah, I passed the entrance exam there and I'm taking Computer Science. My mom asked me if I want to take Nursing too so that I could go abroad. She told me that my aunt, who is in US working as a nurse, asked her to make me take Nursing. I'm not that interested in Nursing but I guess it's okay. The problem is I need to shift course so that I could take Nursing. I already wrote ComSci, IT and Advertising as my 1st, 2nd and 3rd choice respectively. I passed Comsci and IT and I'm on waiting list in Advertising. No place for Nursing anymore. After submitting the requirements, the girl who is organizing the files gave us a copy of tuition fees. Heck, 30,000 pesos per semester! My mom told me to get my requirements back and look for another school, jokingly. *breathes deeply* I don't want to study in other schools. UST is my second choice. I already told my mom that if I won't be able to pass UP, I'll study in UST. She wants me to study there too because it is one of the popular school here but yeah, tuition fee is the only problem. We're not rich. My sister is the one paying for my tuition fees. She told me that I should NEVER flunk or else, it's either I'll go to other school or I'll stop schooling. Ehehehe! Yes, that's how important money to us. Damn crisis...

I wonder what my Economics teacher is thinking right now. Ehehe! Serves him right, he's too strick to all his students. Heh~

To Get Away From You
MustangCowgirl
January 24th 2005 @ 12:46 am

There are things that tie me here, that tie me down.
They're suffacating me slowly, and slowly I'll drown.
But I'd prefer to drown here, then somew where else die.
But I'll be going someplace else, though I've covered the truth with my lies.
I've tried to get away, but there's no escape from hell.
I'm out of luck, I've got no deals left to sell.
So in vain I search for the way out, my key to freedom,
But I'm still without hope, I've nothing left to believe in.
I refuse to submit myself to the painful certainty ahead,

I'd prefer to stand and fight then accept that I'll soon be in hell or dead.
I don't deserve this path that's been chosen for me
But there seems no way out, it seems I'll never be free.
I refuse to let my tears flow, to darkness I refuse to go.
So I'll burn everything that ties me to you, that you've tied me to.
And to escape my own fire, I'll die in a death of blue;
For anything is better then you.

beeedoodeeebooo
emma
February 15, 2004 @ 2:50 pm

im so bored.. =.= im listening to adams' songs.. damn bees is really nice! damn u adam! u pig.. lol. yay guitars.. someday i wanna jamm with you piggy.. when i come to kl.. heheh.. i be the singer.. mwahaha.. destroy the song with my horrid witchy voice.. lolx. ok so yeah go check out piggy's site and look for downloads and listen to bees. realy cool music. man im really boerd that i cant even think of what to blog about.. #_#

i wnt to play ragnarok but its too laggy.. gagaga.. i miss my bunny.. i love you baybee.. he's goin to kl soon..next month.. :(and im only goin either this july or next year!! :(i dunno whats gonna happen to us. this is soo wrong.. soo wrong.. but i love him .. im confused with my self.. my life.. the world.. why the world is like this. life isn't fair sometimes.. but no one said life is fair anyway so no blames will be thrown on life. i know its shiit to say i love hm.. but i mean it.. yea u may say.. you have to have all those blablablabala.. to discover love.. yea i've discovered love.. he is love. hey reader, say what u want. i dont care. if you think im just being stupideedoo mushy and am not thinking properly .. and i am just saying i love him but i dont mean it.. oh whatever. fuck.off. coz i know i mean it. i have never felt like this before. nvr have i felt this feeling that i cant really explain.. but im not saying he is the one.. and im also not saying he's not the one. lets just skip that yucky topic on "the one".. so yea.. love destroys me..love conquers me.. ahhh what the fuck!! why am i even talking about this.. so stupid. i guess im just fuckin bored and cant think of anything else to talk about. rite . oh well i better go have a nap.. wait not nap.. "deep sleep"... lol. i only had 2 hours sleep .. i need 5 more.. or maybe 6.. i slept at 5 in the morning justnow.. and woke at 7 in the mornin.. wuahaha.

i miss you friends. i love you friends. i miss you nita. i miss you piggy. i miss you baby. i miss my friends. i love my friends.. ^^

..pieces..
verucassalty
January 29th 2005 @ 1:53 pm

i left my job as a therapist for a good reason.. it was time.. i couldnt do it anymore because i felt myself becoming numb.. burned out.. too much horror in the world.. and no personal outlet to purge it..

i would spend all day at my old job reading about childern being exploited, abused in unfathomable ways.. the sexual preditors that ruined their precious bodies.. the violence that would kill who they were inside and out.. their rage, fears, their acting out.. i would spend all day on the phone asking questions to their families, to the people working with them... asking questions that were my job to ask.. that no one outside of this field could handle.. asking about the details.. because to treat them.. we needed to know..

i absorbed all of this into my soul.. i became plagued with bad dreams.. hatred.. frustration and anger.. and after 5 years..there became a point where i couldnt see any good around me.. and i left. i had too.

i love the job i have now so much... there is positive energy around me all day. i laugh constantly, i mentor those students that need a lil kick in the ass.. i joke with the ones who come to me just to talk and laugh.. i have students that come see me, just cause they like too.. they let me into their lives.. i also have built a good rapport with many who are going through their own struggles... they come to me cause they know i listen.. they feel comfort enough to share.. and even to break down.. and let me help.. last thursday i had two of my students come in to talk about problems in their lives.. they became tearful... and i talked them through.. as hard as it is to see other people in pain.. this is a level i can manage.. this is where i shine in what i do.. cause this will never be as numbing as where my mind has been..

the people i work with are wonderful.. and ive made friends.. good friends there that i love dearly.. im a different person now.. my family and friends see this.. this blog is only pieces of me ..the neurotic side and full of my exploits.. we all have this side.. tho not everyone confronts it.

...balance...
verucassalty
Monday 01.24.05 [2:31 am]

fine. im not gonna lie to myself and say that i like him just for a fuck. we connected. simple as that. (which truely is not so simple at all) justin let go and let me know who he is. i very much felt free to do the same, tho i am still working on it...

fine. fuck me for wanting this. this conversation. this draw.... this whatever the fuck it is...

i still wish more than anything that wayne would stop the fucking bullshit and reach out to me. but he hasnt. and may not.

i cant life life in if's. i really dont want to. not when i love wayne. and i do. he just doesnt love me how i need him to... it rips me apart inside...

i cant do this anymore. the longing for him... 10 seconds away from any other thought.... is of him.

i cant fucking live this way, love is catastrophically imbalanced. this is hell.

Who do we Blog?
shroom
July 3rd 2004 @ 6:03 pm

I've forgotten why I started doing this in the first place.

I haven't updated in ages, I've forgoten I even have an account. That always happens to me everytime I try something new. I lose interest shortly after.

But I should try to keep this up from now, just to keep my mind from caving in on itself.

Tiny little earthquakes are rocking my world.

It feels good to drivel.

Around
InK
March 14th 2004 @ 10:29 am

ho hum... i got an email from logan... his mom finally left the crap heap of a bf she was keeping but logan isnt doing to well... sounds like he is on he verge of an insanly massivly large break down and he cant get a holiday from things... i feel really worried for the poor guy... i hardly get to talk to him now n i dont wanna lose him as a friend either.. i have too few friends..

im sick again it seems lately not eating much but when i do i get sick n cant eat anymore then just small amounts, my doc is a fuck up made an apointment when i was sick march first till the end of march about the 30ths and she could only take me in may around the 9th... it would take me over ayear to get a new one.. wouldnt really be worth that

school is almost over thank god, im skipping alot recently tho... i cant stand it anymore.. im getting tired like last years of HS when i couldnt hardly go to school cus i would run so encredibly low on enrgey i could only last an hour before passing out from being tired... i dunno whats up with that, when i ask my doc she says its nothing tho

i didnt get my project done i thought it was due friday but ppl are telling me its due tomorrow andi donteven have supplies for this thing... im fucked for that so im prolly staying home to finish (buy the stuff i need) it and then just hand it in the next day to his mail box thingy i cant stand how he is making us buy all this crap with 2 - 3 weeks left and its expencive stuff that we wont even use again! ...

BLARG

Basics
ana_bana
August 22, 2004 @ 9:08 PM

I hate Pre Cal, but I love my friends. Here are the basics of the day:

Church

Vomit

Nap

Pre Cal

Nazi parents.

Cards of Life
Long_Day
January 14, 2005 @ 1:16 AM

Sometimes I get a terrible hand of cards in my life. Well, they seem to be terrible. The situation is all wrong, there are roadblocks at every corner and the way I would like to go doesn't seem to be the way I'm allowed to go at the time. I don't know why we make up so many rules for each other to follow, but I know that if we break these made up rules at the wrong time, someone could get hurt. That's why eventually, after the rules have run their length, the time can be right. I'd like for the time to be right, right now, but God directs in the way He directs. Waiting isn't so bad, really; just calmly frustrating. This sense of waiting gives what you are waiting on the time to flourish. One day, because waitings eventual prize becomes so much more worth it, happiness will come from that simplicity.

My hand of cards right now is both good and bad. There are some things I would like to change, but know that now is not the time and others that I'd like to stay where they are. Either way, I know that the change in my cards is for the best. I'm not showing off my full hand yet, but they're there and they're waiting patiently as life deals what is best. What can't happen now will hopefully happen in the near future. I'm 98% sure of it.

My Dad is in Jail
silver_glass
January 24, 2005 @ 8:44 PM

A-FUCKING-GAIN.

what the fuck what the fuck what the fuck what the fuck.

i don't know what to do with this, but i do know that if a single person utters the words "don't worry" or "it will all work out for the best" or "you don't have to let this affect you," i will shoot him/her in the fucking face.

i want someone to talk to me about this and be real for once.

i don't want anyone to feed me bullshit lies that are supposed to make me "feel better."

you want the honest truth? i feel like shit right now. i feel so fucking shitty, and there's not a damn thing anyone can do to make me feel better.

it is impossible to live a life entirely unaffected by this mistakes of my parents. don't tell me you know i can do it unless you've done it yourself. unless your dad has gone to jail more times than you can count on one hand, don't try to talk to me about learning how to take care of myself and become more independent. i am more independent than 99% of the people i know, thanks very much.

i know how to take care of myself; i'm just sick of doing it all the time.

i struggle every single day to become a happy, well-rounded person. i think i'm losing the battle. this is just a hunch.

i don't know, though. i think i could be happy if i were able to move away from here, but i'm beginning to suspect that isn't going to work out for me. i may be able to get some loans, grants, and scholarships, but those aren't going to be able to cover the cost of everything. my parents are going to be expected to contribute something, and to that i say, AHAHAHAHAH.

my dad's in jail, my mom's running around spending all her money on drugs and crazy pills, and debbie has her own two kids to take care of. financial assistance from them? not likely.

i am so afraid i won't be able to leave this mess. please don't tell me everything will work out for the best. that's not what i need to hear right now. it's too vague.

i want someone to tell me that i can still make it to new york or boston.

but i only want you to say it if you really think it's true.

so if you don't, don't bother saying anything at all.

i'll get through this. i always do. and perhaps that is what is most depressing all.

it's not the first time. it won't be the last time. and unless i'm willing to kill myself, there's really not a lot i can do about it.

and i'm not willing to kill myself.

for the record.

i don't know if that makes me stronger or weaker.

because i'll be honest, sometimes i just want to stop breathing.

it's overwhelming.

i just want to know that i'll be ok.

i don't know.

i pray for my family every night. what does that have to do with anything?

i don't know.

i guess i'll keep praying.

I'm Back... I Don't Know Why... But I Got's Lots To Say This Time...
gumbii
Febuary 4th 2005 @ 6:22 am

so my sister got DSL on this computer... OMG it's so fucken awesome... i can't stand it... the internet experience is so awesome...

and i'm going to start hosting on photo bucket... i was using yahoo, but you people keep saying that you can't view the pics... so fuck it... i'm switching back to photo bucket... i'm not going to fix the previous picture post... i'm just going to leave it that... but i'll post pics later... i don't feel like doing all of that shit right now... plus i'm downloading a shitload of pron... wonderfull wonderfull pRon... i didn't have internet access for like two weeks... i was having sick ass withdraws... nasty... i guess i will start on how my day was today... OMG...

so i wake up about 7am today... guess why... my dad came to visit today... OMG i was so fucken frieghtened... i was awake the entire time... but i pretended to be asleep to avoid him... then when it all passed... i took a shower, and went to say hello... he was really calm... so that was cool... then i hit him up becouse i've been having hardcore heartburn the last couple of months... yes months... so he said that he will bring me some really good pills, that make zantax look like certs... awesome... he said that it actually gets rid of ulcers... and i'm pretty sure that i have a ulcer or too... i can't even eat peanut butter without waking up at night choking like an idiot... that shit sux and hurts... and since i got a grill cheese maker the other day, i've been making a grip of peanut butter &

jelly sandwiches and toasting them in there... that is the shit... but i try
not to eat them really late...

so he told me that he will hook it up with the medicine... then i showed
him how to program a universal remote control that he has been having
trouble with... then he left... tan TAN!... lol... anyways... i took off with
agui today becouse he had to go get some business cards today... he
needs them this week, and he's paying a shit load for them... well, that's
what i think... but he said it's a deal... he wants me to design his shit, so
i'm thinking about downloading some torent shit... maybe illistrator, or
macromedia shit... eitherway, i'm going to hook him up sick... well, this
weekend anyways... i'm really supporting agui and all of his efforts... i
don't want him to fail like other people that have tried to open thier own
businesses and companies... agui has alot of heart for this project, and
i don't see him failing like everyone else... plus, he brought up ATG
company, and he could do it again... i want to work for him too... i kind of
hinted him on opening a rice/performance shop, and he really liked that
idea... but it's going to have to wait...

he also needs to get a truck... he's looking for a 97-below hard body
nissan pickup... i don't think that he's going to find one anytime soon,
becouse no one likes to slang them shits becouse they are really good,
and dependable trucks... and if he does come accross one, it ain't going
to be cheap... but that's what he wants... so fuck it... i don't think i'm going
to graduate this program... i'm behind every fucken work experience...
so i'll just take the knowledge that i got, and take it somewhere else...
fuck the police for fucking up my liscence so bad... why did they have to
fuck with the red del sol... why couldn't they pull over someone else that
night... there were like twenty fucken cars that day... assholes... oh well...
so yeah... agui says that he will probably start hireing people in like six
months... i'm going to be the first to apply... he's going to make a shitload
of cash doing this shit... and for sure he's going to be able to afford me...
i'll be happy with minimum wage... lol...

he's also looking for a spot to have a warehouse, and park his truck... i'm
going to checkout some places for him tomarrow... he has an apointment
to do some papper work tomarrow... so i'll do him that paro... i really
really need a job... i remember when i first started blogging, i was setting
some goals for me... yeah fucken right... where the fuck is my dodge
magnum... let's see... in my fucken dreams... man this really sux... i
also need a girlfriend... i got to clean up first... i'm going to cut my hair
tomarrow, and shave... them i'll go look for some pan somewhere... i

need to stop being a faggot, and walk up to some girls at least... yeah... but i get scared... but just like coco told me when i said that i don't have confidence... he said that that is all bullshit... all i have to do is swallow that fear, and get in thier faces... it doesn't matter how you look, it's all about the way you talk, and the impression you leave... i think that is the best advice i've evAr had... better than "punch her in the stomach so it don't leave bruises"...

damn... downloading at 100KB/s is the shizznitizznizzle... OMG DSL where have you been all of my life... the package also came with a wireless modem, so when i fix the laptop, i will get a wireless PCMIA card... yay for me... i also just discovered how to use bittorrent shit... thanks dreamacyde for the info... i also need to come up with another sticker for our carclub... grass said that he will handle all of our stickers... so fuck it... might as well take advantage of that offer... even if grass does have a reputation of never coming thru... but he has come thru a couple of times with me... he got me a shitload of team sol stickers, and yesterday he broaght me some plexiglass... it wasn't the colour, but i'll make good use of it somehow... i'm crafty bitch... i'm really tired, but i want to wait for the download to finish, so i could start another download... fuck keeping them on the hard drive... they are all going on a cd... i think i have a CD-RW somewhere here... i'll use that instead... they are more durable that my sister's memorex disc...

oh... and for the people that don't know how to turn off my wizard... you are retarded... you right click it, and select hide... i don't know how you mac people do it... thier damn mouses don't have right click... how the fuck do you do it then...?? i don't understand... when i use grass's mac i'm super clueless... idiot is me... but it's not my fault... windows interface is much easier to get used to, and that's all i've ever used... besides linux, and soloris... fuck i need to munch on something... i'm getting neaxious... i don't know how to spell that word... lol... bah... fuck it... that's what i get for eating a shitload of dark chocolate this late of night... lol... yummy... vaca got a bag of the dark hershey's nuggets... those are the bestestests... damnit... i just remembered that we have a test this monday for psych class... damn and i've haven't studied or done shit... i don't know how i do it to pass every class that i get... but i'm so damn good at it... lol... OMG... i'm listening to tool again... reflection is the shit...

so yeah... my sister's friends moved in with us... they didn't have anywhere to go... so they came to us, and we are renting them the back house... i guess this makes us some hardcore stereotypical wetback

mexicans... we have...... .. fourteen people living in a... you could say five
bedroom house... lol... that shit is so fucken rediculous... but at least no
one is out in the cold... i rather have a shitload of people living cramped
up in the house, than know that they are suffering somewhere, or going
from hotel, to hotel... that really sux... and they have six kids... they
are awesome kids though... what's fucked up is that i have the biggest
bedroom in the house, and sleep in there by my self... lol... hooray for
me being better than everyone else... i'm so awesome, and such an
asshole... i truelly am the man of the house... you know what...? i forgot
to count two other people that sometimes stay here... so the total is
sixteen... lol...

but yeah... i don't pay anybills, but i'm still the man of the house...
whatever i say goes... i don't try to be an asshole, but people take my
hints like the word of god... i said... fuck my dogs need dog food, and
they go out and fetch a bag of pedigree for me... i didn't ask them to... i
was going to get them food, tomarrow... oh well... fuck it... i say... damn i
should move those huge pots to this side of the yard, and bam... they go
do that... i said... i always wanted to grow suger cane in the backyard...
and i wake up with huge suger cane stalks in my bedroom floor... lol...
and this was like a week ago, i haven't planted them yet... i don't know
where... lol... and the kids listen to me more than thier parents... and
thier parent's love that... they just give me a look, and i calm thier kids
down with a stare... but that's only if they are acting like little assholes... i
hate kids, and i'm a sagitarious... lol... so i'm uber-asshole... yay...! i love
punishing other people's children... i had to make one of them pick up
buddha's shit in the back yard becouse he got suspended for fighting at
school...

they are also scared that i will hand cuff them to a tree in the scary
dark back yard... lol... that's the best... what a dick... oh well... whatever
works... man the download hasn't finished... it's been like 40 minutes
allready... but i'm downloading 217mb... so i say if i get it done in an hour,
i did good...

gumbii.....

pretty hardcore weekend... six pichers of beer, sports bar, 9 twelve
backs, 4 idiots, one baby shower, one day sobering... equals one fun
weekend...

OMG, this is how i felt when we went to B.J.'s for some drinks... we
had to make up a excuse, so we celebrated burro's birthday... what a

weenie... we planned it a week ahead, and non of his buster friends showed up... haha... fucken asshole losers... so anyways... we show up and take a table at the bar section... fuck making reservations, or waiting an hour and a half for a table... we start off light... we get two pitchers of Jeremiah red to start... i think it has 7.1% alcohal value.... it's some good ass dark beer... it looked like we were the only ones getting dark beer around us... the girl was tripping... i'm pretty sure she's never seen 5 guys pound 6 pitchers of thier strongest darkest beers in an hour and a half... yeah i know... we also got two BBQ pizzas... those are the best pizzas on the planet... i swear to got they are... you go to go to this place... it's called B.J.'s and it's located at cerritos square by the mall... awesomeness... so after we decieded to leave...

gabriel and jose...

jose, and grass...

OMG that cookie was the best cookie on the planet... it had fresh vanilla ice cream on it... and it was all chewy, and hot... chocolate chips and everything... OMG it was so good... i ate the entire thing... the waitress found out that it was gabriels birthday... supposedly... and she hooked it up... so i ate it... everyone tasted it... but i ate it... OMG it was so delicious... i loved every bite of it... yummity yum yum... next time we go i'm defenetly going to buy a couple of those... but i'll try the white chocolate one, or macadamia... last time they offered us desert, but then me and carla looked at ourselfs and we hung our head down and said no... lol... i'm getting incredibly fat, and i don't need it... but fuck it... it's so delicious...

i drove juan's truck becouse the idiot was too drunk, and josé drove his accord... yeah we were pounded... but i still didn't feel that fucked up... but when we got home, gabriels friends decieded to come over, and we made them buy a shit load of beer... take a look...

newcastle, becks, and ¿grolsch?.... WTF is grolsch...???

esgardo, burro, and carlitos...

stupid drunk ass grass...

that's jerry (wannabe gumby) and juan... looks like he's shitting...

carlitos, esgardo, burro, agui, jerry, and josé...

idiots... and yeah these are pictures of us drinking outside my side walk... that is my house... OMG those pics are nothing than what really happened... after we got home... they started drinking again... i didn't... i had to go to sleep early becouse i had to go to a baby shower early in the morning to set up... i had to be up at 7... fuck that... so i tried to sleep really early... so anyways... burro's friends got beer for them twice... OMG twice... even after josé gave carlito's car the "Flying Peanut"... lol... stupid josé gets so drunk he's funny... he threw a peanut at his car, and turned and said... "he just got the flying peanut"... WTF was that about... then before that... we were rapping about that short guy carlitos... he's not my friend... he's burro's friend... and we always rap when we are drunk... it's super funny... i need a camcorder or something... so we started rapping about the idiot... and he started to get a little closer... and we stopped rapping... but then josé "me'd" the song... he did something like... Me me me me me ME Me... i've never heard that idiot do anything like that in my life... we started laughing like jack asses...

juan was super wasted too... he went into my house and started flaunting his cash around... what an nincompoop... i asked him if he had a pearl necklace in his wallet, and he shut the fuck up... lol... that's an inside joke... then he got really close to flo (mag's friend), and looked at her shirt... she had the simpsons... then he started nameing people... that's gumbii, that's josé, that's... when he got to the third "that"... he touched her nipple with his finger... LOL... that was comedy... so he got embarrased and walked outside... then he was telling me something, and he put his lips on my shoulder, and agui started laughing and talking shit... i said... "i'm going to tell josé about this"... and he got really red, and ran inside... he was talking to my sister's and all of the sudden he knocked out on the couch... that was the first time he's ever slept in my house i think... he usually gets all stuborn and sleeps at josé's house... they're related...

jerry was also plastured... he went to my bathroom, and fucked it all up... he did something that i didn't know it was possible... he fucked up my shitter with shit... he clogged it up, and made it chocolodo... lol... idiot... then he goes out, and asks me... "how do you flush your toilet?"... i told him that he has to plunger it... so he started plungering it... and OMG it gets worse i guess... josé comes, and tells him just to leave it alone... lol... so who has to fix, it and clean it up... that's right... me... don't be surprised... it's my friend, i don't mind... but OMG i wish i didn't have to... it was so horrible... i gagged and threw up a little in my mouth... i should of taken a picture... then he sends burro back to see if it's still cloged becouse he wanted to use it again... lol... fucken shit... so i just left to the living room... i didn't want to be around... so i wanted to fall asleep... i turned on my alarm clock... and layed down...

and what happened next... i kept hearing people... "¿where's gumbii?" times a million... then i heard josé come into the room to use the restroom... after he finished he turned around and turned off the light... then he walked out, but stopped... i guess he remembered that i was laying down in my bed... he turns the light back on and yells... "FAGGOT!!!".... lol... i wanted to laugh so hard but i just held it in... that was hillarious... then i tried to go to sleep more... i had a head ache becouse of the stupid ice cream... then 10 minutes later i got a huge nose bleed... then after i fell asleep, i got a horrible shit attack... then after that... i woke up with horrible heart burn... that was the worst... i guess it was the pizza or the beer... damn ulcer... i hate it... why do i have to be plagued with every disease on the planet...??? oh well... at least i'm not gay... lol... josé says i'm half gay... i'm not sure what that means... but i'm okay with it... as long as i'm not fully gay... lol...

so i wake up early as fuck the next day... OMG i was so tired... i only slept like 4 hours... so i get ready and my ride is here... it was my cousin cris... it was his cousin's baby shower... so we start setting up stuff... cleaning... shit like that... then i had a soda break... i started staring at this guy....

yeah i know... it's a pigeon... but this pigeon was tripping me out... he was building a nest from little pieces of dead dry grass... he must have been doing this for hours, or not days... he had a shit load of grass all ready in his hole thing... i was amazed, and inspired by this poor bird... how could something that probably no one has ever singled out in it's life be doing something so increadible... i've never seen it done before... i've seen spiders make thier webs and stuff... but this guy was building his own house... for his family... he was being a responsible parent... then i started thinking about life... i don't want to get into it, becouse i still don't have an idea about it... but it made me think... so i had to take a picture of him... i printed him out and put him on my school folder... i will remember him forever... or at least try to...

so in the baby shower... a grip of people showed up... i know hardly any of them... just a handfull... burned a couple of DVD movies... watched the primus concert DVD in full HDTV and 5.1 dolby surround... awesome... primus is so much talent for one band... i got to check out oysterhead later... so that was my saturday... not much... i was still drinking newcastle... pretty good day... sunday... josé, carla and me went to the starlight swapmeet... it was fun... at least i got out of the house for once... it's been a wile since i've been to any outdoor swapmeet just to walk... josé got dewey a dog collar, and i'm thinking about getting buddah a custom gray leather dog harness... the old man wants 30 bucks for a custom harness... that is so worth it... we're going back this sunday, and i'm going to give him at least $10 so he could make me the harness... he said that he could get any kind of leather, and hook it up... i want to get him a matching leash, collar, and a matching collar for me... with spikes...

today monday, i went to class... OMG it was so fucken boring... but i met some new people... i don't know what the fuck thier names were... but they seemed really cool... i guess normal college people aren't like us mechanicly inclined people... they are much stranger than us... or just not as much assholes like us... lol... this guy seemed really nice, but he didn't come on to strong, or sound like he was trying to hard... he was just a really cool person... he gave us copies of the puzzles we had to do... i wonder why he made so many extras... maybe he did it for that sole purpose... hmm... i wonder... then foot came to my house... he wanted me to put on his stereo becouse it got stollen... check it out....

so i got clarion that i had laying around and tried to install it... it didn't work... i ran all of the fucken wires, installed a amp, did everything... and the damn shit didn't work... i probably worked on his car for like 2 hours straight... with several breaks in between... but in the end the shit didn't want to make a sound... fuck everybody that moment... but it's all good...

lol... josé's mom asked him why he was throwing up and acting like an idiot... she knew he was drunk... she was just beating around the bush... and you know what he said..???¿ "es por qué comi mucho turkey"... what a fucken idiot... he told her becouse he ate too much turkey... LOL... who the fuck would say that... OMG dork 100% 4 lyfe...

well i'm outs... i'm uber tired... i'll see you all tomarrow... if you read the entire thing comment on it... if you didn't don't leave any idiot comments... thank you....

gumbii.........

Who Saids Men Don't Have A Sesitive Side?
Wp2i
September 10th 2003 @ 3:11

A woman meets a gorgeous man in a bar. They talk, they connect, then end up leaving together. They get back to his place and he shows her around his apartment, she notices that his bedroom is completely packed with soft, sweet, cuddly teddy bears. There are three shelves in the bedroom, with hundreds and hundreds of cute, cuddly teddy bears, carefully placed in rows covering the entire wall!

It was obvious that he had taken quite some time to lovingly arrange them and she was immediately touched by the amount of thoughts he had put into organizing the display. There were small bears all along the bottom shelf, medium-sized bears covering the length of the middle shelf, and huge, enormous bears running all the way along the top shelf.

She found it strange for a young man to have such a large collection of teddy bears, especially one that is so extensive, but she doesn't mention this to him, and actually is quite impressed by his sensitive side. All the while thinking to herself… oh bless! Maybe this guy could be the one! Maybe he could father my children?… etc. She turn to him.. they kiss and then they rip each other's clothes off and make hot steamy love.

After an intense, explosive night of raw passion with this sensitive guy, they are lying there together in the afterglow, the woman rolls over, strokes his chest and asks coyly, "Well, how was it?"

The guy says, "Help yourself to any prize from the bottom shelf."

Disposal
basild
January 10th 2005 @ 12:56 pm

I'll admit that I'm something of a TV addict. Old TV programs, sports, cartoons, and especially the news have always captured my attention. Once upon a time, I laughed at 30 year old Scooby Doo cartoons. I watched re-runs of The Prisoner and Dark Shadows. CNN was my boon companion. I could sit for hours flipping from one news channel to another, feeding my desire to keep up with what's happening in the world. TV rocked my world. In spite of this, I gave my $600 TV set to a complete stranger one night, and have never bought another.

My wife Ann and I had been engaged for years in a battle over our TV viewing. She always claimed (rightfully) that we spent so much time in front of the tube that we didn't interact as a family anymore. At night, after supper, we retired to one of the two TVs—usually Ann and Mary to the large TV and old movies, me to the small TV and CNN. It so happened one night that as she was leaving for town with my daughter, Ann made a remark about my being glued to the set all the time.

"Do you have to bring that up again?" I was irritated. We'd been round and round with this subject, and never had come to a satisfactory conclusion.

"I hate that thing" she said. 'That thing' was a new TV, courtesy of our oldest daughter, a present that I had gladly welcomed into the family, and spent much time with since. "I wish it had never come into this house." She walked out.

"Be careful what you wish for." I called out after her. "It might come true."

"Yeah, yeah." She slammed the door, and I sat there alone with our miniature weenie dog Daisy while Wolf Blitzer talked on CNN. I stroked Daisy's head thoughtfully. Hmmm. No TV. What if we didn't have a TV? What if I just got rid of it? Threw it away?

Throw away a new TV set? A brand new $600 TV set? What the heck would Ann do? I reached for the remote and shut off the set. Silence. I could hear the creaks and popping of our old house, and the whisper of the central heating system. There was something ghostly about the room without the yammering from the TV. Could we live like this all the time?

I dumped Daisy on the floor and stood up. I'll do it, I thought. I'll get rid of the damn thing right now. I walked over and began disconnecting the tangle of wires that snaked from the TV to the satellite receiver, DVD player and the VCR. I unhooked everything from the set, pulled it out of the console and carefully sat it on the floor. Wires, electrical cords and coaxial cable dangled forlornly in the resulting large, empty space.

I sat on the couch, chin in hand, and thought carefully. Is this the smart thing to do? Ann will be mad, no doubt about that, but she stays mad about the TV anyway. We all watch too much—and besides, what's it doing to my daughter? Think about the commercials she's bombarded with every day. Think about the racy, suggestive program themes she sees every night on even the most family-friendly programs. I stood up. Nope, the TV set goes, and that's it.

I sat back down. Now, what do I do with it? Throw it in the dumpster? A $600 TV? No, that's crazy. I could sell it to a local pawnshop, but the temptation to return and buy it back might be too great.

Aha! I stood up. I'll give it away. I'll give it away to a perfect stranger. Better yet, I'll give it to somebody who looks like they really need it— somebody poor. What the heck, Christmas is only a couple of weeks away, so why not make somebody really happy? I stooped, grabbed the TV, hefted it to my chest and walked, grunting, to my Nissan truck.

Five minutes later I was out of my driveway and headed downtown. The question was, where would I go to find somebody to give the TV to? I though for a moment while sitting at a red-light, and it came to me. Walmart, of course. Everybody in this town shops at Walmart, and with the typical Friday night crowd there, it would be a cinch to find a suitable recipient.

By the time I pulled into Walmarts' crowded parking lot, it was completely dark. I circled around the lot slowly and looked at the parked cars. Any Cadillac, Hummer, BMW, or any other expensive vehicle was immediately ruled out. I wanted somebody poor, somebody who couldn't afford a nice TV, not someone in a $40,000 Ego-mobile. I saw a couple of broken-down heaps, but as I pulled near noted that they were unoccupied.

After circling the parking lot twice, I had decided to go somewhere else when I spotted it. A dark blue early seventies model LTD, huge, rusting, dented, with a piece of plastic replacing a missing back passenger-side window. It was covered in dirt and grime, and the huge back bumper was wired to the car with strands of rusty barb-wire. I could see the silhouette of somebody slouched over smoking in the front passenger's side. Perfect.

I pulled up next to the rusting hulk, got out and approached. The guy sitting in the car was in his late 40's, wore a dirty baseball hat, a stained chambray shirt pulled over an OD green army-issue t-shirt, and had a cigarette dangling out of the corner of his mouth. I tapped on his window. He rolled it down, and looked up, exhaling acrid cigarette smoke at me. "Can I hep you?" he asked in a wheezing, reedy voice.

"Evening" I said pleasantly. "How are you?"

"Right good. Yer-self?" He bloodshot eyes trailed over me warily. Standing there in my office clothes, hands in my pockets, I probably looked like a life-insurance agent on the make.

"Oh, I'm just fine. I'd like to ask you a question."

"Whut's that?" He was definitely on guard now. He drug deeply on his cigarette, exhaled and suddenly leaned over and coughed violently on his forearm. "Criminey", I thought, "this guy looks and sounds like he's on his last legs."

"Would you like a TV? I have a brand-new one in the back of my truck here, and it's yours if you want it. No strings attached."

The Wheezer went on red-alert, probably assuming that I was one of those con-artists who begin their spiel with "This is yours free, just for the asking." He shook his head. "Aw, I don't need a TV set. I already got 6 or 7."

I looked at him carefully. His clothes were stained, ragged, dirty. His car looked like it was headed for the scrap pile any day. The back seat was covered with empty Coke cans, burger wrappers, plastic bags, and enough dirt to grow a limited cotton crop in. This guy certainly didn't have 6 or 7 TVs at home.

"Listen", I said, "this sounds a little strange, but it isn't a sales gimmick. I'm going to give away my $600 TV set tonight, and it's yours if you want it. This is your lucky day. You've hit the jackpot, man. I don't want to know anything about you and I don't want anything from you. All I want to know is if you want it or not. No strings attached."

His blood-shot eyes focused on me. "No strings attached?"

"Nope." I shook my head. "No strings attached."

"No offence, but is it hot?"

I thought for a moment. Hot? Then it hit me—he thought I'd stolen it! I grinned. "Sir, considering the circumstances here, that's a pretty fair question. Nope, it's all mine."

He suddenly grinned at me, exposing rotted teeth that leaned this way and that way like a rickety brown picket fence. "Well Mister, you seem to be on the up-and-up. I'll take the TV." He opened the door and began to painfully pull himself out of the car.

"No,no. Don't bother getting out. I'll load it for you."

He sat back and sighed gratefully. "Thanks a lot. I been sick lately, and it's pretty hard to get around."

I opened his back door. Garbage spilled out onto the pavement. He looked over his shoulder into the back seat. "Just set it there on the seat" he wheezed. "You ain't gonna hurt nothin."

I peered in. He was right: there was nothing to hurt except a couple of years worth of garbage. I walked to my truck, lowered the tailgate and hoisted the TV again. I wobbled over to the Wheezer's car, leaned over, carefully placed it on the back seat, and stood up. "There y'are. Enjoy your TV set mister."

"Thank ya', sir. I hope you have a merry Christmas." His face split in a rotten-tooth grin.

I smiled and nodded. "Merry Christmas to you, too." I got into my truck and drove off, feeling good. Hey, I'd done my family a favor, and did a good turn for a complete stranger. I drove home humming Christmas songs, feeling full of holiday cheer.

As I pulled into my darkened driveway, it hit me. Damn, there's another set in the house. The one in the bedroom. I shut off my truck and sat there in the dark, thinking. I knew if I waited long enough, I'd talk myself into keeping the smaller, cheaper TV. I heaved myself out of the truck and walked into the house. The smaller TV sat on a bureau in our bedroom. I eyed it for a moment. Hmmm. I had a sudden flash of inspiration. I quickly disconnected it from the satellite receiver, hoisted it on my shoulder, and walked out of the house. Just down the street was a dollar store with a huge green dumpster in back that the local vagrants groped through every day. I stood in front of the dumpster and heaved the TV into it. The set made a satisfying thud as it landed on top of the days' refuse. I slapped my hands together. There. Let whoever gets here first in the morning get the set. The early bird will indeed get the worm in this case.

I walked back to my house whistling a holiday tune, then stopped suddenly. Uh-oh. My wife's green Jeep was parked in the driveway. Time to face the music.

I walked into the living room where Ann and Mary stood in front of the entertainment console, looking at the snarl of cords and connectors dangling down into the empty, desolate looking space.

"Where's the TV?" Ann got right to the point.

"I gave it away."

Ann's lips moved silently for a moment. "You what?"

"I gave it away."

Ann blinked at me. "You gave away our new TV set." She said this in a conversational tone, as if we were discussing the weather or Mary's report card. "Who did you give it to?"

I looked around and sighed. "I don't know. I didn't ask his name. I just found somebody in the Walmart parking lot and gave it to him."

"I see." She pursed her lips thoughtfully. "So you gave a brand new, $600 TV set to a complete stranger. And there's no way to get it back."

"Nope, afraid not."

She wheeled suddenly, her ankle-length coat swirling around her heels, and strode off. Mary looked at me. "Daddy", she said, "I don't think that was too smart. She's gonna be mad at you for a long time."

"I know, sweetie", I said. "It'll be dog food and cold nights for a while."

She reached up, wrapped both arms around my neck and kissed my cheek. "I love you Daddy, even when you do stupid stuff." She hugged me hard. "I'm not mad at you."

I immediately felt better. You can't be down for too long with a kid like that in the house. Ann was indeed angry and I had cold suppers and a big empty bed for a couple of weeks, but like all storms, this one raged for a while and died down. We started spending more time together talking, playing games, and reading out loud. Mary bought herself a TV for her birthday, but we allowed it with the stipulation that it was only for watching DVDs and tapes—no TV hook-up at all.

So that's how things stand today. We don't have TV and we don't miss it. The idea of connecting cable or satellite never comes up, and when I recently asked Mary if she felt deprived by not having television, she thought for a moment, shook her head, and said, "No, not really. Everything on TV is junk anyway."

Everything on TV is junk. Hey, that's my girl.

Crazy Night
dreaminnlalaland
January 17, 2005 @ 1:10 pm

o man...what a day/night..crazy stuff happenin i tell ya..

to start it off..i HATE some ppl...GRR lol im not even kidding when i say this..its crazy how..guys can say shit they don't mean and not "get in trouble" but when girls do it..its this HUGE PROBLEM..whatever fuck it i give up..

i hate being in love with someone who refuses to love you back..or even some what care about you in the slightest..you have no idea how much it hurts to sit here and have to think about him with all these other girls..or.. just that one girl..it sucks like hell..all i want to do is ..make things right.. and i can't..

>sighs< ..im never going to get him...i was crazy enough to believe i could..i think its time i gave up on that dream of having him..and moved on like he has..

well im out..tootles

*britterz

Weekend
mmm_NAKED
January 16, 2005 @ 9:11 am

I was so incredibly drrruunnnkkk, Friday night and it was so nice.

and I was so stoned Saturday night.

i miss the bestfriend i had before she got a boyfriend.

I want someone to cuddle with.

I'm hungry for your lips.

Derick & Lily
xTaKe_My_HeArTx
February 02, 2005 @ 9:56pm

Derick and Lily are sitting alone in the park one night.

Derick:
I guess we are the left overs in this world

Lily:
I think so .. all of my friends have boyfriends
and we are the only the 2 people left in this world
without any special person in our lives

Derick:
Yup, I don't know what to do

Lily:
I know! We'll play a game

Derick:
What game?

Lily:
I'll be your girlfriend for 30 days
and you will be my boyfriend

Derick:
That's a great plan,
in fact i don't have anything to do
much for the following few weeks

DAY 1:
They watch their first movie
and they both are touched by the romantic film

DAY 4:
They went go to the beach and have a picnic
Derick and Lily have their quality time together

DAY 12:
Derick invited Lily to a circus
and they ride through a Horror House
Lily was scared and she thought she touched Derick's hand
but she actually touched someone else's hand
they both laughed

DAY 15:
They saw a fortune teller down the road,
and they asked for their future advice.
The fortune teller said:
"My darlings, please don't waste the time of your life.
spend the rest of your time together, happily."
Then tears flow out from the teller's eyes

DAY 20:
Lily invited Derick to go to the hill
and they saw a meteor
Lily mumbled something

DAY 28:
They sat on the bus, and because of a bumpy road
Lily gave her first kiss to Derick by accident

DAY 29:
11:37 pm:
Lily and Derick sat in the park where they
first decided to play this game

Derick:
I'm tired Lily...Do you want anything to drink?
I'll buy you one.. I'll just go down the road

Lily:
An Apple Juice, that's all thank you

Derick:
Wait for me

20 mins later
A stranger approached Lily

Stranger:
Are you a friend of Derick?

Lily:
Yes, why? What happened?

Stranger:
A reckless drunk driver ran over Derick,
he is in critical condition in the hospital

11:57 pm
The doctor walked out of the emergency room
he handed Lily an apple juice and a letter

Doctor:
We found this in Derick's pocket

Lily reads the letter and it says:
Lily, These past few weeks,
I realized you are a really cute girl,
and I am really falling for you
Your cherished smile, your everything,
when we played this game
Before this game would end
I would like you to be my girlfriend for the rest of my life
I love you Lily

Lily crumpled up the paper and shouted:
"Derick! I don't want you to die
I love you .. Remember that night when we saw a meteor
I mumbled something
I mumbled that I wish we would be together forever
and that we would never have to end this game.
Please don't leave me Derick .. I love you!
You can't do this to me!"

Then the clock strikes 12 ..

Derick's heart stoped pumping..

It was the 30th day

Bad Weekend
TheUnfoundRarity
November 07, 2004 @ 2:15 pm

Okay. I'm offically having a bad weekend.

We went out to dinner last night, and my mom brings up the whole moving thing.She says that if we're REALLY serious about it, she's either gonna have to sell the house, or get a room mate.

So, that really made me think about everything. Like growing up. And right now, I don't want to grow up. I don't want to think about my sister moving out and living alone.

this sucks....And the worst part is, i don't have anyone to share my problems with, or someone to cry on when no one else cares...anyone wanna be my best friend!?

After today I probably won't write in this for a while, due to my shitty computer. i'm sure you all will miss it.

Warning
t3h1337pwnh4x0r8147ch
February 01, 2005 @ 2:04 AM

Damn think I'm gonna loose my job sometime soon. I called in sick and they said it was ok then the next day they were like you need a doctors note. What am I still in fucking high school or something I didnt know I still needed to be treated like a child. Kinda funny though cause yeah I'm lying about being sick but they dont know that, so I guess I'll stay up all night tonight and go in lookin all shitty maybe they'll forget about it, and they'll be like damn that kid looks fucked up.

Mike gettin drunk with you and a few girls is the funnest thing man you are so funny when you are fucked up hahaha man all I got to say is I told you soooo

biatch

oh and just for anyone who was wondering, NO you cant smoke ice infront of my house wtf are you thinking

Peace

Oklahoma
fLaW3d_PERFECTION
January 10th 2005 @ 4:59 pm

oklahoma is by far the worst state i have ever been to in my entire life. but i guess when u bring megan along...anything can be fun lol!

yap so we left friday...we were gonna kidnap chris and bring him but he doesnt have a front door...so ya. lol oklahoma has some weird stuff. for example:

The Wormy Dog Saloon <---wtf is that?

Green Door <--- some kind of night club i suppose

Crabtown <---sounds yucky.

haha yah. and the parking garage was freakin scary...as my mom would say...i feel like a mountain goat. haha we all went er thong shpopping which is always interesting. hmm yah...oh and we got third out of thirty two teams in our tournament. i was purtty happy.

oh...and i know its gay to quote napolean dynamite but i must put this in here just for megan (aka naranja)

i love technology, but not as much as you, you see, i still love technology, always and forever. haha.

i love that nagem.

Last Resort
screwed_up_blonde
February 06, 2005 @ 11:19 am

Hey ppl well i chilled with this guy last night...him and his friend, but his friend didn't even speak english soo it barely counted lol....i tried talking to him in spanish but it didnt really work....lol. anyways we were fucking despereate to get anything.....to get drunk or high. like my friend has an ID that says he's 21....its a real ID and its him....when he went back to his birth country he got a fake thing that said he was 21...soo ya anyways he could buy us whatever we wanted...but the thing was we didn't chill until 2 am...so all the stores were fucking closed....we went to harris teeter and we got all the beer and brought it up to the front and guess what?!!! They wouldn't sell it too us, they're like its past 12..NO! the guy behind the counter went to my school, im like ohh come on there is no one here....say you didn't know the time! he's like NO! so we left....and i was like WAIT i have an idea. so i got cough syrupe...i donno how i did it but i drank the whole bottle...very easily actually. i thought i would be gaggin or something, thats what most ppl do...but i wasn't. So I was like FINALLY i'll get high....cause we were lookin for bud and couldn't find ANY anywhere it sucked. sooo after a long time he was like wait, i know someone i could call. soo he called his sister lol, and we drove up to her house, and she came out in her pj's holding 5 beers..we're like OMG! lol THANKS!!! So we went to this other place, and went to this other guys apartment and chilled....doin nothing cause every1 was asleep, but while we were sittin there this dxm kicked in...the cough syrupe.

OMG i started trippin out, i fell asleep a million times though, lol my friend recorded me on video with his phone...knocked out lol...but he woke me up...but forreal i was trippin like shit, i was really itchy, it was weird like my face, and my shoulders &back....i was SOO ITCHY!!! it felt like i had just gotten a bad sunburn, but it was also extremely itchy... soo i was like burning and stuff and i scratched with all my might. but it was weird like i thought i was burning in my own body...but then i would open my eyes and everything was like in slow motion. so then he was like im taking you home, go get some sleep. so when i was walking down this little hill on the side of my house to get to the back door..its not even a hill just a path that tilts down lol, well there was snow on the top of it near my drive way...and i honestly felt like i was falling forward.... sooo i crouched down and was really freakin out...and when i stepped on it i was shaking...like i felt like i was going to fall down a mountain or something it was soo scary! but after i got through the snow lol, i carefully walked down and into my house...oooo i text messaged from my cell "angelkittycat" and told her a lot stuff that i was feelin it took me forever to type it though. i donno if anyone else has done it too tell me... just curious. ohh its also called robo-trippin...and sum other stuff that i can't remember

aiight bye

amy

149

Someone to Talk To
TheOneIsHere90
January 20, 2005 @4:56 AM

Man do I need to talk to someone right now. Sucks cause everyoens asleep. O well I guess. Some people were wondering why I was in such a bad mood the other day. It's a long story so bare with me. Ten years ago Tuesday was the day my cousin died. That was my boy. He and I connected on a crazy ass level. We were like brothers in the sense that I tried to do everything he did. He was shot walking the streets while he was high. The gangs that were in the area at the time shot him because he was friends with a rival gang member. He fought for his life while in the hospitol for about a week and a half. He couldn't speak very well; but he told me somethings he wanted me to do and some info on his life before he and I chilled. The most surprising was the fact the he had a child. I never met him because he was with the mother most of the time. He told me that I was never to visit him or the mother and that I should stay as far away from his friends because he didn't want me to end up like him. I followed his words and moved back in with my mother. Although I didn't hangout with his old friends, I did keep tabd on what was going on. Anyway I got an email from one of his friends saying that my cousin's baby momma sold the baby to a drug dealer exchange for heroine and cocaine. Most dealers would never do such a thing for a kid, but they're was a lot of people who were willing to pay top dollar for my cousin's kid. So I emailed them back telling them to find the kid and call me when they do. Around 4:30 that morning, got a phone call from one of my cousin's boys and they said they found the kid. He was dead. Whoever killed him cut up his body and spread his body parts over my cousin's resting place with note that said:"Like Father, Like Son." Which pissed me off because that meant that someone had planned this. At that point I was planning revenge and in a big way. Then I remebered what my cousin told me about staying away from his friends. So instead i told them I'd help another way and I did. Then later that day, I his friend called again and told me that they got the guys who did it and that I was lucky I didn't go. Over half of his crew was severly hurt and 4 died. He said that he had something to show me, and he thought the best time would be that day. So I met him somewhere and took what he gave me and didn't open it until I got back home. When I opened it I found 3 things: my cousin's diary, a letter addressed to me, and a hit list. I'm not gonna tell you what was in the letter or the diary, but the hit list was really disturbing. Appeerently my cousin's friends took it from the rival gang that had shot him aand his son after they cleaned them out. The list had 4 names on it: my cousin, his son, me, and my son. I don't have a kid or anything, so I'm guessing they meant my lil' brother. They had been keeping tabs on me even after my cousin's death. This list was obviously new because my brother wasn't born until August of 98. The diary and letter explained everything about why my name was on the list and some more secerts he never told me before he died. I felt better after I read those things he gave me, not the list though. After I read them, I burned them. That was of course my cousin's request in the last entry of his diary. So that's why I was in a bad mood the other day. Well I'm kinda tired now so I think I'll go to bed finally.

Jumped
britishbassist
February 06, 2005 @ 11:37 AM

hmm ok well how do i explain this...lol i got the shit beat outa me yesterday...some black guys jumped me an geo...i have a bruised shoulder a concussion an a broken tail bone..yeah that sucks...first the dude hit geo an i jumped in front of geo because i thought they wouldnt hit me because im a girl...but i was wrong...then all these other people tried to start shit with me an geo an i was infront of him the entire time...that was probably the dumbest or bravest thing ive ever done for someone. i love him. but last night (he was drunk) he kept sayin it was my fault an he hated me an shit...well eventually he did tell me he loved me which was good. and now hes being all like oh my head hurts i have a hangover an rick told me that his way of sayin im sorry, im an idiot with out actually sayin anything... so i mean...meh yeah this sucks tho

My Baby Is Not a Mistake
SXCsweetie10
December 22, 2004 @ 11:39 AM

hey yawl.

I've decided that no matter WHAT i'm keeping my precious baby.

I don't care if i get mocked, made fun-of, teased, i don't get a shit. That baby is MINE! and i'm keeping him/her. (hopefully her!) Now that i know for SHURE that i'm keeping him/her, i sooooo very much wanna

little girl! I`m still thinking on names...i know its WAY tew early for all
that, but i REALLY wanna have my baby now! Nothing will stop me!
Thanks tew everyone whose been leaving me some comments, yewr
encouragement means the WORLD tew me right now. Some of my
friends from school have blocked me off...: (not exactly the LOVELIEST
(sp?) thing tew say, but its true. Rachel, Sonyia, and Jordan have all
stopped talking tew me. Its sad..sorta, but yew know who yewr real
friends are when they stick by ya. Thanks tew Chel.z., Sarah, Rochelle,
Stephanie, Kristen, and ALL of yawl who never left me, evn when i told
yew about my baby. Yew've been awesome.

And tew all yawl young mothers out there, i respect yew SO much!
When yew`re a teenager and pregnant, and yew go thru with it..well thats
enough for a pretty decent award right there. It takes alot. and i'm just
starting tew learn that. And i thank yew guys for being an inspiration tew
me! Yewr babies are G O R G E O U S! and if i'm lucky mine will be half
as pretty. :) I just wanted tew say that tew all yew Young Mothers, yew`re
the heroines of mah world. And i'll be looking tew yew for some advice
later on in the process of mah carriage. And tew help me think of some
ADORABLE names! thanks BUNCHES, yew don't know how much yewr
support has meant!

Emotional
SeXxAyTiFf
January 30, 2005 @ 8:53 PM

something happened this weekend that got me thinking about what
i want out of all of this going on right now...and honestly i dont know.
everything is such a mess and i feel like im so emotionally twisted!...
i cant even think straight anymore. why did everyone realize what was
going on in my relationship besides me? and why me? what did i ever
do so wrong..but love you...i guess just a little too much. how could you
only make me an option..how could ever just want this relationship when
it was convenient for you? was i really that bad of a person to make
you do this to me? and when did you just stop caring...and why did you
stay with me...just to hurt me in the end. obviously it was all just about
you. and now that we aren't together...you still treat me the same. i dont
know who you are anymore...and i dont think you do either. i've lost
you and i dont know why or how long ago i lost you...i guess you just
finally found a reason. you used to promise me the world...and now it
was just everybody before me. that sad thing is i stayed with you....and

watched our relationship go to shit. i tried...but that wasnt enough....what is stephen? what is ever going to be enough for you? when will it ever be convenient for you? but i guess its like you to just push everything aside. atleast when it came to us. everyone and everything else first... then maybe us later. thats how it was.why didnt i realize it until now? sometimes i think maybe i did know...and i just ignored it...thinking maybe it would get better..not knowing that it would just get worse. and of course now you act like everything is just perfect...like it doesnt bother you at all.... sometimes i think that you dont even care. i dont know who you are anymore stephen and im tired of trying to find the old you...and getting used to it. it's not the guy i fell in love with. LOVE...hmm..what is love anyways...something you think you know...and think you should say just because maybe it sounds good. then it just comes and bites you in the ass. its a dangerous thing...and i'm really honestly scared of it. if you didnt mean it then why did you say it...so many questions..and probably never will get any of the answers. i cant even believe you anymore...it makes me sad just to look at you because its just not you...i feel like im looking at someone totally different. maybe one day you will realize...but im hoping that i wont sit around waiting for that day to come... for now..i guess just try and hope to get over you...

it just gets harder...

i'm glad i have met this person...he helps me in so many ways..its just a different perspective on things...somebody that actually wants to tlak to me...to try to help me out. he knows how hard this is for me..and all he does is try to put me in a good mood...thanks...you have really been here for me.

U Turn
rAiDeR_mAmii
January 17, 2005 @ 3:01 AM

today i went to go see coach carter with my cuzin Alysha and my friend Karina. it was a good movie...and i actually drove on the freeway..your probably sayin wow big deal she drove on the fuckin freeway..well its a big deal to me cuz im scared of the freeway..but yeah i drove on it.. so im bad!! LOL!! anyways..my gramma is in the hospital..and when i got home from the movies we went to go see her..shes at that ghetto hospital too..the one by the fairgrounds..anyways..we went there and my mom went in to see her and me and my brother waited in the waiting room...my stepdad comes and was like u have to drive home..i was like yea whatever..i thought he was just messin around to try and scare me or sumthn..but when my mom came out shes all u have to take the car home, cuz my mom had to bring my grammas van back to her house.. so i was like ok...and then shes all go put gas at that gas station across the street...so i did...and when i got there i thought it was closed so i took off..i went towards the juvenile hall and i couldnt make a u-turn cuz there were signs that said no u-turns..so im like okay what the fuck do i do now..so i turn on this street, and made a u-turn..so im heading back towards the hospital and my mom calls me askin me where im at..im like im going back towards the hospital where r u? shes all we bearly left hurry up and catch up..im like ok..so i tried catchin up but i kept on gettn red lights and they were way the fuck in front of me...so then my mom calls again and tells me i have to get the freeway..so im like..uhhh ok..so i got on it..and then im drivin all cool and shit..and then i see a red light up ahead..im like wtf??!! so i stop at the red light and i turned left..by this time i dont kno where the fuck im at..so i call my mom and tell her im lost and i dont kno where i am..so i come to this other light and im on chestnut and olive...in other words the GHETTO..and keep in mind..the car STILL needs gas..so im drivin..and i end up on mckinley.. and im drivin and i find a ghetto ass gas station..so i stop to put gas.. while im pumpin the "GASOLINA" im lookin everywhere to make sure there are no ghetto ass people around..but im scared as fuck..i was ready to fuckin CRY! i pumped the gas and got the fuck outta there... so im drivin in the ghetto still lost..and i come to blackstone..but i didnt kno it was blackstone..bcuz i wasnt payin attention...so i passed it and kept on going straight...and then i turned right on palm and once i got to shaw i knew where i was and i got home...now im home alone..tellin u my story...haha...oh..and all this took place at 10:30-11:00 PM<< i was drivin in the ghetto at nite..ok bye!

Cope
XBIGKILLAHX
January 23, 20053:15 AM

DAmm iz madd late about 3 08 am damm iam keep it real rite now wit sum old skool rap . dammm i kant wait until moday to see her . i hope everything go good an we become sumthing good wit me an her.iam about to go sleep my azz iz tired .me an my niggaes spittin dissin each other . lolzzzz we madd dumb well i got sum beff in skool wit sum cat tryin to test me shit waz gonna pop off wen i found out he my cuz cuzin i aint no dat an i wont want to get a niggae did wrong u feel me being grimey aint cool . so i told my son an he waz lik wer he iama stabe him so i waz lik na son i aint dat serious for stabin niggaes dazzz madd dumb. den he waz lik ight yo wateva i waz lik damm b u gotta chill wen he pop off den we pop off com on G keep dat Folk real only blood niggaes in da VO madd of dem o well u gotta live. ritee now iam tryin to start a relationship wit a speaicl gurl she sum wifey type gurl daz my kind of gurl who cares about u an dont play u for any other niggae . an now iz fukin 3 14 iama hit da sack iz snowin alot in east new fuk an i wanna cope sum new boots and hat and da Army jump off! on da AVE damm . iamma get dat purple dickess suit! aint nody toch dat status! dammm lolz ight peps keep it real and gully jus live and brush dem shoulders off (HATTERSS) Bun Dem 1 good nite yall dream ! good yeah yeah yeah herbS

Scared
x_hollow_and_alone_x
February 07, 2005 @ 1:41 AM

I'm having flashbacks. All I can think about is what they're going to do with me. I'm scared. Too scared to do anything but cry. Then my mom walks in the ER, looking scared to death. They tell me that they're going to put an IV in my arm. They can't find the vain and it hurts so much. I get dizzy and throw up black stuff. It's the charcoal that they gave me to stop the pills. A doctor comes in, long white coat, he looks like Eminem with a ponytail. My mom tells me later that she thinks that he is hot. They keep me there, monitoring me for a while, asking questions. They take me out of the bed and put me in a wheelchair. I don't remember what was in the IV but it made me feel messed up. They unhook the IV from all the monitors and bring it to the elevator that they push me to. They push me out of the elevator down a long hallway of pictures on the walls. Abstract paintings. I get to a big door by a nurses staition and the nurse tells the psych nurses who I am and she unlocks the door. They push me into a dark room and help me on to the bed. What am I doing here? I don't belong here! I'm not crazy!!!! But they don't listen to me. My mom comes in and the nurses are gone. She says that she can't stay for long because visiting hours were way past over and its an hour drive back home. She starts to cry and all I can think about is this mess that I've gotten her mixed up in. She had to leave work because of my stupidity for taking those pills. I beg her to let me keep her cell phone for the night so that I can call her later but the nurses won't allow it she says. I start bawling and the nurse comes in and tells her that it is time for her to leave. I cry harder than I've ever cried before. I don't know what to do. She walks to the door and her words are still in my head, "I love you and don't ever forget that." She leaves and the scary man that is in there too walks the hallways for a while until the nurses tell him to go to his room. They come in and tell me that they're bringing me food. They bring me a Healthy Choice meal thing. I don't eat much of it. I'm too busy crying. The nurse comes back 10 minutes later and tells me to get some sleep because it's been a sad night for everyone. How would she know. I slept and woke up early in the morning. Since I have such shitty luck, I got my period. So I had to go to the nurses station and tell them. They gave me some tampons and I went back to sleep. I woke up a few hours later to the nurses talking to me. They said I could put my regular clothes back on and if I want that I can go in one of the lounges and watch TV. I didn't feel like anyone seeing me so I stayed in my room. My mom comes in. She tells me that the doctor will be here soon to talk to me. Not another counsler, the one I had was bad enough. She brought up shit that I didn't want to talk about. Didn't matter if I cried. She didn't stop, she was part of the reason why I was in there. The doctor came in and we talked. He asked me a bunch of questions about myself. I lied to him. He asked me if they let me go if I would ever hurt myself again and I said no. They let me go eventually. The car ride home was quite, radio volume low. We got home, I went straight to my room and slept. I woke up, Liz called and asked me to come over. I was scared to leave the house. I wanted to go back, I didn't want to hurt anymore. I was too scared to do anything after I got out.

I'm scared right now. I can't sleep because I think something is going to happen. I didn't start thinking about this shit until I was in the middle of the book I'm reading cuz the girl goes the the psychiatric ward. Sometimes I wish I would have stayed there. A lot of shit wouldn't have happend if I would have. I'd be happy.

Problem
cut_my_life_into_peices
February 07, 2005 @10:22 am

1 big problem, 7 trys, 3 relapses......and im stil doing this

i have to go back to skewl tomorrow.....its gonna suck.

Burn
AlbinoKrow
Thursday, January 27, 2005 @ 4:11 pm

Let us burn one from end to end,
And pass it over to me my friend.
Burn it long, we'll burn it slow,
To light me up before I go.

If you don't like my fire, then don't come around,
'cause I'm gonna burn one down.
Yes, I'm gonna burn one down.

My choice is what I choose to do,
And if I'm causing no harm, it shouldn't bother you.

Your choice is who you choose to be,
And if you're causin' no harm, then you're alright with me.

If you don't like my fire, then don't come around,
'cause I'm gonna burn one down.
Yes, I'm gonna burn one down.

Herb the gift from the earth,
And what's from the earth is of the greatest worth.
So before you knock it try it first,
Oh, you'll see it's a blessing and not a curse.

If you don't like my fire, then don't come around,
'cause I'm gonna burn one down.
Yes, I'm gonna burn one, oohhh.

Yesterday
SteveO
January 28, 2005 @ 2:22 PM

Man yesterday was great. The final count was 6 blunts, 9 jays, and 8 bong hits. Man was I fucked up. When I got home, I was passed out like a bear for hibernation. Old cold with no intention of waking up. I didn't even make it to my bed. Passed out right on the floor. People mistake

157

the floor as being uncomfortable, but it did just fine for me. Passed out around 12:30am and didn't wake up til 2pm. That was a great day off. Shit! Now I have to go to work at 5pm today. Fuck me! I have such a weed hangover, it's not even funny. I am really fucked! Later!

Birthday
KottonmouthQueen
February 04, 2005 @ 8:56 AM

—* Hey everyone... *HAPPY BiRTHDAY TO ME* Haha yeah I couldn't sleep last night. This morning I woke up at like 6:30ish and got online and Doug got on about the same time and told me happy birthday, he also left a message on my phone at midnight saying happy birthday making him the first! ! Then when I was about to get into the shower my sister Kaley called and I talked to her for about 20 mins before I had to get into the shower. And then while I was in the shower Clayton called, so I called him back and I hear him, Ashley (his sis), and Tori (his mom) all yell happy birthday !And so I talked with him for about 10 mins. Then Doug came over with 7 roses (all the way from Maine) and a huge vanilla candle, which might I add smelled SOOO good... I WANT TO EAT IT ! And my dad put them in a vase on the table and then he stayed up until 3 making me my birthday card, which was VERy unique. He wrote I LOVE YOU, out of I LOVE YOU'S... lol *Do you get it?* And then there was a poem next to it. It was really awesome. He said he messed up a lot. Oh, the the "O" in the LOVE was a heart instead of an "O", made up of I love you's which seemed like it was be very hard to make. Then I actually got to school early and Jarrod, Sean, Jen, Adrienne and Kyle all said Happy Birthday, and that Jen's getting my present after school... *The Kottonmouth Expeirence CD* and then Doug's getting me the *Kottonmouth King 10 year's deep DVD* (I want it because it has some of their FIRE iT UP TOUR, and they ran the camera on me for awhile at the concert because I was front row and Daddy X pulled me on stage, so I might be on it!!!) Then Adrienne I think has something at her house... I think I'm going to smoke at lunch today, I normally don't at school, but hey it's my birthday! And after school Jen, Doug and me are going to go and smoke with Larry. Yeah so it's only first hour and a lot has already happened. I'm not feeling to great tho, that's the only downside but I'm trying not to let that get in my way. I knew I shouldn't have ate this morning, but I haden't eaten in over 24 hours, so I guess I figured I would so I don't like faint or anything today *haha* So tonight, Doug and my family... and me obviously, are going to Crown Center to go eat at the Cheesecake Factory, Shopping, and Ice skating. ! I'll probably write back late tonight. Hope everyone else has a good day! AH I'm 17, feel like I should be 18 but at least next year I'll feel like I lost a year.... in Hannah's words to me, "Happy 17th birthday Kayla! Just one more year until we are legal and can be sluts and get out tounges peirced!!!! " Haha I know and I can't wait! Well thanks everyone who's wished me a Happy Birthday or got me something, you guys rock and I love you all! MUAH* —i LOVE MY COKE * Later babes. XOXOX

XO:KAYLA .:.*RUM*.:. -;-LEGALiZE iT-;-

—* I LOVE PENGUiNS! *HAH*

(iF YOU DiDN'T KNOW, RiGHT KALEY!)

Life Is So Confusing
hangingonbyathread
February 06, 2005 @ 9:59 pm

Today has left me feeling strange. I'm not sure exactly what I like about myself and the world. I think my problem is that I just need to prioritize a few things. I've never had really good morals and values but i do have priorites... i just tend to forget about their order of importance sometimes. I think that's what gets me in trouble. I need to start thinking about where i place the people i love among the other distracting things in my life like drugs, boys, impressing people, friends, work, money, and my reputation. I give too much thought to all these things and end up doing something stupid which i later regret. Especially boys. They are my downfall. Like for example, why did i start drugs? Boys. who do i want to impress most? Boys. The majority of my friends? Boys. Do you see a pattern here? sigh Life is so confusing =(

~day day

Wishing Plant
PreppyBeater69
February 06, 2005 @ 10:33 pm

If i had a magic wishing plant i would grow it up big and tall so i could cut it down and smoke it all. Then id wish for an s.u.v, so i could get in the back and roll the windows up. Then roll four joints and a fatty ass blunt.

Smoke that shit streight to my head, smoke that shit till my fucking brain was dead. Smoke that shit all day and night, smoke that shit till the world was alright. If i had a magic wishing plant Id wish for a million dollars, but that wouldnt be enough to solve all my problems. So id get in my s.u.v and smoke a fat ounce streight to my dome, smoke that shit tilll i fall out and have to crawl my ass home.

Up All Night
XxThe_Vampyric_LoverxX
January 22, 2005 @ 8:25 AM

Hello. It is like 8 in the morning, and I stayed up all night. I had fun with everyone of course... they all crashed around 4, and Jess was the last besides me standing until about 5. Tis was fun though. I love them all so very much. Jess, Amanda, Jackie, and my little sister all mean so very much to me... I love them all so very much and they are all wonderful in their own way. They keep me alive, especially my little sister, because I know I have to make it for her. She is a big part of why I am getting help and going through all of this change and trying to change the way I live. And my buddies are there helpin me along the way. Jess, Amanda, and I have the best times just fuckin laughing at nothing over a buzz, and sometimes even without a buzz. And Jackie cares so very much, sometimes I believe it to be too much. She worries alot about everything when she shouldn't, but tis only because she cares for us more than she does anything else. I can't help but love her for that, just as I can't help but love Amanda for being an honest hippie, and Jessica for being... well... Jessica. I wouldn't change a thing right now.

Outside of them though, there are some more people I know I have to thank... like Kym. Her and Arick have done a hella lot for me. They've came to my rescue when I needed someone to help catch me as I fall and I will be forever thankful for that. I know I do not always quite know what to say... I'm not always the best at getting across how much someone means to me, or how I feel about... well... anything. But I know in my brain how I feel, and that is enough for me right now.

My Dad and Lisa are also on the list... they give me so much freedom to do as I please, and they adore my friends. they'd fight for me and they are doing everything they can to get me the help I need to be ok... They joke around with me about smokin pot and partying and being a stoner, because they are too and I love it. Dad can walk outside like he did this morning at 6 AM to find me sitting out on the patio smoking a cigarette and just sit beside me and talk and have a cigarette with Lisa. And when I tell them I'd been up all night, they don't get angry or over worry or anything, because they listen to me and let me explain. And they understand... they really do. And it's awesome, and I, again, after the way things have gone and the way they have turned out, wouldn't change it... because after all the shit I've been through, I've grown, and now that I am almost a senior and getting ready to be on my own with this great advantage to most other people my age because I have lived, I appreciate the hard shit I've lived through in knowing that I've made it here. And here isn't that bad because I know I have a support at home again, and I can talk to them like real people, like friends or like parents, and they listen and they communicate, and they understand.

Wow... staying up all night gives you a shit load to think about. I was just thinking about all the reasons why I am still alive, and what I have to be greatful for... when I reflect on it like I just did, it makes me realize what might have happend if I had actually gone through and killed myself those times I tried... I'm glad I chickened out. I'm glad the overdose and cutting didn't send me to the hospital. I'm glad that night Kym had to come and redeem me I was able to get myself together and realize I need help... because even though I may not make an impact on the world if I was to leave it tomorrow, I know that the people that I do have would be deeply and forever affected, and I also know my little sister would be stuck here alone and without me, and she wouldn't make it... I'm glad I had a night to think about all of this... it really helps.

-diNah-

BK

XxBLeeDingMascara05xX

February 06, 2005 @ 9:34 PM

wow i've been high since tuesday...it's a great feeling...i'm expirementing with myself to figure out how many days i can go being high until i can't take it anymore..so far i'm all good with my school and everything..i'm more happier but the worst time to get high is before "school" or "work"... plus on top of that my store manager would fire me..hah..

this crazy feeling inside of me is pretty weird...it's like it's a warm mutual feeling and now i don't know what i am talking about... anyways yesterday i went for a stoner cruise with a couple of people..with "damien"..a kid i work with..it was great...we stopped at bk before though and as i'm a big stoner...i was sooo high when i saw "donnita" she's a store manager for east paris bk...anyways yeah it was sooo funny i swear it was sooo funny...and i didn't even know why it was so humorous..lol

but after we all left then went to a church place and smoked some weed.. yeah i know sounds bad but we couldn't find any other place..then we stayed in my van for 4 hours..just chillaxin and driving to other parking lots..it felt like a party in each parking lot and we were listening to the radio the whole time..we all felt like we were clubbing..but the truth was it was a trip..we were all so high that we thought we were clubbing when all we did was stay and lay down in the car with our seats tilted back... whooaaaa..it's crazy.

Robotripin'
XxBellARaceR420xX
February 03, 2005 @ 7:27 PM

OMG last night was so weird.... i think i took too much nyquill, robitussin!! and then i took my allergy meds.... my whole body was really numb, and tingly, and my eyes kept rolling into the back of my head.... god damn!! wow that was so weird!!! then dave called.... and all i remember was him yelling at me and then he was like "good- bye!!" and hung up on me..... and i passed out!!!......... hmm it was really weird..... i hope it doesnt happen tonight when i take all that shit!!!........oh well!! anyways......

well let's see.... work as pretty good today.... my back is killing me though.... i got to know Justina a lot better.... god shes really pretty!! lol we had to clean the cooler.... eww it was so nasty!! but i'm semi- starting to get things down.... lol i have answering the phones down...thats easy... its just the damn computers!! lol ya then on my way home i drove through like a gang bang gun shooting or something i heard all kinds of gun shots and people screaming and running..... hmm not going that way ever again!! lol ya so my mom came into work tonight to give me gas money.... lol and she told me her and my dad were going to the country club for dinner and that i should drive up there after work..... so i go home to change.... and their here WAITING for me.... ughhh "we're all gonna drive up in 1 car" welll.... fuck that!! lol i had already made plans to go smoke a cig with jamie and then go up there.... ughh so ya i have no cig's left, no jamie, daves mad at me i think, i smell like a god damn rose... sheenas babysitting so i cant get anymore cig's, jamies in kennett...cant risk driving all the way out there..... sunoco has NO strawberry daquri SOBE's!!!!! AHHHHH FUCK THAT!!! my dad got in my face today about my cell phone bill and how i'm grounded and that if theres any calls on there that shouldnt be there im in big trouble....Oops!!

did i mention that my back is killing me?!?!? now would be a good time to take those LP's..... but i wont... i know i know.....

oh god and then my boss asked me if i could work on sunday.... Sweetie thats SUPER BOWL SUNDAY!!!.... Fuck No!! haha

okay well im gonna go take something.... my back just hurts soo bad it's not even funny.... i almost wanna cry!!! no joke

<3 ya chrissy

Wake & Bake
TickledPink420
February 02, 2005 @ 5:21 PM

MAN

I still feel real sleepy. A bowl will wake me up more. So um...Mollys bitch ass called me at like 215, and of course I woke up. I didn't answer that shit tho. I juss listened to the message. She called to tell me that she seen my "x" Josh on like 27th workin on constrution..or somethin. Hmf...I miss him! But there ain't nothin I can do now! He has a cunt of a girlfriend. A baby by her. And hes juss usin him for his money since he has alot of it and plans on building a house out in the country. ANYWAYS...So I'm watchin TRL and I think its soo fuckin funny how the have Lil Jon playin with the "groundhog".

My dad told me that if I installed and read through this little book about billin people for his work, then I'd get $100 a month...HA I told his ass you betta give me $100 every otha week! See...he makes this magazine, called Homemart Magazine. I've bet some of you have seen it at Super Saver, Kwik Shops, yanno, anything with a newspaper rack like that, my dads mag. is there. And one week, he delievers the papers, and gives the bills to people, and collects money. Then the next week, he makes the magazine, and picks up ads and shit. So I would be doin what he wants me to do every otha week, so I deserve to get paid every otha week! LoLz..

Speakin of money....my daddys going to get me a new ring for Vday since when I got in a fight with my bro, I punched the wall and my ring bent and the ruby fell out of it. So hes going to go and get me a new one. I told him he should also give me $50(which would be $100 for vday) so I can go shopping. I bet they have new clothes at Charlotte Russe n Vanity. I might go to AE but my dad has a card for it, so I dun need to spend ne money there.

Ight I'ma wake n bake now...

xoxox Sara

I'm not looking forward to Valentines Day

American Porn
MegTheLesbian
January 23, 2005 @ 5:16 PM

Sex.

It's a natural, curious thing. If people tell you it's not interesting (to do or watch) - they're lying. It's a human thing. People build a fantasy for sex. Look at Amreican culture. Look at American porn. Look at what we put out there. Young, tight, pretty, skinny girls. That's who we want to picture ourselves having sex with. They're not the odd, funny looking women we're used to seeing in our everyday life. They're not the widow who lives next door, or your high school teacher, or your own mom. No, of course not. If that were the case, then we'd all be mother fuckers.

Small Town
Wake_n_bake_that_hydro
Sunday, February 06, 2005

sry this is long, i havent posted in several weeks so

im here in hooper, colorado, town of 88 ppl. its not to far from alamosa, which is small, but big enough to have a walmart, grocery stores, whatevr u need, movie theater (no mall though). i think it also has a small college there too. anyays, i talked to bill, n he said he ardy knew 'bout me getting in trouble for mj b4 he talked to my rents so he wouldnt have been telling them anything new. the reason he wanted me to come live here is so i can have some time to get aay n think bout where im going w/ my life, and man, let me tell u, there is plenty of time for that. there is so nothing to do here. i watch movies, bills got like over three hundred dvds, so i watch bout one or two a day. i got a part time job at the local dinner (the only place to work in town), well its a gas station, with a breakfast and lunch dinner in the back, paying 6 bucks an hour. it also has a laundrymat and u can pay to take showers there (its a truck stop, but most of the ppl who take showers there are local, 'cause the have no running water). ya, this place is a fuking third world country. alot of ppl dont have running water, those who do run off there own septic tanks, the city doesnt provide it. theres one old lady who lives several miles outside of town, no electricity, no running water, no heat, no car. stuck in a trailer home out in the middle of nothing. the church has a wood service, were they chop wood and give it to ppl who need it to eat there houses. the church drives out to pick her up to go to church, or take her to wash her clothes or get her water when she runs out, and bring her wood. they got her a couple small heaters to put inside incase she runes out of wood. the other day she had wood outside, but she decided it was to cold to go outside to get more wood for the fire, so she burned so of her clothes, she does that sometimes.

most of the pp here are weird, like somethings wrong w/ them. there r a couple ppl who r cool, but pretty much no one my age.

i was supposed to go skiing today but ive been sick lately so i cancelled. im starting to feel better, all i had was a sour throat, no other symtoms, but it was the worst sour thoat ive ever had in my life. i couldnt evn swallow my spit w/ out dying in pain. i wasnt able to eat, and the only lquid i could drink was hot tea. i went to the doctor, she gave me some amoxicillon, so ive been on that the past couple of days.

so i decided being born in americas isnt good enough. im so thankfull i was born in a big city, it would so suck to be born in a small town.

i wasnt able to bring my computer up w/ me, thats y this is the first time ive posted since ive been here. bill lets me use his occaisionally, but since its a laptop he takes it evrywhere w/ him. all my music is on my computer, i brought my cds w/ me, and the somehow managed to fall out of the car on the way down here when we swithed drivers. ahhhhhhh, i cant live in this silence like this!!! bills got alot of old music, like old skool rock, (ie zeppelin, aerosmith, s n roses, the who, billy idol, the beatles,) theres some good stuff in there as u can see, but i miss my music, its sooo much better. i found out the other day that the guy that was going to bring my comp up, (i have all my cds copied onto my comp) see i would have brought my computer up in my lap if i had to but i guy we know was coming up here at the end of feb so he was supposed to bring it, well i found out his trip has been delayed so i have no idea when its going to get here. i axed my rents to see how much itd cost to send it up here, i figure itd be worht a days work to have it a month or more sooner, but since i think they me right now, they didnt answer my e-mail.

i feel so issolated from the world here. we dont get tv here so i dont really know whats going on in the world. i was in the krocery store in alamosa the other day and picked up a mag about bushes speech he gave when he was sworn in, apperantly it was pretty controvercial. this is just an example of something important going on in the world that i know nothing about.

well not much else to report, the super bowls tomorrow go eagles!!! were going over to my bosses house to watch it (well acually bill is the pastor here and he also manages the cafe side of the gas station, but were going ovr to one of the two sisters who owns the place's house).

Depressed
xXtoxic_dreamsxX
February 03, 2005 @ 9:09 am

ok...well...first entry..

im so depressed right now. so much stuff is going on..i cant take it anymore. my dad is so stupid, i can believe he won...i hate everybody that believes him. my sister is really sick, and my step-dad came home last night and him and my mom were screaming at each other at like 11:00 at night, i am soo pissed...i cryed myself to sleep last night, when i did get to sleep it was like 4:00 so i only got an hour and a half of sleep. i woke up, and our fucking phone was shut off. i was soo pissed...i went to call my friend to tell i was coming on my step-dads cell, and i didnt know the volume was off, and the phone operator came on..and he like fliped out on me...so i just left...i cant take him yelling at me like that he pisses me off so..bad.. and my mom does not do anything about it, she just sits there..and GAH!!!....i hate her so bad. so many of my friend are depressed and sad, and i was just reading my friends xanga, and i didnt read it in a while, i was like crying when i read it. i just feel so empty and lonely inside. i hate this feeling. i have not eaten in 3 days, i dont eat breakfast ever....i dont eat lunch and my mom has made dinner, then went upstairs so i told her ate but i didnt, i just put the left overs in trash...

or i put it away for my step-dad when he comes home from work. i dont know...i just cant take much more...i may go crazy. latley i have been thinking about somethings....things having to do with suicide...what it would feel like..and how i would do it.......i just GAH!!.....

~Unwanted Soul

New Year
Elricmadefromblood
January 01, 2005 @ 1:07 AM

HAPPY NEW YEAR!!! BULLSHIT!!! its just gonna be another repeat of last year pain, suffering, false hopes, and me with a knife against my throat.

3 More Days
Enigma317
February 03, 2005 @ 11:43 AM

im not sure what to do anymore, i mean i cant be here but i cant go, i hate them, but i still i dont know i feel something for them, i just i want to run away, somone please take me away from here, i cant be here any longer, please, i jsut cant stand it, i cant deal with this, why do they hate me? why dont they listen, why cant they see, everything i have ever done was for them, i just want to make them happy i want to make them proud, but never have i once been good enough, always i should have done better, i should have gotten an A+ instead of an A, i should have written it like this instead of like that, i should have done this before i did that, i should hang out with them cuz they rnt good people, they have no fucking idea what they r talking about, they dont look into others souls, they cant see thier essence, they dont even bother, they dont want to know the truth, they want to be content in thier small little bubble of perfection that will never exist, i hate them i hate them so much, i wish they would go away i wish i didnt have to be here with them, i cant stand being around them, they are the reson i feel the way i do, they make me want to die, they make me hate myself, they tourcher me, and the worst part is that they dont even know that they're doing it, thats why i hate them, but still there is something there, thats why i cant stand to see them cry thats why it kills me to hear the arguing about me, how im so bad, where they went wrong, how im so ungreatful, how much i suck, but you know what im trying my best, i truly truly am, everything i do revolves around making them happy, yet never am i sucsesful, why cant they see me, why cant they hear me, why dont they understand???????????????????

What to Write?
heavenslanguage
February 07, 2005 @ 5:14 pm

i feel like writing something depressing, but nothing comes to my lips or finger tips. when loneliness howls aorund you, you want to express emotions all the more clear. i havent found a word yet that describes the bottled up, comfused feeling inside so many of us that are fearful of being found out. im just like everyone else.. trying to live this life one day at a time.. trying to found out what we're all about. this life is meant for something, yet the meaning is hid. i see the tearful eyes full of pain everyday. most people are just like me but are just afraid to tell how the pain inside them grows. if only more people would, i wouldnt feel so alone. like im not the only one. but tahts just me being self centered once more. if life was written in a poem, maybe then i could comprehend it.. all the ways the winds and waves or trials toss us. i just dont know about this.. so much for not writing anything depressing.

I Just Want to Sleep
sweet_despair
January 25, 2005 @ 3:46 PM

So yet another day of life has passed and I am still here gazing at this computer screen wondering what to type. I feel like I did this morning in front of my English class...I had to introduce myself and all that good stuff. "Um. I'm Cassie. I'm fifteen. I have 3 sisters, 1 brother and yeah... that's about it...I don't lead an interesting life I'm sorry..." Well, since you are here to learn about my life I'd best make it a little more interesting!

Well, I'm listening to Chevelle right now. They rock. None of my friends can go to the Slipknot concert, which sucks, but still...I wanna go.

I still want to learn how to play the guitar. I have my acoustic (which is a sorry thing...), but I have absolutely no idea how to play it correctly. I should get some books on it or something since I can't teach myself right. I know I'm gonna have to seriously start cutting the nails on my left hand so I can hold down the strings between the frets correctly, because that is my biggest problem. I also have had no previous musical teaching so I dunno what the hell a chord or a note is or how to play one.

School is trying to kill me, I swear. I feel horrible at school. I hate looking at people for fear of them staring back at me. I hate it. I'm afraid of what crosses their minds when they see me. Sick. Disgusting. That's what crosses my mind when I see me, why should they be any different? I'm so afraid of people sometimes, not to mention tired. I get so tired of seeing them, exhausted really. I don't really remember being happy. I'm paranoid of everything, what I'm wearing (is it good enough, no...), what I say (I'm so stupid...no one cares), what they say to me...I sound a little self-pitying sometimes, but goddammit can't I be allowed even that? Just a little pity for myself, because no one else cares...

Everyone thinks I'm conceited and stuck up just because I'm quiet. It's not fair. I just want to crawl into bed, pull up the blankets, and stay there for the next four years...sleep and sleep and sleep.

Happiness
Jamesjr218
February 07, 2005 @ 5:26 pm

Happiness. A friend once said to me that true happiness doesn't last forever. You live most of your life sad. We all know that problems don't go away. You'll always have something going on in your life, but I can honestly say that when you get what you truly want everything is so much easier..

People are pathetic. A lot of them anyway. Especially in the love department. Maybe I just live by such high standards that I expect too much from people. I don't want to go out having sex (I'm a virgin) with every girl I ever date, because when "the one" comes around, I'll be "dirty". If I'm dating a wonderful girl, she deserves more than some pervert guy. Maybe I look at sex and love differently than others. I don't say "Underage sex is wrong" for the reasons people think I do. Parents say it because they don't want their kids having kids at young ages. I say it because it loses its meaning. Sex is supposed to be an expression of love. If you have sex with every person you've ever dated because you "loved" them, it lost its meaning. How many people can you truly love?

169

I want my first time to be with the girl I'm sure I want to spend the rest of my life with. I want it to be perfect, in the right mood, and to know we're losing our virginity to each other. Maybe I'm old fashioned, but your actions speak louder than your emotions.

If I love someone and they care about me but don't love me......it's hard to explain. Let me give you an example. Let's say James is in love with Corinne. They go out but after a while Corinne feels she doesn't want to be with James anymore. She loves him but she's too spoiled and stuck up to care about his feelings. Hers come first of course! Anyway, she breaks his heart and awwww it hurts her. Poor baby. Having to suffer knowing James is hurt. Yeah, right. James is suffering, deeply. Corinne meant a lot to him. He loved her with every inch of his heart and she broke it off for stupid reasons. Now he's suffering and Corinne feels bad and that's it. No consideration whatsoever! Eventually she moves on and hopefully kills herself and rids the world of her filth.

Of course, that was just a made up example Anyway, things like that happen. People watch as others suffer from their actions. They love them but just sit back and go for their goals. "So-and-so loved me but i loved his friend. Anyway, to cut it short I was a slutty motherfucker and ignored So-and-so's feelings and went striaght for the friend. He suffers inside and I know it. I'm not going to do anything though. I'll just sit here like the waste of life that I am and think about it and babble." If you haven't noticed, I feel strongly on this topic. Anyway.

Got a 2 page paper to write. I went asleep and missed a chance to talk to someone special I miss her. I'll stay up tonight and talk to her though That's what gets me through the day...And the day isn't too bad though. Not as bad as it used to be. Yay. Let's see how long it lasts. I better go and write that paper. Bye bye!

Your So Gay!
lifesoup
January 28, 2005 @ 12:23 am

I had a great night. I talked to Ty and he was in a good mood even though he sent me a text earlier today that said he was tired and that he had a bad day and that he was just going straight to sleep tonight instead of calling me. Which doesn't bother me cause I know he's tired... he should be, he works all day long and still finds time to work out. But... it was a good talk, and things are back to normal.

I went to Wal-Mart today with a couple girls and I guess I said something "gay" because one of them was like "I swear you're a homosexual" but then she said "it's ok, cause I love you." Then the other one was like "it's cool if you are, I have loads of gay friends" and then I guess I turned red cause the other one was like "HE IS" but I quickly changed the subject by saying "Hey look, granola bars!" So that's my story. In a weird sort of way I felt accepted, and that maybe I could tell my friends and maybe they wouldn't care. Then I thought about my family and the feeling of acceptance vanished. Blah...

Then tonight, like 15 minutes ago, I had a great Bible talk with my friend Julie (yeah, the one who had a crush on me). She basically explained to me about God and Jesus and how we get to heaven and how to please God because we have this free gift of eternal life. And I don't want to ruin my free gift. So basically I figured out that I don't want to feel bad for the things I'm doing. I feel like our talk just wiped away like all these homosexuality vs. religion thoughts that have been going through my mind. Because people focus on homosexuality way too much...even if it was a sin (which it isn't IMHO), it's just as bad as any other sin. People that are SO against homosexuality are usually sinful people themselves... I mean, everyone is sinful, but... I'm not trying to judge, I'm just saying that...so what? It's not that big of a deal if you really think about it.

I just feel like...refreshed. And it strengthened all my feelings for Tyson. I feel so free and I want to be more involved in my faith and that's a good feeling. I've been focusing so much on the bad things that I don't take enough time to look at the good. I have the most amazing boyfriend in Tyson and we're so perfect for each other...my friends are so cool even though I didn't want to give them the chance...my family, well, they'll come around, they love me and support me for who they think I am so maybe they will once they know the real me too. And school...ya know... I have a major, I love it, and I finally feel like I have a path, a goal. Things are falling into place and I know in a couple days I'll probably be all depressed again...but...right now I'm on cloud nine and I'm not gonna let anyone bring me down for a while!

New Jersey
Jigga_where
February 05, 2005 @ 12:38 am

Pam ditched me tonight... what the fuck?!?! She asked me to hang out with her... then she ditched me. When I wanna hang out, or talk to people this week, it seems to me they are ditching me or not available. what the hell? fucking shit.

In Enviro today the teacher said "People don't like New Jersey, so they pollute it." hahaha.

Boom! I Need To Cut
SCREAMING_UNHEARD
January 21, 2005 @ 10:30 pm

Wow...What a rush. It just came out of no where..and I just had to cut. So I did. Gonna have to go wash off my knife now, though. That was so wierd. Just BOOM 'I need to cut'. I've never felt anything like that before. This on is closer to my shoulder than the last one so you can't see it as easily..and then a lil on on my side....That was kinda awesome.

Perplexed
InNeeDhG
February 08, 2005 @ 3:22 pm

well that hott guy i like is still staring but i cant tell. u kno all i want is to kno whether he is bi gay or str8. then it will take this huge wieght off of my shoulders. i mean i cant stop thinking of him. and at school i sometimes feel like introducing myself b/c he doesnt kno me and he or any1 else doesnt kno im bi but i just cant . i dont want to jus go out with him i would like to just get to kno him. my life sucks i wish i stopped liking him but itz not gonna happen. like he says he isnt gay online but i would say the same thing if sum1 IMed me asking me that. i thnk he is in the closet. but its kinda suspicious the way he stares at me in school and he doesnt stare like that to any1 but me. for example i saw him yesterday and he stood right there talking to his friend and looking at me like every 2 seconds and when i walk behind him in the hall he slows down and wlks at my pace. so i figured he might be Bi but u never kno i could be wrong! well i will write again soon bye.

My Day
Liquid_Rain_81
February 03, 2005 @ 12:27 am

I always hate getting sick. When I woke up Tuesday, I felt really bad. I was light headed, stuffed up, and I had a sore throat. So, I stayed in bed until noon. When I was finally able to get up, I did my dishes (because they needed to be done) but I had to sit down on the couch because I was getting really light headed. I sat there for a couple of hours. The world began to spin. Man, I hate feeling like that. However, after a nap, I was so much better. The world had stopped spinning, I could breathe through my nose, and my throat did not bother me that much.

Kristy came over to drop off some apple kuchen. I had to return a dvd to blockbuster and she suggested that we go so I would get out of the apartment. On the way to blockbuster, we were behind an ambulance which went past two hospitals, Meriter and St. Mary's. We decided we were going to follow it to see where it was going. The ambulance was not in a hurry and the lights were not on. We followed it all the way to Univeristy Hospital. Kristy commented that it was my first time chasing an ambulance. And, frankly, I hope that it is my last.

We then returned the video and just started driving around talking. We do that so often. Usually when we drive around we have such great conversations. Last night was no exception. We finally decided to head to perkins to grab something to eat. We were there for a couple of hours just chatting with one another. It was a very revealing night for the both of us. I'm glad that we had our discussions.

So, when I went back to my apartment I was tired. I was ready to go to sleep. But, when I layed down in my bed, I had a problem. It actually turned out to be a major problem. I laid there thinking. What was I thinking about? Well, let's just say that I covered the spectrum. I thought about my future. I thought about past events in my life. I spent a lot of time thinking about my friends, parents, and brothers. Thinking about this occupied much of the time. I thought about friends who I had when I was younger and lost contact with. I thought about friends who I have grown close to recently. I have thought about where all of my friendships are going. I thought about my relationship with my parents and how it has evolved in the recent months. I ruminated on the task that I have given myself involving my parents. Then, I began thinking of my future. What is going to happen to me?

So, I do this sometimes. What usually helps to end this long nocturnal ordeal is to turn on some music and focus on the music instead of the ideas racing through my head. So, that is what I did. I turned on some jazz to play softly in the background. Alas, that did not help. Now I began contemplating scientific ideas. What should I do to keep my scientific knowledge intact? Am I going to find a career that will be fulfilling and rewarding? Then, I began thinking of my friends again. I began to think of all my undergraduate friends, friends to whom I have grown extremely close, friends who are little more than acquaintances... I look up at my clock, it is 3:30. I need to be up at 6 AM. I roll over...there I lay, listening to the jazz...trying to put these rampant thoughts out of my head. I laid there, with my eyes closed, trying to meditate. After what seemed like ages, I finally dozed.

I was able to get up at 6 AM with no problems. The thought of just sleeping in crossed my mind, but I quickly dispelled it. I loaded up on some coffee and trudged out the door to get on the 7 AM bus. I was able to maintin focus in all of my classes. The haze and laziness wore off during property. I felt like I had all my sleep. This focus continued as I volunteered at the LIC. I convinced myself that I was going to work out since I didn't yesterday. I had focus then. I didn't feel tired. After my workout, went to look at apartments (they sucked). I was good yet. What was going on. But, I needed a nap.

So, I went home and climbed into bed. I looked online and started talking with some friends. I quickly began involved in a deep conversation with one of my undergraduate friends. I finally told her I needed to take a nap. I closed my computer, and laid down. Then, I decided that I must try once again to find a summer internship. So, I opened up my computer and started looking again. There I sat, working diligently and productively on my computer until 8 when I turned on the State of the Union.

9:05 PM I went outside my apartment and waited for Kristy to pick me up. We went to Patty's to have some strawberry daiquiris because Patty had a stressful week. We just hung out there for a while. It was a good time. Unfortunately, Kristy decided to do the tickle torture to me. Unfair. It is so unfair that I am so ticklish. The lack of sleep suddenly hit me. Yet, on the car ride back to my apartment I had enough energy to dance to the songs playing on the radio and serenade Kristy with a heart moving rendition of Enrique Iglesias' Hero.

Good Times had by all.

Home
eyes_ofXa_tragedy
February 08, 2005 @ 6:47 pm

so today was good until i got home

my friend chris is like overly emotional and worries about me so god damn much. yeah its nice sometimes to have someone be worriedd about you but that's all he evers talks about. how he cares and worries.... ugh....and he says sorry all the time for stupid things...he's pissing me the fuck off. today he asked me if he was smothering me..and i said yes b/c i'm an honest person...so he's all freaking out like omg then i'll leave you alone i'm so sorry but why is it bad that i care?! UGH just take some drugs..chill out..

ugh...i'm SUCH a screw up...

my "best friend" dumped me to go get drunk with her work friends last friday. yeah well when she quits that job and doesn't hang with those work people anymore...who's she gonna come running to? ME...and who's not gonna be there? ME....treat me like shit and ignore me..be all selfish...hm...why are we friends again?

my boyfriend for 3 years is totally wonderful...i'm only 16 so i've been dating him since i was 13. and i never really had any b/fs before him.... but anyway....he lives in PA and i live in FL...but he's 2 years older than me..so he gets out of high school this year and might move here! if he doesn't...then i guess i'm gonna have to say..let's be realistic this is over...i really hope he does move here...i've pretty much based my life and future around him...so he doesn't come here...and i'm more of a nothing than i am now. i know i'll never find anyone again that i feel as comfortable with who loves me so much.

what have i eaten today.......a few cheetos.....a few bites of ice cream..... water water water water.....2 mints.....and that's it. i would go look to see what i weigh...but i'm too afraid to.

my dad hasn't called me in a over a week...my mom is too busy for me...my sister has things to do...i have no best friends anymore....my boyfriend lives a million miles away....and everyone says i shouldn't feel alone....screw everyone....

i just cut tonight for the first time in a long time. i don't think i'll be able to quit. ::sigh:: but i did quit pain killers....oh well..doesn't matter..i'll probably end up killing myself anyway!!

Seeing Red
CrimsonXScars
February 08, 2005 @ 1:11 pm

Ok so last night i went to work with my father... and that sucked... cept for when sam gave me my pay check... ya know thats always a good thing. um.... i found out that a really good friends who worked there got fired. so i was pissed off about that.

today has been very boring... i did school.... and i dont think it went all that well cuz i still feel like shit... then i cut my legs.... and my cat i think wanted to help so she scrachted the fuck outa my arm... it was funny... she did a good job.. there was blood driping off my arm... so no complaints....

anyways tomorrow isnt going to be as boring... i have to get up and go to O.T. then take the computer to get fixed (also i wont be online untill at the earliest friday) then i think im going to work with my mom... then church. woohoo.... anyways im going to leave you guys with a song. Later

Dad
sr388samus09
February 05, 2005 @ 7:34 pm

If my "dad" was to die tomorrow, I'd be the first in my family to celebrate.

I wanna fucken stab him to death.

Right Now
Nextgen
December 22, 2004 @ 6:03 pm

right now i just want to break down and cry...

People don't die from sucide... They die from saddness.

My Situation
ViolentScreams
January 18, 2005 @ 1:43 am

Well i am a human and i am still learning........ ill pick up where i left off anf keep on walking down the road where my life was ment to be at.... i will keep on waling and walking intil i reach the end of the road...

i need to be more responsible.... that was my new yar resolution but i cant help but to look blindly at it..... it something i just dont have... i wish i had it... really i do..... but i guess im not ever going to be for my mother..... and my father... fuck my whole family.......

Finals are soon...... im getting out realy ... ha my parents dont know but who gives a fuck....

I talked to mayra over the weeeked god she bores me sometimes... well she has good luck with guys i guess. so far she has like 3 guy that like her....... i dont know why but they do... lmfao.... that good i guess... i just hope she wont just on the first guy what would ask her out.... she would be jumping on someother thing later on... and got i just dont want to see her parents jumping on her because she has her belly a baby that she cant ever take care.... well yeah.... i hope this will neve happen to her.... to enyone....

kill you all later Die-Ana

Lord
tink70
February 04, 2005 @ 1:41 pm

Hi! How is your daily quiet time with the Lord? Do you have a corner set up with your Bible, notebook . . . in my case, cd player, candles, keyboard . . . Do you race to the secret place, and if your time is cut short feel somehow cheated and not completely with it the rest of the day? I sure do!! How does God lead you to structure your prayer time? I read randomly right now but need to get a new Bible with a study guide/tracked readings . . .Ask God to carve out a time of day for you to rest in Him, see what you receive. Each minute stokes the spark of longing in your heart . . . for more . . .

King for a Day
superflywebpimp
February 03, 2005 @ 2:02 pm

gleaming light of the morn' doth shine, brake riders united against my punctuality, my attention ye have gained, stay out of the fast lane you mini-van bastards.

"let's get one thing straight, i never asked to be king of the idiots." - superflywebpimp

I Hate Life
This_Is_My_Little_Secret
December 31, 2004 @ 11:46 pm

i hate that im crying...this really suckss i hate life happy new year if they say the way you spend your new year's eve is the way you're gonna spend the rest of the year...i guess i'm gonna be miserable writing on this and crying myself to sleep every night...i really dont wanna be here right now...why cant this be my perfect world? just for a day...i wish everything could be perfect...just one day where i could be for once genuinely happy for the entire day...i want a hug so badly right now...thats all im asking for...just a hug

Piss On You
happy_go_kramer
Sunday, February 06, 2005

i want to piss on all of you. those are my feelings right now. i left my wallet over at my dads and he cant bring it over till later tonite. my nites gunna suck my mom is in a fuckin pissy mood so fuck that because i wasnt hungry so she threw her fit and i came home. my birthday has been great. actually i dont give a fuck... i wanna go out and do something tonite but nooo i had to leave my wallet at my dads. i playedwith my new puppppy alot over at my dads that dog is cool. hes like a redish brown color and tanish itsa doberman. some one call me if you wannahng out to nite im bored.

i havent masturebated for 3 days. i wanna go to best buy and get a cd but noooo i had to forget my fuckin wallet. i want next weekend to come because ill have a fuck load of money. a loooooot . and i just spilt beer on my pants.

school is gunna suck for some reason friday went by so fucking slow. then friday noight i had fun. i cmae home then went to dads. he got me a funny birthday card. i laughed.

any one wanna hangout this week or weekend im free all week and im getting paid again!. bitched im out

Turkey Break
PriNsEfLy
November 29, 2004 @ 11:28 PM

what's goin on people??!! i trust every last one of you had an awesome, filling, eventful turkey break like myself. if not.....well then.....sorry?? anyway, i may as well get down ta it. ***public warning*** this is gonna b a long post, so you might wanna get up, go ta the bathroom, make yourself a sandwich er somethun ta snack on, cuz you'll b here for a long time (that is, unless you X me out riiiiiiiiiiiiiiiiiiiiiiiiiiiiiiiiiiiiiiiiiiiiiiiiiiiiiiiiiiiiiiiiiiiiight....
......now) but anyway, here we go....

Tuesday

we start out tuesday after my last post. i decided ta bust outta hurr later in the evening cuz like i said, no one was gonna b round. so i got home round 7-7:30, decided not ta let the masses in slatington know i was home, an just chilled wit the parents for the night. i wound up finding one of the 435794876439643 (yeah, seriously that many) home movies we have in the TV cabinet. popped one of those in an laid out on the couch. i watch thansgivings, christmas', bowling / chuck E. cheese b-day parties (HEY!! you know you had one at one time er nother), easters, an everything inbetween. i never realized how RIDICULOUSLY HUGE my fro was back then til that night. HAHAHAHAHAH! anyway, there was tuesday.

Wednesday

wed started out wakin up round 10 er so (this was the only night / morning i actually got a decent amount of fucking sleep). went ta visit the good ol psychiatrist for a refill on my meds. got back an laid round the house for much of the early afternoon. then i decided ta call the masses an let em know that i was home an ready ta spread some havoc

about. steph was the first ta get at me, tellin me that she needed ta
talk ta me bout some stuff that happened since we talked last. so she
stopped by, filled me in on the current situation wit the guy that she was
seeing (keyword: was) an how that fell apart. told me bout her random
trip ta SC that she was gonna embark on for the break an that she was
sorry ta bail out on me (which wasn't really a big deal cuz i figured i'd
only see her at best once over break anyway). she also needed some
advice and input on some bipolar stuff too (for those of you who don't
know, she's basically right there wit me on the whole bipolar / ADD
wagon). it's strange when we talk bout that stuff cuz she alwayz tells
me bout situations that i've already gone thru myself, so it's kinda like
she's two steps behind me in all these little twists an turns that life just
loves ta throw at us. i can relate to practically everything she's goin thru
an it sucks cuz it made me realize a lotta shit that i guess i tuned out
or purposely overlooked. i don't wanna elaborate on this cuz if i think
anymore bout it, i might just havta scream cuz i've been thinkin bout it
ever since her an i talked an i'm goin fuckin nuts. aight, time ta get off
of the subject cuz it's ruining the whole flow i had goin, an i can't fuck
wit the feng shui (right kuhn?) aight, so after steph leaves, lerchy gives
me a call ta watch the varsity b-ball players play against the alumni. god
damn, i wish i would've played senior year. i was in the best shape outta
all the alumni, an most of them coulda wiped the floor wit me in high
skool! but anyway, met up wit jared there (cuz he was playin an all....
lucky bastard!! NOT!! HAHAHAHHA) an that was it, which goes into....

Thursday

thursday started nice an fuckin early (try 7 am......yeah.....break what??
) my dad volunteered me as bitch boy @ the golf course, so naturally
they stuck me wit the shittiest job of them all.....recharging the batteries.
now you're probably thinkin "what's wrong wit that? all you havta do is
plug em in, right?" well, you're half right. **random piece of info that you'll
never need ta know in your lifetime unless you golf** electric carts have
6 batteries each that they run on. each battery has three "cells" that are
submerged in distilled water as to help electricity flow through. well, if the
water gets low enuff, the batteries fry, an they're expensive as shit (try
80 bucks.....EACH!). so naturally they saw this as an "oh let's rape dustin
in the ass an make him refill all the fuckin batteries". so let's do some
math....64 carts...6 batteries each....3 cells to each battery....40 degrees
out.........what do you get?? HELL ON EARTH! that took a nice 7 hour
chunk outta my day (an my lower back, which is still fucked up from all
the bending down) so after that, i came home, got showered, changed,

an my mom (biological), sis, bro, an uncle showed up for turkey an such. me, my uncle butch, an my bro devoured everything. an then came mama supp's chocolate peanut butter cheesecake ...mmmmmmm!! after that, E called me, an i headed over there for a bit. came home early cuz.....

Friday

i got ta wake up @ 7 am again!! YAAY! an guess what?? i got ta do....you guessed it....more batteries and carts!! double yay. but then after that was all done, i could FINALLY relax. wound up goin over ta ryczak's that night an playin pong wit his friend from work getty, rick, an his "friend" ally (ally.....ally's sEEEEEster ....if you don't know what that means, then don't worry bout it cuz it's dumb..HAHAHAHA). it was good times. i was on fire for pong. it was until getty made me shotgun two beers straight that the night started goin downhill. oh yeah, an those two beers.....natty ice! key piece of info: don't shotgun natty ice.....EVER!! anyway, it was touch an go there for a bit. every sip i took felt like it was goin against the current, but i didn't puke, so hurray for that one! wound up stayin awake til 5 am while everyone else was passin out round 3 cuz his rents came down in the middle of the night an witnessed our drunken debochary, so i hada play it off like i was the one in control (which i still dunno if i pulled it off er not, but i was the closest ta sober out of all of us, which is a suprise, i know) an then i passed out into.....

Saturday

uneventful for most of the day. woke up wit a nice hangover which was swifty kicked by the aleve. ate my day old Sheetz hoagie, met ryczak's newest band member vince (kewl guy...found out he's cousins wit brett evans, so i found out the scoop on that kid) did jack shit when i got back home. then E called me up bout 7ish, told me that beva, billy, an jared were goin over ta visit him @ ESU an wanted ta know if i was in. so they picked me up, an we headed over. on the car ride over, we got ta talkin bout all the chicks in our graduating class (don't ask me why er how, it just happened). it was funny as shit hearin bout some ppl that i hadn't seen nor heard from since graduation. but anyway, finally arrived @ E's place (which is def. a nice ass house i might add!! props ta you, buddy!), chilled, watched dazed an confused, an closed out the night by playin risk on PS2. this takes us into...

Sunday

we all got up. drove back (uneventful car ride back). chilled at my house, watched the eagles game. i was gettin ready ta head back when all of a sudden, my dad's like "we're goin out ta eat wit your grandmother". so that delayed me like two hours. so i didn't get back here til late last night. unpacked my shit an hit the sack.

which leads us up until this point. my AIM's fucked up. for some reason, it's tellin me that my name isn't registered er somethun, so i'm tryin ta fix it (hence why i haven't been online...so if you're lookin for me, know that i'm still alive an well an you should give my cell a call er stop on by). i got finished wit a 9 pager like right before i started this post round 11ish, so thank god that's over wit. too badd i got nother 5 pager due on tues an i dunno what ta write it on!! next week's gonna suck major donkey cock since it's the last week of the semester before finals, but thank god this semester's almost over!!! anyway, i'm dead tired, so i'm gonna make this NOVEL come to a close (SEE??!! told ya it was gonna b a long one!) i'm gonna chill out wit my journal, vent some stuff, an pass out. til somethun else happens that's worth talkin bout, laaaaaaaaaaaaaaaaaaaaaaaaaaaa aate

This Pen
ransom_notes
January 24, 2005 @ 6:56 PM

This pen turns the paper black,black hearts never fade...only break, i wish you would tak this black and understand it's all i have to give, it's not like i could fake that i have something better to give

Asking myself if i want better,truth is theres nothing more i could want, if only things went two ways nowadays

take this offer it's the only one you'll get, for the frear of being hurt will hurt the most, the choice is yours they all were so take your time and make and honest decision to

*that's mine i really do have to much time haha well that's all

Diary
AC_201
February 06, 2005 @ 11:44 PM

HER DIARY

Tonight I thought he was acting weird. We had made plans to meet at a bar to have a drink. I was shopping with my friends all day long, so I thought he was upset at the fact that I was a bit late, but he made no comment.

Conversation wasn't flowing so I suggested that we go somewhere quiet so we could talk. He agreed but he kept quiet and absent. I asked him what was wrong; he said nothing. I asked him if it was my fault that he was upset. He said it had nothing to do with me and not to worry.

On the way home I told him that I loved him, he simply smiled and kept driving. I can't explain his behavior; I don't know why he didn't say I love you too. When we got home I felt as if I had lost him, as if he wanted nothing to do with me anymore. He just sat there and watched T.V.

He seemed distant and absent. Finally, I decided to go to bed. About 10 minutes later he came to bed, and to my surprise he responded to my caress and we made love, but I still felt that he was distracted and his thoughts were somewhere else. He fell asleep - I cried. I don't know what to do. I'm almost sure that his thoughts are with someone else. My life is a disaster.

HIS DIARY

Today the Rockets lost, but at least I got laid.

Life Lesson
RockFreak13
January 27, 2005 @ 5:56 pm

wow, so it has been an eternity since i have written in here. not much has really gone on since my last entry..um, i cut my hair..thats about it. yeah, its short and clean cut again...i guess thats a pretty good thing, feels weird without it though, cause it was pretty long for me.

after some deep soul searching, i have begun a new path on life. i am tired of whom i used to be, and now i have a new plan and a new outlook on life. i am trying to surround myself with more positive people and i just dont feel like suffering with people who are constantly over run with emotions. sure, you have to let your feelings go, but you cant let everything get you down. shit happens, but it all comes from how you deal with it. it all deals with new signs of maturity and the need to grow up and realize what is truely important in life. i just wish this lesson had been learned earlier in life, and it sucks that it has taken me this long to figure out what the difference is between what is wanted and what is needed.

I think i have learned my lesson now.

The Ball Stops Here
darketernal1226
February 01, 2005 @ 6:13 pm

So, I am sitting here and thinking about some people, and realizing how much I absolutely hate this area. What the fuck is wrong with people anymore? I know i m not perfect but i am damn near done with this petty bullshit. It is rediculous anymore. I am tired of it, and if you have something to say, dont be a little fucker and whisper around say it to me, what the worst I'll do? Tell you to fuck off, heaven forbid. Believe it or not I do things with others in mind, until they piss me off then i could care less. Maybe if you took into consideration other factors, and had the gumption to say something to me, it would have been resolved. But no, no one ever does that anymore. And if you think I am being hipocritical, try me, come up to me and ask me my gods honest opinion or what i think of you, and I will. I personally dont give two shits who i offend anymore, because i tried to be nice, so you know what, fuck you! My view of people changes on a daily basis, so if you need a reinforcer every now and then, just ask, I will be more than happy to tell you what I think that day. That's the only thing people seem to understand anymore. Fuck this.

Yeah, so when I was having a rough time, mayn people showed a legitimate concern, and others could have cared less. Also, the mother fuckers who like to talk amongst themselves and try to divide and cause problems, grow the fuck up! Oh yeah, and if I tell you something, and tell you not to tell anyone else, you little shits, that means keep your good for nothing pie hole shut. And then you wonder why I don't tell you anything and get all pissed off. Wait.... Yeah, and people who continuously pry into my life, or don't believe what I say, I dont give a shit. You dont belive it fine, but dont second guess me, because that pisses me off more than most things. Two-faced people. I want you dead. I am beyond tired of you fuckers. And people who drop off the face of the earth, then expect me to jump at the first opportunity to do something, stop that. There are three people that I would drop shit for, and more likely than not your are'nt one of them.

One last note, dont give me shit, expect me to take it and then be like whatever, cause the ball stops here.

Where Did I Go Wrong?
Archangel_Thames
April 18, 2004 @ 10:49 PM

Who am I supposed to be? I don't know. No one seems to be able to accept me for who I am. Everytime I have an opinion I seem to be shot down and given dirty looks because I'm wrong. I don't know who my friends are. I don't know what I'm supposed to do with myself. I don't know why I'm hated so much.

Would it just be better without me here? Should I just disappear and not return next Fall? I don't want to abandon my commitments and loyalties but I have found myself to be questioning whether or not my "loyalties" want me to continue working with them. I do not wish to seem contradictory to what I have said in the past and say maybe I should have faith in "Gods" plan. I just can't continue to accept that I'm supposed to do something beyond just die.

Where am I supposed to go and what am I supposed to do? As of now, I'm just ready to say fuck it and give up on life...because really, what additional purpose do I have here? I know of less then thirty people who would be distraught if I were to just drop dead and even then it would only affect them for a month at most.

Where did I go wrong?

Guess What?
Diffy
May 05, 2004 @ 8:31 am

IM NAKED!

Actions
sep00426
January 22, 2005 @ 2:13 pm

recently i just cant belive the things i have been seeing and hearing.... common girls get a man that treats you right... no one deserves to be used and hurt and thrown around like there not worth shit, you are worth somthing and its a hell of alot more than what hes worth... we all know who im talking about. You keep going back to him so he thinks he has the right to do whatever he wants, he dose it becuase he knows no matter what you will just keep running right back into his traps and lies. Why would you let yourself be cheated on stolen from and disrespected by someone who hasent giving you anything back except the words i love you... you think he loves you... think again, actions DO speak louder than words and his actions have proven everything i just said, belive what you want... obviously the truth dosent matter, what you want to belive is all that matters... living in the moment will not make you happy... take a moment to take a step back and look at the whole picture, are you willing to risk your friends and most importantly your FAMILY for someone who says i love you but dosent mean it? your friends and family DO love you and always will, why would you risk that for someone who says it but dosent mean it... ignoring the truth dose not make it go away...

High Ramblings
xF_ckingxEmoxSoul
January 30, 2005 @ 12:43 am

I'm sittin here... tis Saturday night and I am stoned as a mother fucker. I'm alone in my room now... so yeah... it's all good I guess. I don't have any cigarettes or b&m or anything to smoke though... and that is bad because I really need to smoke. But what can you do I guess.

Yesterday I had an interesting experience hanging out with Kym and Jess. We had a good bonding time when we got drunk, and we were so drunk, and I got so sick as fucking always. Thus I don't like to drink like I like to smoke.

So yeah I puked up everything possibly in me and ended up having dry heaves and puking up bile and it was disgusting.

But then I got better because I ate chicken noodle soup and all that jazz... And then I smoked 2 bowls at Amanda's that were blunt roaches so that helped my stomach settle perfectly. But yeah... then we bought a half. First time I've smoked since Wednesday. But yeah...

I was supposed to see Connie tonight... but then Jess couldn't get me home on time and then my leg got hurt... We had just pulled in and Harold was backing out but his lights were off and Amanda asked me to get her jacket so I had my legs out the dorr and was sitting down and turned around and the next thing I notice is sharp pain in my legs and Harold had backed into Jessica, wedging her between the door and his car, and that pushed the door closed on my leg and hurt it bad... and it was stuck like that a few seconds and then I had to be helped intp the house and to the seat. It sucked. But yeah... thats what had happend... I probably won't be able to walk well tomorrow... -.-

But yeah... I'mma go. Just thought I'd update my high ramblings.

-diNah-

He Told Me He Loved Me
teenage_heart
February 05, 2005 @ 11:10 am

I was on the phone with Jeremy allll night yesterday, and he was really drunk, so he was telling me the truth about everything. It was so nice to hear his voice, that fucking mental place his dad put him in is horrible he says. He tries so hard to be good and come bak here but it's no use.

he told me he loved me<3 it was so sweet. and he's gonna get a car and come see me sometime this week when he's by his moms. it's crazy with all the shit he does there compared to when he's here. i miss himmm.

Good Day
Dark_Princess9
February 03, 2005 @ 9:08 pm

I'm getting pierced again on Friday, I think . . . not quite sure what I'm going to get pierced yet. . . any ideas?

I'm sooooo sore after last night. I've taken the skin off my hips which really really hurts (boned corsets are bitches) I've also completely done my back in and most of my muscles. . . don't ask me what i was doing because I'm not entirely sure.

I'm trying to get rid of negative people - ie those who make me feel like crap. So far this is three people who I will do much better without. As for the boy element . . . god I know how to pick them!!! Although current ideas are either to seduce a monk (there's quite a few of them around here) or to become a nun without any vows of silence, chastity or any relation to god etc. . . second thoughts I may need to think about that one . . . I want my Jack tho . . . I'm still a true candy cane child which has resurfaced amazingly strong recently

We picked out pieces of paper for rooms earlier . . . I got the attic room whcich I'm so so so excited about!!! I've got a floor to myself he he he I've always wanted an attic room - I'll be like a princess in a tower!!! (Even if it is one flight of stairs from the bathroom, two flights of stairs from the lounge, and three flights of stairs from the kitchen)

I've been downloading lots of videos from the network thing here which is cool . . . but i've managed to download a load of vids in French (including cold mountain with the gorgeous you-know-who) which is annoying as it means that I have to concentrate as I watch them.

I sort of didn't sleep last night lol . . . I went to sleep (eventually) at about 6am . . . after lots of intriguing conversations on the internet and with Mike, and also one point of walking downstairs in my pyjamas to find lots of people there, then turning round and falling up the stairs - ooh how classy!!! Earlier today I also managed to follow in Meg's mis-footsteps and fall down the stairs too.

Having a good day overall today - woo hoo!!!

Bad Karma
some_day_I_will_fly_away
February 08, 2005 @ 8:33 PM

my mood has slowly went down the drain! I'm in a state of paralysis and cannot move. I miss Fluffy but also do not. i don't know why i'm posting because i don't want to share really what i am feeling . I do i guess in a deeper level but i cannot seem to find reason for putting my feelings out in the world too. I had a really odd bus ride home tonight which just shot me into misery. It's funny, I can be happy one minute and then i can sit and think for five minutes on my own and by the end of the thought pattern my brain has already thought about ever bad thing that has, or is going to happen. As usual i'm just confused and scared . I need alone time but then at the same time i need others. O well as usual i will say "lifes a bitch" because it is. I guess this whole feeling sad has been created froma lack of love. And i know their will be a few of you out their who will automaticlly post that you love me. but it's just not so. I couldn't actually think of anyone who truly loves me. I me i sat on my bus thinking about htis for 15-20 minutes. I pictured in my brain that all the people who loved me wouyld have glowing lights some brighter than others. I pictured that everyone who didn't love me or like me or hated me were filled with black . I searched for the lights but it was consumed by the darknes. This all sounds really whiny and probably like every other teen out thier but I's consuming me and i cannot find those lights. Don't post that you love me, don't post that lost of people love me because i will not take it for truth. I feel alittle bit flustered rgith now as the waves of hate hit me but all i can think about is how much i love a lot more people and that no one (truly) loves me back. I love my friends i care about the world and i feel sad that their are so many people who do not love they just sorta like people. I don't think love should be something found from just one person i think it shoudl be everyone who cares about someone . I love you all who read this (alot more than any of you know however) and i hope that you all just think about loving someone (not boyfriend/girlfriend love by the way). I'm done I'm through i just said everything that i did and dinot wan tto say. Do not post your comments on how much you love me if you think i will feel better because it will just make me feel worse. Well toodloose.

Also i feel lately that are group has been down just as other i think have noticed (nicole specifically and katie). well i think taht we need to do something brach off or split up or talk or somethign however i don't know why i'm saying this because of late i've felt like oan out sider. well anyways something needs to to happen and i don't think that positive energy is jsut going to fix it no matter how hard i hoped it would . The group feels stagnate and old and decaying. It's got a bad vibe or karma or something. One way or another something has to be different.

Draft
NetZumi
January 09, 2005 @ 2:55 am

Fuck it... FUCK IT ALL! I'm all for anarchy now what the hell does our goverment think it's doing lets draft again!!!! I'm not some damned pawn... I'm not an easy man to make angry by any stretch of the imaginatation.... but i'm going to protest, people have to know whats going down...

No Reason To Stay
DemonicNecroeater
November 21, 2004 @ 12:32 am

ive reached a point in my life where you can look back and realize what kinda person you are analyze your right and wrongs and realize that you've done more wrongs then rights and that you have repeled ideas of society that would turn you into another mindless follower of the same idea people believe in becouse "it's the right thing to do" becouse then everyone will think that you are a bad person. why does religion have to do with everything in my life why does in have to wrap me in a sort of uncormftable way that if i move anywich way i will up set the balance between me and somebody i know. i know i am happy with atleast half of my life, i may appear happy superficialy. but deep inside there is great sadness and frustration, feeling like there is something else i have to do to be happy, it seems all the self reflection and all the crying in the world isn't doing anything to help the pain go away, drowning it out with alcohol seems to help. there is only one person who can truly makes me smile who truly gives my heart a ray of hope to continue and not to break down. is the life i've built around me to the shape of my mind and to the needs of me. i love becouse im not sure of what to do anymore. and when that is gone.........i will have no other reason to stay mentaly alive. god helps not, if being the outcast of your whole family becouse you can't force your self to be a sheep, the way of god, i want no part in

190

it, i have that part of me wich is still flourishing inside a pit of raw hatred and bottomless bone pits, but yet people insist on taking that much away, i will not have it, such goodfriends they are, waiting like dogs for the first bone somebody throws out. let us pray to a place where nobody cares, where the god you praise selects only a few.. if only i knew how to pry this leech from my life draining the happines within me growing restless with sides of sleepless nights and pulsating hangovers.

Kaitlin you hold more in your hands than you realise. i love you so much and i wont let anyone between you and me. to all those who try to come between us... I have not yet begun to fight

Just Me
martian4adam
February 06, 2005 @ 2:08 pm

i lay awake each night, staring up at my ceiling, just wondering
i'm so lonely, and it makes me sick just remembering it all
in my mind your face appears, and i wish i could just reach you
i imagine all we could have, but my dreams don't ever come true
do you ever think of me, like i think of you, just before you sleep?
if i could just change your mind, it'd be the best thing in the world
i'm drowning in my own lack of faith.. thinking the worst so much
will i ever find the happiness in love that i'm terribly lacking now?
here's a letter to remind you of all that i've continually felt for you
at least i know i'm a friend, at least i know that i matter somewhat
sometimes being a friend's not enough, cuz i know i could be more
this is just my world, my disfortune, my pain, my grief... just me

Doves
dragon13356
February 04, 2005 @ 4:43 pm

DAMN LIFE! While it was nice of my body to pick today to be sick, it was also very cruel...my mom told me I couldn't do anything today... maybe I can convince her I feel better and that I need to go do stuff tonight, but it's doubtful. So, I'm sure you guys want to hear the lovely story of the sick....well, it's pretty boring. I woke up, ate some cornflakes, and proceded to purge them from my body (in the BLEAH way). Been randomly hot and cold and slightly feverish at times. Anyways, I'm gonna have to talk to peoples and find out things, but I most likely won't be able to go anywhere today, although I haven't thrown up since early this morning and I slept for a long time, so maybe I'm better. Anyways, I decided to change my layout (to Gundam Seed, whether you like it or not), so I'll be doing that, and by the time you people come back and read this, hopefully I'll be done with it.

"The dove is a symbol of peace. It is not born with the kind of sharp beak or claws which could inflict a fatal attack. So they say that if these birds were pitted against each other, it would undoubtedly be a long gruesome battle."

To Helen
pewee
August 12th, 2004 @ 7:10 pm

I don't want another pretty face
I don't want just anyone to hold
I don't want my love to go to waste
I want you and your beautiful soul
You're the one I wanna chase
You're the one I wanna hold
I wont let another minute go to waste
I want you and your beautiful soul

Ending My Pain
Lost__inmyworld
February 07, 2005 @ 10:21 pm

my heart is fighting....i'm completely in love and it hurts...

tears burn in my eyes as i try to understand....i try to understand what i'm missing....what don't i have?

Father, you've given me everything i've ever asked for. you've protected me when i needed protection. something is happening and i don't know what it is. i hate living in fear....i hate not knowing what's going to happen. father, i want to see your plan for me...i know i can't control it, i know you have all power over me...but i just want to know. i want to know that i'm not losing my mind. father, what's going to happen? why do i feel like this? why can't i get rid of this sinking feeling? why can't i sleep enough?

i can't i get out? my only time of peace is in his arms....in the arms of the wonderful man you sent to me. but what is it haunting me? it's not mom anymore...it's not my guilt, i let that all go. it's something new... it's neglect...it's being naive...it's being blind. it's aching for things to be normal agian...it's a longing for a perfect life...i want to leave the horrors of this world. i want to spend eternity in your arms...i love the world in which you've created me, yet father, the beauty is tainted by evil... shadows follow me....my nightmares have left me...but this feeling has not. take me now...end my pain.

My Mother
drowningyourselfinantifreeze
February 09, 2005 @ 9:45 pm

Now it's time for a rant.

My mother is a dumb, useless, dope-whore bitch. And I plan to to tell her that. If you were one of my friends you would know what I mean. I have been silent for far too long and it's about god damn time that someone stood up that bitch. I love my sister, Bailey, and I would kill for her, but I know she will never call my mother out. And no matter how much my family tries she will never listen. So someone has to give her a reality check..and I am volunteering.

Why do I call my mother a bitch? Hahahaha long story. But to make it simple:

"Kathleen you were an accident, I don't know why I even kept you in the first place... you will never be like me and you will never be my daughter. I am completely washing my hands of you. Don't talk to me, I don't know you." - my mother circa 1997...

"Katie I am know I was a bad mom. I have changed. I promise, I just hope you can come up sometime so we can 'bond' and I can get to know you better." - my mother circa 2003 (note how she didn't say sorry... she hasn't for 6 years)

"I am pissed at Katie. She won't talk to me and she hangs around her Aunts like a fucking dog. I don't know why I even try... she didn't come to my birthday..she's hasn't spoken to me."- my mother last weekend. (I was by my aunts so I didn't have to talk to her... but I did to make my aunt Misty happy. I just told her 'happy birthday mom. I'll see ya around.' And besides where has she been on every birthday I've had since I was 8? oh yeah...get strung out and leaving me at home. Silly me, I forgot.

so that's why I hate Sheri (there are also other reasons, but they are far too personal to put up here.) I know my life is not that bad and it doesn't suck as much as it could, but I feel like my mother is pulling me down and I need to cut loose. This has been along time coming and I am ready to face the consequences. But if I disapeer or come to school banged up... you'll know why.

What is Going On With America?
BillyDomCrazy
February 09, 2005 @ 9:43 pm

School is really starting to get on my last nerve.

A. They have teachers that have NO idea what the fuck they are doing or what in the hell they are teaching.

B. Teachers can't control the class, always calling up the principal.

C. Students wasting MY time and the TEACHERS time chattering away and acting out....

D. The learning enviroment is really not helping me.

I know I'm being selfish and all, but I rather just drop out or get fucking home schooled...so tired of looking at people's faces...each day a new girl's arrive with a belly, as in she's pregnant. None of them are above the age of 17...WHAT THE FUCK IS HAPPENING TO AMERICAS 'FUTURE'?

You Don't Know
TrustMe_ImOkay
February 02, 2005 @ 6:55 AM

You don't know. It's all just speculation. Hell, I don't even know.

I know I'm hypocritical. I know that after all my bitching about you cutting, I started cutting again. But you don't know that. And things should stay like that. I deserve this. I hurt you. I'm leading you on when I'm not even sure of my own feelings. Something I didn't want to do. I see now why you stopped talking to me, tried to push me away before. It would seem easier. But that hurt me so much. We were best friends. I found out you loved me, and it hurt even more. But now I think I understand.

And "I'm sorry" doesn't even begin to cover what I want to tell you...

Hips
tryin
January 23, 2005 @ 11:57 am

cutting on your hip is easier than cutting on your wrist.

People can't see it as well

Messed Up
l3laze_x
January 18, 2005 @ 11:38 pm

oh my god i dont think anyone gives a shit really this is messed up about what i say, how i feel or anything . its like im not even there, makes perfect sense why things are the way they are. its been like this all my life, why didnt i realize this. the way people are with me. everyones just fake, and best friends right thats a joke what are best friends? i wont even talk about the gf thing, its just messed up basically.

Dreams
xDreaMz_aRe_oVerRateDx
January 22, 2005 @ 11:04 am

I wish that I could sleep every second of the day. When you're asleep, you're never overwhelmed by life itself. Dreams overtake you while you sleep blissfully and unaware. Problems never occur.

Dreams, however, are overrated. They always end too soon. You never get to finish your dream. There is never a happy ending. Dreams whisk you away, off your feet, to a whole different world where no one commits suicide, no one is alone, and fear does not exist.

I want to dream twenty-four seven. Life is not fair. Life is what makes dreams end. Life makes dreams overrated. If only dreams lasted all day. I wouldn't have to worry, I wouldn't feel pain, I wouldn't be so scared of the world that surrounds me. I would always feel safe, something I never feel anymore.

Everyone judges. No one can see past the lies that surround the exterior of the human body. No one can see the truth. When they see a shooting star, they make a wish. I'd never wish upon a shooting star. Because somewhere, there's a falling star that everyone thinks isn't as a spectacular sight, and then someone catches it.

That someone.

Is me.

They don't know the half of it.

I wish dreams lasted all day long.

But dreams are overrated.

Miss Spelled
TickledPink420
February 06, 2005 @ 4:40 am

hello all! I'm sorry if I don't write all this shit corect because I'm kinda fuckin waisted and i duno if im spellin shti rong or right so juss ignor tha bad spellin lolz...itll be alot better tomorrow when im sober lolz..

so i went ova to annas house...andher couise was tehre...he couise is real cute...i think im curshin hard...i might only be sayin trhis because im drunk...and kinda high...but still...hes real cute and he smokes and drinks...so its not like we dont have nethin in commen lolz...he listens to gangsta shit too which is pretty tight because we have mjsuic in commeon too! woot bitches! lolz..i duno is he thinks im cute but iuts all good...i can still think hes cute...

welp im fuckin waisted and im typein all this shit weith my eyes closed... and it hink i need to go to sleep...wow...what did i just tpe? loz...im such a fuckin loser...NOT wow...ok im going to go nbow...tonight was uckin aweoms

Last Night
BaNg_BaBy_BaNg
January 29, 2005 @ 1:54 pm

omg last night wasnt a good night at all.. god damn david.. what an asshole.. why does he always gotta be like that.. hes saying too much shit and now he said we cant even be friends and we dont even kno eachother which is total bullshit and my friend zach give him a piece of his mind.. oh let me tell you a piece of his mind!!! lol it was great! but yeah............ i cried forever last night.. im done with this bullshit.. why does everything bad have to happen to me.. but im not surprised it happened like this because david is an asshole.. derrr!!! anyways david and me arent talking and he hates me and i hate him but i think this was just a reality check for me because now i kno that i need to watch out for the assholes who are disqused as nice guys... im tired of being used and abused... physically and mentally.. and im tired of my "false hope" relations.. this year is gunna be different im gunna make an effort to change this... change it for good.. im not gunna sit there and be blind anymore im not gunna sit there and take the shit from people i used to because i dont deserve to be treated like this and almost every other guy or girl agrees (except the assholes) people are so surprised when they hear what i have gone through and i have gone through so much its horrible and this isnt gunna happen anymore.. i am prepared for what will happen and what is coming and what is going on right now.. because i will NOT be used and i will NOT be taken advantage of.. im done with the shit.. and i apprecatie my friends more than ever now because they have been there with me through so much shit... and they truly do love me and they truly do care about me because they have always been here and i will always be there for this is my life and this is how im gunna live it.. spending the last couple days crying really makes you look at yourself and really ask am i the person i want to be? and i dont kno.. am i where i want to be? and i dont kno again.. i want to say yes but my mind thinks no.. and i dont kno where to go in life now because i have become so frustrated and insurcure about myself because of what has happened between me and some people.. and not juss david.. so now i feel insurcure and frustrated because of people either saying things or doing things and so now i have become afraid............

this has only been a reality check

for this is my life

and this is how i will live it

i love my friends forever and ever

and i love myself and one say i will come to relise it

<3 always

danielle

Job
forbiddenxdesires
Febuary 10, 2005 @ 4:49 pm

Yesterday, my baby didn't go to work so he could see me, and he never got to. So he's at work right now and I don't get to talk to him until he either calls me or I call him at like 8ish. That really blows. I don't like him working, it takes up all his fucking time. Oh welll, he has to have a "legitimate job", he can't just be a dealer. Whatever.

In other news, I think Mel has already left. That sucks my left tit, because now it'll be harder for us to plan this weekend. Which i'm not even 100% sure I can go out. (Kaylan, if my boyfriend wasn't such an angry douche bag, you could come. I wish you could!!! Love you bundles!) Bah, so yeah, I have to wait for her to call me.

Fuckness! My phone just rang and I was hoping it was Adrian, but it was some chick asking for Ron Lewis. Thats not me. OH MY FUCKING GOD!!!!!! The most terrible thing happened to me today. Those of you who know me well, hold on to something.... I lost my shirt!!. That white one I carry around?! Its fucking gone. I lost it at lunch somehow, and now I wanna cry. I'm about to fucking kill someone. Thats like, my fucking sanity right there. And I left it in the cafeteria. Woohoo, my sanity is in the cafeteria.

Kaylan comes back on monday. I wish I knew what her 2nd period class was so I could send her a flower, but I don't know where it is... I'll buy her one and give it to her. That'll work too. Anyway, i'm gonna go lay down, wait for 8er to call, and grieve the loss of my shirt....

Real
sicandblind
January 26, 2005 @ 9:23 pm

You know. alot of the time it seems like nothing is real.

It's all a collage of dreams, images, noises, memories, and deju vu. And then. You remember what it was like last time you talked with someone who made it all real.

...

I Do
DaniDanger420
February 07, 2005 @ 12:30 PM

seriously...who goes and gets up and chills with dad and then goes and smokes up...

I Do.

thats who.

bitch!

Nothing Hurts
Indescribable_Thoughts
February 09, 2005 @ 2:54 pm

Today, heh it sucks. That's all I can say about today. My kidneys hurt so bad that in 8th period. I started to cry because it hurt so badly. Before all that though in Lunch Michael and I were talking about girls showing their boobs and stuff like that I for one thing think it is really disrespectful to do something like that just to get attention. I don't know I just think it is even if you love your body so much you want to show everyone do it in a respectful manner. Then I said something like "it doesn't matter." He went off talking and when the guy called us for our table to go up I just left and went to the line. He didn't say a word to me in the line so I got out of line and sat back down at the table b/c I didn't feel good. Since 4th period (lunch) he hasn't talked to me. And before activity's period came around he put the 2 bracelets things in my locker and was like "I got to go to homeroom." That's all and it makes me feel like shit that he doesn't even want to talk I guess he just wants to wait until we get home or something like that. I'm really not too sure. I just ugh I don't know I hurt like ultra bad, and I don't want something like that break us up, which I highly doubt that. I'm just telling myself by the end of the night everything is going to be all right. Everything is going to be all right.

I have had time to think about everything, but I need more time to think on this I'm not sure this is what I want. But I want to move down with my parents I do not want to stay up here any longer. The only reasons why I stay is for my happiness with Michael. Because he is my world, I don't know what I'd do with out him, and the silly thing is he knows all that. Heh

The night falls down as everyone sleeps I awake to my love next to me. Kiss him gently and slowly run to the bathroom sit in the bathroom and cry, cry for what? Pure happiness.

Nothing hurts more......

Never
vixmarie420
February 10, 2005 @ 7:39 am

Fuck this shit, im goin to school all angry and shit.

She lied, i knew she did, she got pissed at me and lied to someone else about me.

When is it gunna end.

When are they all gunna realize how childish they are and that they need to grow up?

Never.

Thats why i shouldnt have friends like that anymore, but they always wanna tell me different.

God i hate this!

grrrr

Someone help.

Forehead
TheInfamousNothing
February 09, 2005 @ 11:50 pm

This guy I know tried it, so im gonna, lets c if i can tpye my name with my forehead.....

cu7nhjtrpovidaxzsw its in there somewhere

Cu7nHjtRpovIdaxzSw (look at uppercased letters)

More Then Enough
MustangCowgirl
January 10th 2005 @ 10:44 pm

My mind goes blank,
And I want to run.
Into darkness I sank,
Someone turned out the sun.
Everything's spinning.
I'm so afraid.
My world is dimming.
I'll never get saved.
A force unseen,
A sudden pain.
Hands rough and mean.
Locked down and chained.

I'm on my way to hell,
And there's no way out.
No one can hear me when I yell.
What's this all about?!
I never did much wrong.
So many times I've been hurt.
The pain's been going on so long.
Been treated like nothing more then dirt.

And I'm sick of it.
I've had enough.
Ready to start that fire I've been planning;

www.bookofblogs.org

Ready to get it lit.
Gonna get down and dirty.
Gonna get tough.
'Cause I've had way more then
Enough.

Ain't a soul who can stop me
Not now, not anymore.
You just wait and see,
I'm gonna find that door.
The fires gonna burn bright.
It's gonna set me free.
I'm gonna set it all alight
And my past and pains will burn with me.

'Cause I'm sick of it.
I've had enough.
I've started that fire I've been planning;
Ready to get it lit.
Gonna get down and dirty.
Gonna get tough.
'Cause I've had way more then
Enough.

I've proved yall wrong.
I'm stronger then you.
I got away, and it didn't take me long.
Maybe now you'll see it's true.
I got away.
And now I laugh in your face.
I'm free today,
Of me you won't find a trace.
'Cause I hit the road
On my new Harley.
Carrying a new light load,
I'm finally free.

'Cause I got sick of it.
I'd had enough.
I started that fire I've been planning;
It's alread lit.

202

I got down and dirty.
I got tough.
'Cause I've had way more then
Enough.

Yeah,
Way more then enough baby.
So I set it all on fire.
My past is burnt to ashes,
And my pains are just mere memories.

'Cause I got sick of it.
I'd had enough.
I started that fire I've been planning;
It's alread lit.
I got down and dirty.
I got tough.
'Cause I've had way more then
Enough.

Tough,
Yeah baby, tough.
Stong,
Stronger baby.
Stronger then you'll ever be.
I'm free.
Yeah, baby
Do you know what free is?
Yeah, it's me.
I'm free.
Free baby,
Free.

Grim Reaper
venomous_braincloud04
February 07, 2005 @ 12:25 pm

Couldn't sleep at all last night. Kind of weird. But anyways, went through all of my sister's stuff from high school. It was kind of interesting. Really didn't pay much attention to anything except her old papers from english and art class. It was then I realized where I got my talent from which is pretty fuckin' awesome considering that my other older sister sucks at drawing and writing and all that other creative/artsy stuff. Finally a trait not all 3 of us have a trace of! Well, if you want to count sucking at school and not getting straight A's through your whole life a trait then there's one I def don't have a trace of. 2 of us suck at math yet I'm the only one that can't just pull off an A. So annoying. Not that I feel the need to try and be perfect and be as much like them as possible hell I'm far from being like them as far as personality/clothes/sexuality stuff like that goes which is cool since we still get along pretty good. Back in my Junior year I had to join this group and make a movie thing about this book we read. it was For Whom The Bell Tolls and after begging they finally decided to let me play the part of death. I won't go into the whole story so to keep things short I fell in love with that black grim reaper robe my mom made me. I couldn't find it for the longest time and I thought she threw it out. I was upset but eventually got over it. Last night...hanging in the very back of the closest...there it was...more beautiful than ever before. All I need is a scythe and it looks perfect! So excited! Don't know where to wear it to though. I was thinking I'd walk around here and knock on the houses of the amish and scare the shit out of them and run like hell before they can catch me...who wants to come?!?! Classes tonight. Hopefully I'll find out how I did on my test in study stratigies and how my paper was. Then off to math. Hello Mr. F! Maybe this will turn out like it usually does and shit from high school will come back to me..hopefully....

Monster Inside
Bro_keN
February 10, 2005 @ 11:32 pm

I think it's crazy. there are people online who are sick, really sick. anorexic or bulimic, and wasting away, destroying themselves, and then there are these blogrings, and these people who treat anorexia like just another diet; "Ana Luv" and all that. people die. it's a deadly, horrible disease, and people die. it's like cancer or something. it takes over your body bit by bit, until you're too weak to fight it anymore, and then you give in...

why do so many people act like it's a good thing to be? like it's something to be admired for, like it's a group thing. I just don't think that's right. if someone's anorexic, and so unhappy that they're willing to starve themselves to lose a couple of pounds, because they see fat in the mirror, even when the rest of the world sees bones, I don't think it's right for people to pat them on the back and say "well done, you're amazing, ana luv!". that just seems wrong, and a little bit twisted to me.

I mean, I understand that people want support, but I think so many people on xanga are getting the wrong kind of support. people need the "let's beat this together" support, but all they're getting is the "wow, let's lose weight together, ana luv!" support, which isn't really support at all. you're all guiding each other towards death, towards the destruction of such already-beautiful bodies.

it's the saddest thing I've ever seen.

I really wish that this anorexic cancer, this bulimic monster, would go away.

none of you deserve it. none of you.

I just wish you could all see yourselves from the world's point of view. because you're all beautiful.

all of you.

<3

Sux
radarlove
January 20, 2005 @ 11:41 PM

Another day another dollar. Not! I'm adapting to the schedule change. Waking up early sux but my energy level has finally began to adjust. Chemistry wasn't so bad today. It was nice to see those connections of formulas. Trig. was great, not for the math of course but for the guys. Jamakin Bag sits next to me now. So every Tuesday and Thursday I have Jamakin Bag distracting me to the left and Signing Boy Michael distracting me at the front of the class. I have to literally keep myself from looking at Michael because everytime I do I get this fat grin on my face. Melani knows that look I get. lol I'm starting to forget what Santino looks like and what his voice sounds like know. It really sux. Loving someone that you can barley remember. I haven't seen him in 5 months maybe? God this so sux, I'm 19 years old and I don't even have a boyfriend. It's not like I'm not approach it just that those who want me I have no desire for. It's irony in plain site. Sux.

Sorting Me Out
Enlightened_Youth
February 08, 2005 @ 10:42 pm

Ok so I'm back from my shower. On the whole lesbian thing now. Like I think I'm more of a bisexual really and here is why:

1. I still think guys are hot

2.I have never had sex but in order for it to be enjoyable a penis seems necessary

3. I like have feelings for guys

But the thing is I'm really confused . Like sexuality doesn't seem like something you should be confused about. Like they say you are born gay. And I really do think that is the truth. Ever since I was a little girl I like wanted to be a boy. Then society told me this was wrong so I kind of grew up to be more girly. And I still pretty am girly. Well I mean its not like being girly has anything to do with it but it's like this. I have never felt comfortable in my own skin, like I should have been born someone or something else. I mean I know I'm me but I just feel like I should be diffrent but there is something holding me back inside. If that made any sense at all. Like I'm not like a total man....I think I'm really pretty (lol) and my basic dress is black jeans with a tight white shirt cons and like 3 spiked belts. But then like I've always wanted to cut my hair and wear it in like a short boy cut. I know how you look doesn't make you a lesbian but like, this one time at a party I was dared to freak dance with a girl, so I got behind this girl and we were grinding pretty hard (mind you we were both drunk) but like I really enjoyed it. More than I ever have with a guy. And I didn't mind her like rubbing on my boobs and stuff and I was rubbing hers (I know all the guys are like turned on now lol, but I'm serious). Like I just don't know if I'm a lesbian. I've always have had these feelings. In 2nd grade I had a crush on a girl and I drew a picture of us married and I was the guy. I've kind of has always had like crushes on girls. But I think this society has told me that is wrong so much that I forced myself to like guys. Besides I think it runs in the family. My uncle was gay (R.I.P.) and my aunt is a lesbian too. So I don't know. If you can help me leave comments please...

Fading
MustangCowgirl
January 16th 2005 @ 10:03 pm

I woke up this morning,
With tear already in my eyes.
I guess somehow I knew what was coming;
Geuss I could see through the lies.
I wish I had known then,
What the pain was that the day would bring.
'Cause maybe if I had known
I could have lived it up; had one more chance to sing.

If I had one more; one more hour, one more day
I would live life like it should be.
I'd have fun my way.
I'd go wild, yeah, wild and free.
I'd tell you how I really loved you.
I'd take all the chances.
I'd live like I used to,
Yeah, Like I used to.
With the risks and the chances,
With the love and the glances.

But I won't be seeing tomorrow,
For I know I'm fading fast.
Please, for me don't feel sorrow.
Let my life lie in the past.
Remember how I loved you,
Then just forget.
I know it's hard to do...
But just forget we ever met.

Your hands in mine and you're crying.
I want to tell you I'm ok, and wipe them away...
But then I'd be lying.
I try to whisper I love you,
But now I can hardly move.
I start crying too...
You're trying to sooth.

I'm losing blood fast,
A red pool spreading out on the pavement.
Your jeans are turning a shade of black,
I'm trying to wave the pain back.

Now you're yelling ad loud as you can.
"Someone help us please,
Please someone save her man."
You're yelling that you can't live without me...
I want to tell you that you can.
I want to tell you that now I'll be free,
But I can't.
I want to tell you I'm ok...
That I'll get up any moinute now.

But I won't be seeing tomorrow,
For I know I'm fading fast.
Please, for me don't feel sorrow.
Let my life lie in the past.
Remember how I loved you,
Then just forget.
I know it's hard to do...
But just forget we ever met.

But I can't anymore.
Everything's black.
One of you're tears lands on my cheek.
You're yelling "Please,
Oh please god,
Send her back."

But I won't be seeing tomorrow,
For I know I'm fading fast.
Please, for me don't feel sorrow.
Let my life lie in the past.
Remember how I loved you,
Then just forget.
I know it's hard to do...
But just forget we ever met.

To anyone who actualy took the time to read this:

Thanks. It means a lot to me. I'd love it if you'd comment, because I really don't know what to think of this one. I've had mixed comments, as well as mixed feelings. I want to find out how it really is.

~Nicole

My Walk With God
lilhopey007
February 01, 2005 @ 4:48 pm

Hey! Well, today, i actually listened to the bible studies, i mean i've listened to 1 or 2 of them, but otherwise its simply a grade to people and its deathly obvious. Well, you know its bad when someones all describing a trait or a person with that trait negatively and you posses the same exact one, maybe not under the same circumstances, but the same basic principle. My heart is hard, and supprisinly i like it that way. I appologize if i've offended or hurt any of you in the process, but i'm just trying to get by life without worrying about every little thing. Sometimes hardening your heart for a while is the only thing that can help you get by. I'm still a Christan though, yes my walk with God isn't exactly perfect, but i try my best. I'm tired of feeling like because i don't profess God all the time, that i'm not as "good a Christan" as other people. And its hard not to care what others think, it being second nature and all. I'm just tired of feeling judged for certain aspects of who i am. If your going to reject me, at least get to know me. Instead of taking one look and decided your better than i am. I'm who i am no if's and's or butt's about it, but i have feelings too. Atleast somtimes that is.

hOpE

I Wish
suicidal_fag
February 11, 2005 @ 8:12 PM

I wish you wouldn't yell at me. I wish you'd be calm about things. I wish You could love me for who I am and not how I look. I wish you wouldnt hit me i wish youd understand i wish youd come home and appriciate the dishes i did i wish i wasnt your slave i wish youd hate me i wish youd did me why you did bong i wish wishes came true i wish youd tell me your boyfriends names i wish youd listen i wish we had a perfect family i wish i could behave how you wanted i wish i were like my brother i wish i had friends who truely cared i wish i could fit in i wish youd hit me so id have bruises i wish youd tell me to runaway i wish you apprieciated the things i do i wish you didnt acknowledge me bad traits i wish youd stay out of my life i wish i could have a journal with out yOu reading iti wish you didnt call me a freak i wish you werent so mean i really wish i hated you

4 Days
encrptyer
January 14, 2005 @ 1:08 AM

it's amazing what 4 days can do.

so tuesday, i was roaming around on the internet, looking through some blogrings i joined. and i was looking at the latest posts and stuff, then i see a girl's picture that reminded me of someone from a while back. for some reason that picture just pointed itself out to me, something drew me to click it you could say. well i clicked it and as it turned out it was the old friend of mine i was reminded of. i was dumbfounded honestly, it took me 2 hours to believe that it was her. it took some searching but i found her name, and it was the same so yea, then it took a little while for me to get the balls to leave her a comment on her page, and might i say that i was nervous pushing the "submit" button, but i got it over with, and it turns out a couple minutes later she left me a comment on my page. i can't tell you how happy i was, it was like learning that if you wish hard enough things can come true. honestly i think there's something out there that's on my side now, or at least something is making up for all the unhappy times i've had lately, and i've had plenty, so this makes up for them all...ten fold.

so she posted me late, and she left her sn for me to message when i wanted i guess. so i was like...anxious the entire school day wanting to go home and get to talk to her. it was like i had to go find some gold or something, i was excited, o so excited. yea well, when i got home she was signed on, so i opened up a text box and typed in "hi", and once again i was scared to contact her, so an hour later i pressed "enter". and a couple seconds later she IMed me back, asking how i was, how i found her, and what not...I WAS SO RELIEVED, honestly, i was so happy that i got to talk to her. i haven't said a word to that girl in like..almost 12 years (not counting 1 or 2 random encounters where i ran into her and said hi).

goshhhh, i remember for a LONG while that she was the VERY FIRST girl i had a crush on, seriously, even though i changed schools during first grade all i did was wish i was back at the old school, so i can play with her. she was like my best friend, she and i would speak in our own language and leave everyone out of our inside jokes, once and a while i'd go to her house before school started and play games with her then get a ride with her to go to school. man i miss those days, back when the only things i had to worry about was shitting my pants and calling the teacher "mommy" haha.

i had a crush on her for the longest time, even if i didn't see her so often. i'd see her like once a year because of the filipino celebration in the church and whatnot. man come to think of it, the only time i actually got over her is when i thought that i'd never see her again. but that was when i was more ignorant, closed minded to the world. i can't tell you how much i've grown.

but anyways back to the story. i've been talking to her a couple times now, and we're getting to know each other again, and i think i'm starting to like her all over again. gossh haha

so now since i found her again, i haven't felt so empty, i'm happier now and i can think clearly without hesitation. it's like i found what i was missing, and i think it's been gone for a while. since re-connecting with her, i dunno, it's just, the place is looking alot better. man...i don't know if i should believe in fate, luck, karma, religion, destiny, hell, i don't even know if it's real, all i know that i can surely believe in is that i'm pretty happy now, more than that, i'm estatic.

My Apology
mimijess2006
June 30, 2004 @ 5:34 pm

I am sorry that you feel that I am a pathetic person. If I hurt your feelings I would like to apologize now. My page was only directed at you due to you nonchalant attitude regarding my feeling. I guess your letter only proves me right, but in any case I guess I was wrong. It wasn't your fault no one showed and you don't owe me an explanation. I guess I just figured if we were in fact friends you would at least say something to me ahead of time. Also I did express my anger a few weeks after the fact, I suppose I did because I ... tried to forget that no one cared ... or that not even you bothered to tell me you weren't coming. I guess it made me feel a little worthless and it well hurt my feelings every time I thought about it. I guess that does make me pathetic because I surcame to my feelings and over reacted with emotions. I guess that does make me a bitch. Well I can't think of anything else that I would even like to say to you but umm If you didn't like the way I treated I am sorry anytime that bother you or hit you I was only playing, its not like you didn't do the same. Well I hope that your as over this as I am. I hope that you have a great summer I sorry that it all happened this way. Thankyou for readig this and helping me realise...

Unhappy
Nymph0514y3r
February 11, 2005 @ 11:07 pm

there are things you think about alone, and in the dark, that shouldnt be thought. must be why i avoid that dark. yeah i fell to sleep this afternoon and had a terrible nightmare, like all my nightmares i have all the time all in one, geeze. now im all wiggin and alone and realize that im so stupid. but what can u do? home alone on a fri night becasue you canceled all your plans to be with someone who dosent wanna see you after all, yeah that stings a bit. oh well. tomorrows another day... why cant i just be a happy person?

My Day
masoCHISTIC_tendENCIES
January 28, 2005 @ 3:14 pm

Well, isn't today the day of coincidences. >_< Matt was giving Crissy and I a ride home, and as we were leaving school, we saw these two girls and a boy walking on the sidewalk. And Crissy goes, 'God, I hate that boy! Every time I see him I just wanna punch him in the face!' And immediately after she says that, the girl walking closest to him just slams him into a car, he trips over himself and falls flat on his face. Wow. So we rolled down the window and laughed at him; Come to find out, Crissy doesn't know him at all. Now I feel bad.

But THEN. So Matt drops me off at my house and as I'm unlocking the first lock on the front door, I was thinking to myself, 'Gee, wouldn't it be funny if my mom locked the deadbolt?' Because I don't have a key to that. Well guess fucking what, she did. So I'm all like, 'Hey, it's good, I've got my window which I always leave open a crack.' Nope. The ONE TIME I close my window all the way is the one time I actually need it open. Anyway I ended up popping out the screen and almost breaking my window (it's got a big crack through it now, but it's not all the way through the glass). I was in the middle of trying not to knock over my candles and not fall on my laptop while the Sandalwood kids started walking down my road and staring at me. Yeah.

But still, today was really good. I got all my work done (and read ahead in English) and went to Taco Bell for lunch ^_^ Then afterschool Jessi, Adam and some other kid came to visit. It was so nice seeing them! :D Adam had on a shirt that said "I'll give all you emo kids something to cry about" with "Goonie and Floywitt" on the pocket. Eee. So yeah, that was my day.

Septum
baranoir
January 27, 2005 @ 7:27 pm

hi all...

bothing has happened cept i pierced my septum again.. but the pincher was WAY too long to flip insode my nose so we decided to change it to a curved barbell and that stupid ass well goes "its fell out" aww i would go into detail but im still pissed... w/e

well carol told thar azn dude i like..that i like him... she asked his name but i didnt hear him.. he talks way low... i think hes scared of me now.. damn .. w/e i have to go the same way he does for like 5 periods so he'll have to deal w/ my fat ass...

i think he has a gf? dunno i saw him at a football game one time w/ a chick so... w/e i use to being rejected or w/e.....

i got a test tomorrow so betta go study...

i wanna go to a party... like ill be invited lmfao

ja......................

Por Nada
Dismal_Invisibility
February 03, 2005 @ 4:48 pm

Stressed doesn't even begin to describe how I'm feeling. I'm way behind in all my classes after missing a week of school. Not to mention a depression for the first time in about 3 months. "There's nowhere left to hide, in no one to confide." A line from a song by Muse. It's starting to feel like I have no one left. After Drew said what I mentioned in the previous post and a lot that I didn't, I couldn't stop thinking that the whole friendship was a complete waste and I should have ended it the first time he fucked me over. I told him everything for nothing. I think I need to find new friends. And you know how that will end up. Well, no you don't...but I do and it isn't very good. Por nada.

-Ghostly hauntings I turn loose

Coupons
Openroad
December 13 2003 @ 1:11 am

...they cut our wrists like cheap coupons and say that death was on sale today...

Back Talk
killersrquiet
January 10, 2005 @ 4:43 pm

hey, yesturday me and my dad got in a huge fight because i was "backtalking" him...he kicked me out and i think i have about a week to find somewhere to live and that really sucks cuz i dont kno where im gunna live cuz if i go with my mom i cant go to my school and shit but i dunno i miught just stay here but never b home when he is exept when he is sleeping but yea if u kno where i can stay let me kno cuz i really need a place to stay but neway everything pissed me off again today so im going to the mall with holly to get away from it all becuz she is the only 1 who really understands me and right now i feel like no1 cares and if i shot myself in the head right in front of every1 they would just b like " my god ambers dead...so neway about that kid in math hes so hot..."

its like they would care for .3 seconds and then completly forget about it but whatever u proly dont care so i dont kno y im complaining to u about it cuz i hate it when ppl complain to me so i guess im a hyprocrite but i g2g...ttyl byebye

Lock
BaBiiKiMiiEx3
February 08, 2005 @ 3:40 PM

hmm.. before ii start a bitchin entry lemme tell you bout yesterday. sat around did NOTHING, who would of guessed? lOl — uhmm Samantha called mah sweet ass nd her nd Sammii came nd got meh. we went to see Brad nd then to get iced tea nd whatever ii dont remeber. lOl but we got Kevin; we went up the park nd meh nd him smoked a bowl, then we drove around nd met up wit Westell, ii chilled wit him for most the night. hes a funny kid, well he isnt a kid lOl. but uhm yah then we went down caste to get Stephanie, Sammii took her home, came back nd Westell nd Zachery came down. we kinda juss chilled Sammii took Samantha home nd Westell nd Zachery took me home.

today was fine at school, OH OH ! BUT..SOMEONE PUT A LOCK ON MY LOCKER? II GO INTO SCHOOL, ND THERES A LOCK. JUAN WAS LIKE U TRYIN TO KEEP ME OUT? im like ii didnt do it? soo we go to the office to get it cut, nd Sammii was in ther etoo... im like wat the hell u in here for? shesz like theresz lock on my locker? WOW PPL R LAME AS HELLLLLLLL.. kinda funny tho. so yeah we got em cut but other than that... iim tired tho. uhmm.. ii gott kinda lot of work to do tonight, ii wont have time tomorrow since ii work, soo ii should try nd get that shit done, uggggh — presentations are horrible! but yah we had Mr. Tietsz for like 10 min in 8th period, he asked me to babysit soon nd ii was like hell yah, ii <3 Tietsz!!! hes mah BOY! lOl

well Willie decided to tell me his liddle girlfriend CRIED all yesterday bcuz of me nd Sammii.. nd to PLEASE STOP SAYING things to her. UHM NO? sorry babe, ii would do that if she didnt wanna call meh out again. nd ii would shut up if meh nd Sammi'sz name didnt appear in her mouth like your dick does. so lets see... ii think iima juss stop talkin to Willie, since his liddle girlfriend is way more important cause he turned into a pussy nd claims hes in love... but itsz cool cuz when the girl fucks you over... dont expect us to care. when you wanna tell us bout how you fingered her, please keep it to urself. cause no one wantsz to hear about her... when she cheatsz on, dont cry to meh. juss like how ii dont cry to

you anymore. honestly dont expect me to be your support anymore. fuck
you. you changed, we all hate it and we all hate your girlfriend. but itsz
ohkay, cuz it aint nothing against your girlfriend.. its against the fact ii
dont approve of half the girlsz u talk to. juss like you dont approve of half
da guysz ii talk to; nd well looksz like ii didnt listen to you nd u was right,
so when uu find out she ISNT THE ONE for you.. ill laugh cause lemme
tell u someone that is always callin you STUPID nd DUMB nd all them
niice niiiice wordsz really is someone you should beh wit. but its coooool
cuz ii juss aint gonna talk to yah ne more go beh wit ur liddle girlfriend..
nd oh if you gotta problem wit, please tell me. nd ii aint scared to say
shit to Bree.. its juss shes scared nd will call the fuckin copsz [again]
since shes a pussy — kinda funny? its ohkay Bree.. no one likes you.
nd funny how your going around sayin that YOU ND TONY both didnt
say anything to Will'sz girlfriend, but somehow his g/f said you did? ha...
funny :) sooo sweetheartsz if you gotta problem wit me.. call me up...
ohkay!? Will gotsz mah cell number in his wallet — call it!

<3 peace bitcheszzzzzz

Just A Thought
Pimpmasterwosh69
February 08, 2005 @ 9:56 pm

How would things be for other people if I wasn't here?

How Come
ViolentShadeOfRed
February 06, 2005 @ 5:25 PM

If I am your best friend then how come you cant even include me in
anything. You say you hate her so bad and you talk all this shit on her
and you hang out with her more than you have ever hung out with me.
But I guess it is just me you know, thinking nonesense again. Well, I am
sick of everyone using that excuse on me. I am sick of being there for
everyone. And no one can even call me to see if I want to go and hang
out. I guess you all figured I am too busy getting stoned or cutting myself.
Well I wouldn't do that as much if you would have me as someone to
fall back on. I am just the person you call after you are done hanging
out with those people who dont want me along and tell me how lame it
was. Well... don't fucking call me and tell me how lame it was. I dont care
anymore. Hell I would probably be fun to me because I would finally be

good enough to be around. But I guess you cant have it all. Not everyone needs a best friend.

Rambling
yeh_i_live_in_a_car
February 10, 2005 @ 5:25 am

well, it all began when she took my bike away, and then ....cry said the sheep but the brown goat had to run around a light pole cuz he forgot to pack his compass. so gary the allegator had to find a giant watermelon to feed all of his rabbit friends, he also had a friend who was a goat, named rufas, he was a lesbian, but still drink 40 oz's for breakfast and had kegs for dinner, but all of a sudden a lolly pop hoe came out of the bushes and ate everyone!!

holy shit watch out thiers a rabbit in your sock ahhh no watch out for clifferd the big red dog!! sometimes winny the poo comes up to me and offers my crack, i figured that i'd do the right thing and give in to temptation this time. then this elephant with purple lips a nd a big belly butten came up to me and told me that i was under arrest. ding dong ding dong ding dong, wow ,i was flying with an alarm clock, then brown goat found his compass and lived happily in the forest with lions and tiger and other stuff that would eat him. omg they killed.....oh wait he's in the clouds with me still!!!!! damn why did my mom have to take away my car!! no way i never had a car??? crap, i that i saw rufas with my step mom, it was just a horse, or was it a leprachaun ? naaa it was a pillow. watch out for the crazy crack head sock!! g-g-gg-g-g-g-g—g unit. talk is cheap motha fucka! no, i cant ride a chicken up the mountin! i know what your thinking................mmmm.................who is his dealer. i was right! right?

So Cold
coyliter
January 24, 2005 @ 4:23 pm

You say you know all about me.

You know the inside of my world.

Then why the fuck do I feel so cold?

Why I Do What I Do
XxScarletDismayxX
January 25, 2005 @ 9:58 am

0. do you cut? yes

1. who do you hide it from? mostly everyone especially my mom and harry.

2. who knows about it? anyone who reads this and Jess

3. how long has it been since you last cut? Yesterday

4. have you ever tried to commit suicide before? three times

5. where do you usually cut? wrist, ankle, hips ,and shoulder

6. when you cut, who's usually the first to find out? my cat?

7. what`s your worst experience with a fresh cut?when i used my nail to scratch myslef and it still hasn't fully gone away.

8. do you have a fascination with scabs? sure

9. do you like scars, yes or no? yes and no

10. do you name your razor? no

11. what other methods of SI do you use? burning and not eating

12. do you dislike the term "self mutilation"? no but it sometimes sounds worse than it seems.

13. what various ways do you use to hide cuts? bracelets of course and never wearing shorts and tank tops.

15. ever been institutionalized/hospitalized for SI'ing? no but my mom said she would if she found me doing it anymore.

16. do you ever run into problems with hiding cuts? when getting ready for bed.

17. what`s the best part about cutting to you? iit shows something I can't explain. For just a moment I feel relief.

18. do you know of any songs that talk about SI? Papa Roach "Last Resort" Marilyn Manson and Kittie "Do You think I'm a whore?"

19. have you ever been caught cutting/burning, etc? Harry caught me once and I in school twice.

20. what instrument do you use to cut? pins, razors, my nails, w/e

21. what causes you to cut? boyfriend, lack of friends and seeing people in my family suffer and die.

22. what do you feel afterwards? maybe I should've cut deeper and if it will ever be my last cut.

23. what is your closest Close Call? I have a big scar on my wrist from when I cut on my main artery, it didn't stop bleeding for hours but it finally healed

25. do you keep a razor in your bag? yes

27. do you have someone like a therapist you talk to regularly? no i did 3years ago

30. how long have you cut for? five years

31. why did you start? when my ex b/f broke up with me and from so much death in my faily, my pain had nowhere to go but onto my skin

33. what did you use? glass, and a disposable razor harry has now

35. have you ever tried to quit before? yes i was clean

36. what`s the longest time you've went without cutting? 4 months

37. have you tried alternative coping methods other then cutting? coke & heroine

38. why do you like to cut (if you do)?fascination with blood and feeling more calm

39. why don't you like cutting (if you don't): it hurts other people i love

40. have you ever needed stitches before? no

41. have you ever been to the hospital for cutting or issues relating to cutting? no

44. would you advise people to stop or start cutting? no

45. have you ever talked to a professional about your cutting/issues relating to cutting?yes

46. do you like the taste/look of blood? yes

48. what is your opinion on cutting? addictive and embarrassing at times

49. have you ever taken pictures of your cuts/scars, if so why? no but I've made a few pictures in my skin (stars, X's, Z's)

Fuel
Swimmer182
February 08, 2005 @ 10:15 pm

today I ate:

1 slice of pineapple

3 saltine crackers

A Thing Called Life
chicagopunkchick
February 02, 2005 @ 7:37 pm

right now i could just fuckin die for real. i dont know what i did this time but alls i know is i guess i always fuck up the best things that i have going for me god for real i just keep crying cuz i dont know what i did. i know i shoulda got fucked up last night i had coke being just waved in my face on a quarter with someone sayin here just do it. and i was like no im not gonna do that shit anymore cuz i dont wanna i want to actually have a life. and i guess i was wrong i shoulda just fuckin did it again line after line but i chose not to cuz i had better things going for me but now after thinkin about it and a few other things i guess that i just shoulda done it for real im done with this so called thing that people call life

Man Vs God
420lover
May, 2004 @ 2:02 pm

Man made beer, God Made pot, who do you trust?

72 Hours
xSyk0x
January 30, 2005 @ 10:14 pm

(1/28) Friday - Was good. I had a hell of a fuckin time friday night. The news was, that Dan was "sort of" off probation (basically he's off), but he has one more IEP meeting with Sedore. Right after school Dan smoked and i went over around 6. It was boring because we didnt have anything to do until 8 or 9.. And his mom and dad were home. So luckily Dan got a boner, okay.. and i decided that there were definatley much more exciting things to be done than just sitting there. Actually, it was a mutual desicion but, things can get kind of interesting when it's not .... I fell right asleep after that. It was that good. It always is. Not every female is as lucky as me... But it's O.K. with me. After my nap Dan wanted to go straight over Shawn's. But he wasn't home yet so we just sat around and waited for his call. We ended up goin over there around 10:30 and we stayed for like a half an hour or something. We were supposed to be at Brea's at 9.. but Dan was really thrilled about the shit he was getting from Shawn so i didn't mind going there Friday instead of Saturday. Blueberry isn't always that easy to come by (just a random fact). We stopped at 7-11 on the way there cause Dan promised to get me raspberry tea from KFC but it wasnt open. Shawn's was straight. We werent there that long. And then Dan's dad picked us up to take us to Brea's. I am perturbed of being around Dan's parents high (another random fact). It was a long ride. But once we got there i became alot more enthralled with everything going on around me. Upstairs; Brea, Emily, Lisa, Mandie, Kristen, Crystal, Rae, Nate & Dave Payne were already there. All Star had just left and throughout the night other people ... started ... dissapearing. Huge smoke fest. People were drinkin too. I didnt drink though. I was so fucked up just from smoking. Then i did some of the shit i already had and made a buisness profit . More like a trade. Dan did some of that with me too but not the hardcore hardcore stuff. I was trippin hard core... fuckin freakin out. It started out where it was supposed to be like an end-of-probation-free-to-do-mass-amounts-of-drugs-again-reunion for Dan, but it was more like a reunion for everybody. I dont remember alot from Friday.. Mandie and Crystal puked. Everyone layed down around 3, but i doubt any of us slept (except Mandie). I "slept" with my face dead center into the pillow, all curled up in a fetal position, laying in a pond of saliva. I had no idea. I was comphy as hell. My entire body went numb (which was good because lucky for me.. i got my period) I "woke up" at like 5 (even though i was awake the entire time) and from there just waited for everybody else to get up.

(1/29) Saturday - The morning started off at Brea's.. without any sleep. Basically still fucked up (it wouldnt suprise me if i was).. Some people went back to sleep, most people went home around 12. Around 1:00 PM Dan's dad picked us up and brought us home. He was asking what was wrong with me.. and that's when i started feeling really strange. I dont know what the fuck was wrong with me. Outside of Friday night.. and everything there, the only thing i could have been sick from was my period.. but my cramps were over. My mood was chaotic. I havent fucked with my meds so the only likley cause of that would be my period (which hadn't been bothering me) or delirium (from lack of sleep). I didnt actually have a "mood". I normally dont. But i felt so blank. Like i didnt even exist. Literally. My body was numb, slowed down, anxious, i had blurred vision. In my mind; i was still having slight visual and auditory hallucinations.. and massive mood swings. I guess to point out the obvious i was being a bitch. Aggrivation. I dont know why. I had an appetite too.. but i wasnt hungry.. even if i wanted to eat i couldnt. So when we got back to Dan's i decided on taking a nice nap for an hour and maybe that would being some life to me. I couldnt fall asleep.. mainly because i kept hearing things and i kinda blamed it on Dan for heating up some pizza and doing some other things before he came to lay down with me. By the time i wanted to be awake, i was just dozing off. So i was like fuck it and didnt sleep at all. Cause then the day would have been wasted. Poor Dani. He had to put up with my shit alll day. The day ended up being a waste anyway because of the snow. Oh yeah, and then i thought i left my shit at Brea's (my personal section) and i scavengered around for it for about an hour before i gave up. Didnt find it. We were gunna go to the mall or somethin just to kill time.. but oh well. Maybe its best i was kept inside. We found something to do anyway. An old pastime of ours... It was a death defying, ruthless and audacious jouney through subzero temperatures.. to the Great Garage Tundra of some person we dont know's back yard! It was a risk we had to take. But no one saw us. So we smoked a bowl and walked home. It was straight. Me and Dan think up some crazy things when were high. I never made out with anyone before yesterday when i was high. (I mean really high..) Maybe i just forgot. Its so fucking ..SEX. grrr.. Apparently, weed makes Dan horny. Like he'd fuck a venus fly trap.. if one happened to be laying around somewhere... No wonder Dan used to always smoke excessivley around July . Hah. I couldnt believe it though.. Dan.. last year.. last year we were getting high in the same exact place as we were sitting. His face and everything still looks the same but its almost like i know a whole different person now. And everything i thought he was or had potential to be then, has all been proven to me over the past 6 months. It made me feel comfortable. The comparison between last year to now. I just couldnt believe that i have someone so perfect ©. Somehow i knew way back then that this is the relationship we'd have if either of us were ever motivated (or desperate.. sorry to say) enough to do something about it. Well.. anyway then we went downstairs and i made soft pretzels. And we watched Comedy Central. Then our high wore off.. and we started getting bored again. Around 11:30 we left to go with Dan's dad a few places and then he was taking us to the Pink Floyd laser show. We planned on smoking another bowl before the show but there wasnt enough time. Dan's parinoid as fuck anyway. I hate that. The laser show kicked ass like always. They played The Wall (I never got to see comfortably numb until last night and i wanted to see it high) ..There were madd people in there who were trippin, freakin out and shit. When we went back to Dan's we pretty much went right to sleep.

Today - We woke up around 11.. I did. And Dan had to work at 12. So we took Dan to work and his mom dropped me off at Brea's so i could get my shit i assumed i left there... but i had it with me the whole time. In the exact same hoodie i was wearing all weekend. Im kind of glad i forgot i had it though. At Brea's we were talkin about all the crazy shit that happened last night and then we started watching Mrs. Doubtfire. I didnt pay too much attention to it because i had to leave. My gram picked me up around 2:00 PM and all day ive been sitting here. My ass hurts. My gram and pap are watching a special on face-eating tumors.. haha. Today was my first dose of birth control. Prepare for boob enlargement (maybe..). Well, ive been writing this entry for 2 hours now (off and on) so im gunna go. Bye

©I LOVE YOU SO MUCH DANI!!!©

This Morning
XdeadlyXintentionsX
February 09, 2005 @ 7:44 pm

This morning I found out Mrs. Pug died....

I've been so depressed today between that and my mom's screaming. I wrote this:

I am on the brink of despair,
I beg you, end this affair.
Stop the pain,
Before I go insane.
Can't you see me cry?
You can't deny,
That it's entirely your fault.
Is this meant to be a deadly assault?
What must I do,
To get through to you?
You're killing me,
Why can't you just let me be?
All of this
Is so amiss.
I need to feel
Something real.
You just don't realize
I need to get away from your lies.
I need to feel inside,
I don't want to have to hide.
You're fucking killing me,
Just let me be...

Tired Of Drama
jessica128
November 20, 2004 @ 9:06 pm

Friday sucked, today sucked, we went and ate at Ryan's then went to Great times. I am so sick and tired of where I sit at lunch, and all my "supposed" life. I hate it sometimes. I always get crapped on. Alisha doesn't fully understand the things she did to me on her xanga. Everyone told me she talked shit and that whole time I just sat back and didn't believe them. I can't even look at her now. Alisha just dont apologize to me. And if yo know who sxe-for-ever is why couldn't you tell me? Will I hope you will tell me in person on Monday.

Im just so fed up with my life right now. The only classes I am passing are Languge and Journalism. I dont particularly like my lunch table anymore because there all Alisha's friends and they don't like me. She doesn't like me. And I dont really fit anywhere else in the cafeteria. I mean I can't go sit with like ahsley kelly and megan tye and all them-they hate me, I can't sit with the druggies cuz they beat me up or something, i dont really want to sit in the senior section with shelly and laura cuz Im not for sure if I really fit in with them, and I dont really belong with the preps, I dont belong with all the freshman, God/ there is no where I can really go in the cafeteria to get away from everyone I sit with. I still want to go to lunch, unfortanetuly I cant change my lunch because I have Journalism then, and I cant do anything about it. I dont want to skip lunch-I like lunch-plus I dont want people to think Im snobby or un social, but I am just unappy with they kids I sit with.

Im tired of all the drama and Im so fed up with all the kids that I thought were my friends. I want to move or somthing so bad. I dont have anyone to really talk to or be good friends with at school cuz no one really interests me. Im just depressed- all my teachers hate me as well. they think im a failure. I hate derek I hate him so much -I dont even want to look at him or know he exsit. I never EVER want to have another thouht about him. I hate patrick, i just cant stand him sometimes.

I hate spanish, i hate science, mr. curts hates me, i hate math, but mr. hensley's alright, languge is cool sometimes, i like journalism from time to time, but mrs roberts intemidates me -still, i hate health, i hate ceramics, i hate cleaning up when im done on the potters wheel. i hate trying to stay awake in class when all you want to do is say screw it and fall asleep. sometimes i get so mad at people i just want to walk out the door.

i know now that the people i once knew, loved like a sister or the guys i used to like, g/d i i i i just cant even look at them anymore. the only place i feel safe at school is my locker. like the moran twins are cool, their near my locker, zacks a punk, but i like picking on him, sammy next to my locka-shes cool, josh is cool-their prettty funny when his friend scott comes around cuz he jokes alot, but besides that i got no where to go or no one to talk to. no one likes me anymore. alisha toke the best out of me, or whatever joy i had left in me. im just not happy anymore, and i try so hard sometimes to be happy but its like i cant.

im just tired of feeling like im constatnly alone, my parents hate me, my friends, my teachers, neighbors.

Being Irish
NYHCKATe2
January 29, 2005 @ 6:02 pm

"God made whiskey to stop the Irish from taking over the world." I think thats so true. I love being Irish, I couldn't imagine not being it. I love alcohol even though i don't drink it anymore, I love bagpipes, I love reels and jigs and penny whistles. I love having irish luck, the entire world against you, even yourself. I love that I'm Catholic and my entire family is still Catholic even though the English tried to make us all anglican. The English even made us change ourlast name, and you'd think your heratige would be lost after that, but its not. I've known my Gaelic roots since I was a kid. I've always known how we had to change our name to sound more English even though all that shit happened at almost 200 years ago. Bagpipes always play at weddings and funeral, and when I hear them I can picture the green hills of Ireland. Green is my favorite color. Beer is better black. And leprechans, though scary, are still cool..

What Should I Do?
MamiMorenita
January 29, 2005 @ 1:02 AM

I wanna be rich. Im fat, i need to lose weight. I started doing cocaine recently. I started off doing it in a party. I passed out because I was already drunk and high. I did it the second time to stay up because I had to catch up on school work. The third time, just to have energy. I started off doing two lines, now, I can do 3 and it wears off fast. I havent been doing it that much but I think I'm thinking about it too much. This can turn into a problem. We'll see. I kinda only wanna do cocaine because I want to lose weight fast. Dumb I know, but I'm obese. I was willing to do liposuction but they won't operate on anyone under 21. I'm in debt by $5,000 from previous things my ex put me through. What should I do?

Bags
dangerousADRENALINE
December 28, 2004 @ 10:23 pm

aiiiiiight bitchez...............i still am all geeked n shit bout this rave! im gonna ta 1 2nite but i still got a long while. so this mornin i got high as fuck. x is a bitch! everytime i take that shit i get all horny n shit, good thing my babygirl wus with me thenn. she got high too we wus fucked up on it. but we ended up fuckin like to jack rabbits, i tore up her walls man hahahaha shit it felt like i did n the way she was moanin made me harder n more hornie so i had to keep poundin at her pussy. she said it her but afterwardz she was a happy camper so wus i. i wus such a happy camper that as soon as we stopped my dick got hard as hell n we had to fuck again. she loved it so did i so w/e w/e. christina keep playin me mann, she aint goin to the rave 2nite so lame ass excuse. but nah she told me how it wus, she wont hide shit at all. she been talkin bout this bitch ass hoe ashley or sum shit. that ugly bitch is like shanes new gurl or sumthin. christina aint say she was a ugly bitch or a hoe or nuthin I DID i dont give a fuck that bitch is ugly LOL! ne way jus remember christina u look MILLIONS x MILLIONS x MILLIONS timez better! that fuckin hoe LOL i left a comment on her webpage i said she was smart, i hope she didnt mistake that for a compliment. get this: she all happy to be havin his baby. BOY I TELL U!! shane wouldnt have nuthin to do with that bitch if she didnt get pregnant, and u c how ugly she is?!?!?!?!?!?!?!?!?! u know shane jus wanted sum pussy. he prolly put a bag ova her head while he fucked her, im sorry but i couldnt do that mann -too ugly- ne way peace

My Thoughts On the USA
jaketherake
November 03, 2004 @ 4:12 am

Fuck the USA.....Fuck you Bush.

Ruthlessly Absurd
ThESiRE
October 29, 2004 @ 9:54 pm

Wednesday morning...7:45 am...in my first period class...Earth Science..
Teachers...Ms. Vargas, Mrs. Hughes...my head was down on my binder
when someone tapped me on my shoulder...yea it was a vp...ms. fucking
shepherd...never saw her before...she tells me to walk down to the
nurse's office with her...i ask her "can i call my parents?" she says no...
i proceed walking down to the nurse's office when she says something
to the nurse about "Here is the suspected" again i asked..."May i please
call my parents?"...oh no i was denied again..the nurse examines me...
saying i was uthargic (in other words a fancy word for tired) she also
said my eyes weren't dilating correctly..***Enter Ms. Eberley*** (School
Drug Counselor) Yea she came in and i asked for a third time to call
my parents when she said oh we are already contacting them now..so
then my parents come...(I Still have no clue what is going on) then ms.
eberley tells me everything that i was a suspected user of drugs and
that i have to get a physical and drug test within an hour...my parents
come to school so pissed off but defending me...we then leave to goto
the hospital to get my drug test and my physical(s)...so i pissed in the
tiny cup thing...and then went across the street to the other place to get
my physicals...all three of the doctors said i was fine and all three said
that my blood pressure was very high and my heart was beating too
fast..i replied "yea...i'm a little pissed off about this bullshit"...i go home
at like 12 o'clock and talk to my parents and they ask me if i wanna
get transferred to another school cause they can't stand this bullshit
anymore i said yea sure..then my dad gets a call at 1 from the clinic
place saying i failed the drug test..and was positive for marijuana..so
yea...how are your guys' lives' going?

Tweeken
sarah1607_milz
January 30, 2005 @ 6:12 pm

Ah interesting weekend.

Thursday night Tiffany and Joyce stayed the night. We got drunk and
stoned in the woods by our house with green haired/pierced lip/fucking
hot Brandon (who I don't even fucking like, and he thinks I'm obsessed
with him) and a bunch of other guys. What ever happend to our GIRLS

night, Joyce? Then we migrated up to the church to hang out and watch the boys skate. Me and Joyce were so fucked up. Us girls were acting so stupid! They prlly all thought we were retarded. Seriously we were fucking acting like little kids. And Joyce kept fucking taking Brandon aside to talk about me, which is why he thinks I'm obsessed with him. I'm like his new stalker now or something and I just think he's hot! Wtf??? I already have a kind-of boyfriend. Who I'm not going to say.

Anyway we went home later and at about 4:30 in the morning Jeff calls me up and wants me to sneak out so we can chill so I did. And I fucking got caught to cuz I didn't come home til like 6:30, when I KNEW my parents get up for work at 5:45/6. Whatever I was all weird off of air freshener lol as stupid as that sounds. And huffing's not even a hard drug so I'm good with that, even if it is dumb. But I need fucking something to do besides smoking pot. I can't tweak or do coke anymore.

Before I went home though Jeff used the hollow needle I brought and pierced the left side of my lip. My face was numb so it didn't hurt at all. I'm not sure if it looks ok or not but everyone says it looks hot.

Friday night my friends from Oak Harbor came. We went to a party at James' house. We all spent like a half hour in the bathroom with a can of Oust air freshener and a rag and by the time we were done the can was almost empty. Our heads felt so funny though (had to pay for it the next day though, felt all retarded and had a killer headache).

Besides that I got drunk and smoked quite a few bowls with Ashlee and Josh, so I got pretty fucked up that night. Me and Ashlee kept on writing notes to eachother and Jeff, and I wrote this AMAZING poem to Ashlee about everything going on that night, and you could so tell I was out of it. Lol I never ended up going home that night either, so THAT, on top of getting caught sneaking out, AND piercing my lip after three years of my parents saying no whenever I asked if I could, I'm in trouble right now. Not as much as I thought I would be though.

Finally, last night: Me, Joyce, Tiffany, and Aleesa hung out with Hot Brandon, his brother, and some other guys. At the church of course. It wasn't all that great because I was tired (hadn't slept in two days), hungry (hadn't eaten either), and fucking FREEZING cold.

Anyway I weighed my self yesterday and weighed 113/114. But I ate a bunch this morning (the girls practically forced me too) SO I probably gained a few pounds back.

K well this is getting too long. Gotta go.

Stop The Comments
AntiLife
January 21, 2005 @ 12:11 pm

I just wanted you guys to know that I'm a fat dyke-slut-whore. Now EVERYONE knows ariel. so you can stop the comments. thanks.

Seeken Employment
keko18
January 26, 2005 @ 3:57 pm

twas a serious problem.

hard drive was completely destroyed.

price estimate on new hard drive installation along with service charges...$200+

bowell...such is life.

i'm looking for a job. trying like mad to get an interview set up with undertow records, but i'm not getting any responses from Bob. a simple "No" would be fine. not that i'd be happy about not getting the job, but i'd like to get some sort of response. i'm putting all of my other job searching on hold with the hope that i land this one. i guess i should start applying elsewhere, take a job if i can get hired anywhere, and if the job with undertow is ever offered to me, i'll quit the current job and go with undertow.

i'm still trying to figure out how i will manage my time if i work and have school. its the second week of classes and i'm drowning in projects, papers, quizzes, and homework. throw a job in that mix and i'm dead. however, the money is sounding all too good at this point for me to even care about that. i'll find a way.

i had to buy a hacksaw the other day. the key to my bike lock snapped off inside the lock. we can thank the frigid weather for that little blessing. so i had no choice but to cut it off. it worked well...sucker came right off. you also get some priceless looks from people walking by as you are sawing off a bike lock. i didnt think to wear black clothes and a ski mask. that wouldnt have been suspicious looking. but back to the hacksaw...so i bought it to help me with one task. then i finished that task. now i have a hacksaw sitting here on my shelf. what a waste of talent. that sucker could be cutting through all sorts of things. but there it sits.

i've been hearing that our basketball team is doing ok too.

goodnight bloodsucker.

sleep tight.

Drugs Are Funny Things
DrugsR4ME
January 12, 2005 @ 3:15 pm

My brother came home again last night. its weird to see him. but its good to know hes still alive. the doctor said that the drugs are frying his brain. litterally. he wont be able to live much longer if he stays on them, especially doing how much hes doing right now. He's supposed to start rehab today, but then again he was supposed to go yesterday...so that doesnt really mean anything. and since hes 19 hes the only one that can check himself in. I hope he gets better soon before he completely loses his mind.

Its weird tho. drugs are a funny thing. when he was here last night, he was on the drugs, its so obvious. and i sit and watch him and i see the way they affect him negatively and how fucked up he is, but theres nothing i can do about it. i just feel bad for him. then he says something funny thats really random, and my brain starts shouting 2 different things. One side starts thinking how sad that is that he cant even hardly form sentences, and the other side starts laughing and saying "dam i wish i was high". so then it gets me thinking....can i stop doing drugs? i mean i have never tried.... what if its too late? i feel like im fine, no addictions i could stop if i want. but how do i know that i really can?? i should try. but then i dont want to because it seems pointless if im not addicted. ive been good lately tho. being a designated driver sucks. my goddam friends need to get their goddam licenses. Driving is BS. But i have a lot of drugs. in my room. i could do them right now if i wanted to....but i wont. save them for this weekend...the end of finals...the start of a whole new semester. YAY!!!

Peace in columbia~~ Sam

231

Skin
eatMe_innocent
September 04, 2004 @ 12:49 pm

i feel as if my skin is the only thing keeping me from going everywhere at once

Glowsticks
ShyaFeiP
February 09, 2005 @ 3:08 am

Sigh, i dont feel happy.

woo yesterday nite.........hm....

at first everything was totally fine. until one of my frd got arrested. FUCK. we were so afraid, rushed into da toilet, took all the pills we have. well... damn i threw away one of my 5 jai (fuck which made me still cant fucking sleep now) but dropped 2 E jais... damn!!!! then i went really fucking bao. bao dou hai...diu never tried one nite 2 e jais. fuck i forgot to bring the god damn glowsticks down. ai..................... if my frd havent got arrested.. i guess we would have a even greater nite. anyway, exclude this incident. everythings fucking gd. deco.. suen la no expectation, better than dj hyper one tho, well lighting n sound system really okay wor. adam freeland fucking rocks, so fuckin handsome, live show much better than his albums, hernan... good as well but no big surprise.. david lam.. all my frds say ng ho, but frankly if tht time im already " bao-ing", his music r good for bao too ga wor.

friends... go to rave siu sum d. sorry ar taylor..

fucking tired, but cant fucking fall asleep. ding. nin chor 2 wui have a party i sun hung kai.. dou ng g go ng go ho. saturday shall be heading to Bling, the parties SOUNDS kool as breakbeat, tribal house n progressive house will b spinned (my favortie tit-3-kok)

p.s. please dont take the words that i say during im "bao-ing" so serious. as many i just mo liu say it, or just kau kei say it, ng goi......... gong ha ga ja. not 100% true ga.. dai lo..... ng go gimme so many " responsibilities" just becos i bullshitted during tht time la.

I Hate Myself
xXBlackVelvetXx
January 09, 2005 @ 1:35 am

Some days I just really really hate myself. I mean truelly hate myself. Hate isn't disliking. There's a difference. A lot of people will dislike something and say they hate it, but I seriously doubt people feel hate very often at all. When you hate you know it immediately and if a person has felt hate any time in the recent, they wouldn't be over using the word as people so often do.

I've only felt hate a couple times and far between. It's a bit different everytime but I couldn't say how. It's not a thing you like to remember. I remember feeling it, I don't remember why, when or how exactly I felt. But I'll say one thing, the hate most people think they feel has more to do with [violent] anger than disgust. And true hate, to my knowledge, has much more to do with disgust than anything else, especially violent anger.

That and a certain vile element that leaves you feeling something like the stench of death and the taste of rancid vomit all. over. you. INside and Out.

That's mildly put, without thinking too much about how to describe it because there really is no way to describe hate accept as Hate.

This is one of those days.

Can You See My Pain?
xxfallenangel88xx
February 11, 2005 @ 6:12 pm

Agony today. My parents don't understand and my friends never notice that I am distant. I bet they wouldn't even notice if I died! It rained today and I felt like crying from all the sorrow in my heart. These demons that haunt are too much to bear! I can't take this anymore! I just wish I would die!! My parents don't even notice that I am dying. I have attempted suicide twice and they still don't even know about that. My friends can't see the pain behind my smile. I am slowly dying and wish the end would come soon enough. If the eyes are the window to the soul why can't anyone see my pain?

I Am Stuck
iseriouslyneedhelp
January 12, 2005 @ 1:45 am

Isn't there a point where everything's ok again? I cant get there... im stuck.. in pain.. and there's no one to help me out of here.

Crampy
morbid_misfit_girl
February 04, 2005 @ 3:28 pm

hey....i got my period today,in school actually so thank god i was prepared!! this explains everything!! i'm fed up with having leftover feelings that won't go away from my ex : (...that seems to be one of my many problems...my dad and i keep fighting again : (....it's not so good, i'm not exactly a morning person so that explains the fights before school....my individual therapy was cancelled last night because i got there late : (and now she's like maybe you should just go to group and not individual anymore...i was like what the hell, i've only been to see you individually twice!!!! oh well, my other alternative is the school therapist but during school i am busy in every class now!! it's weird to get used to and this time i don't have anyone helping me with slack so it's even doubly hard.....i felt empty a bit today, i have to do laundry today but i may not becuase physically i feel crampy.....i have homework this weekend : (thats odd too last semester i didn't really have any.....oh yea one of those girls is still talking to me a little...but i have my gaurd up so it's ok.....i;m kinda insecure again but usually during this time i feel like this so, yea it's my period...i go through intense mood swings already and then the time of the month comes and ahhhh!.....this weekend should be ok, i'm probably not going to do anything though....

Black Cloud
scars_of_pain
January 08, 2005 @ 9:36 pm

I'm so angry. I feel like I have to hide everything from everyone. This year, I made a resolution to keep it all inside. And that's what I've decided to do. I don't care how much it hurts me, or how many times I'm going to have a nervous breakdown. But I don't want to seem like the type of person who depends on everyone to help her own. That's the last thing I want. I think you guys will be the ones who I talk to the most. lol. I don't even know any of you, but I feel like I can talk forever. Maybe because you all feel the same way I do. I mean, don't you ever get the feeling that you're a burden? And everytime you want to talk to someone about a problem, they always think to themselves, "omg, she just won't shut the fuck up!" Or when someone specific knows about the cutting, and you want to let your feelings out, you think that they're tired of listening to you ramble and complain? Maybe they really are....I don't know. All I know is that no one I know will be aware of any of this. It may kill me slowly inside...but then again, it might be the trick to getting better. Anyway...do any of you ever feel like that? That you're just that black cloud that follows them all over the place?

Some Days
DarkCrimsonStar
November 17, 2004 @ 5:45 pm

I wish I could say that I haven't cut since my last entry, but I would be lying. However, I am not really freaking out over it and hating myself for it like I used to, back in the days when I was still addicted. I would slice my skin open for the littlest reason...if someone didn't talk to me or someone looked at me the wrong way, even. If blood was tears, I always would have been crying. Since my two big attempts to quit, I have learned not to let things push me over the edge like that. If I cut now, it is because I really can't take something. For example, living with my parents. Who wants to be abused and berated until they feel like nothing? And they honestly have to wonder why I want to go as far away as possible for college.

But I don't think I will really feel better until I quit for good, which at this rate, will be never. I want to believe that someday everything will get better, that everything will work out for me, but most of the time I can't. I'm living a day at a time so I can get through this mess...some days are better than others.

Some days I just want to shoot myself. I am way past the days of telling the few people I trust that I am feeling like killing myself. What they can do? Put the will to live back in me? Make me happy?....doubt it. People have never made me happy, even at the best of times. I don't want them to think that I am searching for attention. It's too bad that if I kill myself, I wouldn't be able to see the looks on all their faces when they found out that I was dead...

Digital Bathroom Scale
fallen_from_grace_772
December 08, 2004 @ 10:11 pm

U BLEED JUST TO KNOW UR ALIVE. sooo..my mom caught my brother stuart smoking weed a couple days ago, n so she's all freakin out 24/7 cuz of it... had to c my shrink today, that wuz ok.. my dad's gettin out of the hospital in a week, nd then moving in w/ my sister, cuz he cant live here cuz my parents divorce will b final january 6th. i ordered sum apple cider vinegar pills, cuz i cant stand drinking it, n the succes stories say stuff like "i lost 32 lbs in 28 days" hopefully it will help me lose this huge disgusting layer of fat covering up my beautiful bones... in addition to the other 3 natural formulas i'm taking for weight loss. i wuz wearin shorts today nd looking at my thighs, nd they r sooooo fucking ginormous, i took a razor blade nd carved FAT and WEAK on my left thigh, nd CONTROL and UGLY and a star on my rite. i also cut a couple times on my stomach, but not really bad. todays total calories wuz sumwhere around 800...the sad thing is that is after purging..god i'm never gonna lose all this fat if i dont stop eating.... its kinda weird too, that during my shrink session, it wuz near the end, nd like always, he asked me if there wuz anything else i wanted to talk abt, n i wuz sooooo close to tellin him bout my ED...i dont even fuckin want ne adults to know, cuz they'll shove me back to generose...but then again, i hate how i feel abt myself....i've always hated myself, but even after losing 16 lbs,i think i hate myself 10x worse....life is just fucked up i guess... mayb i wuz just never meant to b happy. its makes me fuckin angry i cant even weight myself when i want to, seeing as our scale is fucked up- f.i. i stepped on it this mornin when i woke up nd it said i wuz 94 lbs, which is definately not true. then i stepped on it again after i took a shower, nd it said i wuz 189 which cant b true either....so its clearly fucked up..howeever i asked fer a digital bathroom scale fer christmas..i hope i get one.. my adjusted gw fer christmas is 143 lbs, instead of 138....jesus,i cant believe i'm changin it.. i can never fuckin stick w/ nething.. neways, if i'm gonna get up fer skewl tmro, i should go to sleep now. nite gurlz much ana/mia luv **camilla**

You Rock My World
x1_800_ana_4evax
February 06, 2005 @10:43 pm

i'm so tired, so sick, and so confused! i think i need a day or so to let this be..

i'm sorry..but you guys still rock my world and i love you all tons!

i need to pray and see what happens, b/c everything is so mixed up in my head and i'm really overwhelmed! i'm sorry...stay strong all of you, and i'll prolly comment tomorrow, i just can't tonight!

...i'm sorry

This Can't Be
BitterDays
February 10, 2005 @ 4:50 pm

THIS CANT BE HAPPENING

He was so perfect and pure...he never deserved this at all...today was a day that no one will ever forget....

Today in first block the most horrible thing had to happen...A support counciler came into my spanish class and told us the news tht had happend the night before..He died...he was gone and no one understood how this could be happening

My friend...Martin...the nicest guy you could ever have laid eyes on...a smile so big and the most beautifulest eyes had passed away Wednsday February 9th at Sanit Lukes hospital...he went in with a fever and his heart began to fade....and he didnt survive...

They told us in the morning..and tht was the time everyone just became silent...my jaw dropped to the floor...he was the same guy who said hi to me everyday in school when he saw me...he was so nice cute sweet and pure all at once...he had no enemy's only friends...

I went to science class and i just broke down..i cried so much..he didnt deserve this at all..and to think about his family...his sister everyone who was close to him, .it was the worst feeling ever..

But wht made it even worse....so many ppl didnt care..there were senors and others who were saying " hah a freshman died" and they began to laugh...to hear tht ppl were gonna go to his funneral just go get out of school....tht is the worst thought tht went in my head

Do you have no heart.....Wht are u thinking...

If you ever had the chance to meet Martin you would understand why so many people have had their heart broke. He was taken before he should have been and no one understand why. He was a baseball player and a basketball player, he was healthy, he was happy, and he is gone.

i will miss him forever...nothing can change wht had happen..no one can bring him back, he is in heaven watching over us. High school will neve rbe the same, life will never be the same. Martin showed everyone that we should all live life to the fullest an never give into the stupid things that the world throws at us. He would want us all to be happy and live life, just like he did, happy nothing less. Know that at any moment you could be gone or you could lose someone so dear to you without a chance to say goodbye

Today was a day of tears and heartache..that will never end

R.I.P MARTIN....I WILL ALWAYS LOVE YOU...YOU WERE A GREAT FREIND

Fuck Food
icouldnttellyou
February 10, 2005 @ 9:18 pm

just gained 2 pounds from a binge. after several months of srtuggling with my weight, ive just realized what it takes. i have finally learned something good from a binge.

I HAVE TO EAT NOTHING TO HAVE CONTROL.

so i am not going to eat tomorrow. or the day after. unless i have to. and it wont be sugar. sugar and bread are what i binge on and go crazy for.

if i can steer clear of any shit like that, ill succeed. i am not as strong as you girls. i cant just have one roll. i cant just have one cookie. i have to have ten.

so i will not eat. screw everyone. im not gonna eat even if they think i have an ed. i dont care anymore. whats the diff if they think i have an ed? they wont do anything about it anyway. one girl knows about it and she didnt do fuck all yet.

i am not going to eat. in ten days, i will have lost a great amount of weight. my punishment for todays binge: wake up at 4:50 am and exercise for one full hour. and restrict for ten days. i can do this. i just have to not eat.

ill time myself for when im in the kitchen. ill allow myself 2 minutes in the kitchen for some soup if my mom wonders. shes the only one who will do something about this if she knows.

im not eating anymore. if i do i might as well kill myself. eating is like suicide. ill be obese and die anyway. i rather be thin when i die.

ana has turned her back on me, and frankly i dont give a damn. ana doesnt love me, nor did she ever. i have depended on her to save me.

i realize i can only save myself

ana never helped. screw you ANA. SCREW YOU. go fuck yourself. you are a piece of shit. i dont need you even though you make me think i do. fuck you ana fuck you. screw MIA too. your just a lazy exit... im not lazy. ill prove it to you both, you bitches. i can do this on my own.

NO MORE FOOD. FOOD KILLS. Statistics reveal more poeple die from obesity these days than starvation. if i die any way related to food, ill starve. never from obesity.

FUCK ANA FUCK ANA FUCK FOOD.

I CAN ONLY RELY ON MYSELF and ANA wont help. shes just something in my mind. a voice that doesnt help. and she hasnt been there. FUCK ANA.

Hi My Name Is
Annalizze
February 08, 2005 @ 9:04 pm

Allow me to introduce myself. My name, or as I am called by so called "doctors", is Anorexia. Anorexia Nervosa is my full name, but you may call me Anna. Hopefully we can become great partners. In the coming time, I will invest a lot of time in you, and I expect the same from you. In the past you have heard all of your teachers and parents talk about you. You are "so mature", "intelligent", "14 going on 45", and you possess "so much potential". Where has that gotten you, may I ask? Absolutely no where! You are not perfect, you do not try hard enough, further more you waste your time on thinking and talking with friends and drawing! Such acts of indulgence shall not be allowed in the future. Your friends do not understand you. They are not truthful. In the past, when the insecurity has quietly gnawed away at your mind, and you asked them, "Do I look.... fat?" and they answered "Oh no, of course not" you knew they were lying! Only I tell the truth. Your parents, let's not even go there! You know that they love you, and care for you, but part of that is just that they are your parents and are obligated to do so. I shall tell you a secret now: deep down inside themselves, they are disappointed with you. Their daughter, the one with so much potential, has turned into a fat, lazy, and undeserving girl.

But I am about to change all that.

I expect a lot from you. You are not allowed to eat much. It will start slowly: decreasing of fat intake, reading the nutrition labels, cutting out junk food, fried food, etc. For a while, the exercise will be simple: some running, perhaps some crunches and some situps. Nothing too serious. Perhaps drop a few pounds, take a little off of that fat tub of a stomach. But it won't be long before I tell you that it isn't good enough. I will expect you to drop your calorie intake and up your exercise. I will push you to the limit. You must take it because you cannot defy me! I am beginning to imbed myself into you. Pretty soon, I am with you always. I am there when you wake up in the morning and run to the scale. The numbers become both friend and enemy, and the frenzied thoughts pray for them to be lower than yesterday, last night, etc. You look into the mirror with dismay. You prod and poke at the fat that is there, and smile when you come across bone. I am there when you figure out the plan for the day: 400 calories, 2 hours exercise. I am the one figuring this out, because by now my thoughts and your thoughts are blurred together as one.

I follow you throughout the day. In school, when your mind wanders I give you something to think about. Recount the calories for the day. It's too much. I fill your mind with thoughts of food, weight, calories, and things that are safe to think about. Because now, I am already inside of you. I am in your head, your heart, and your soul. The hunger pains you pretend not to feel is me, inside of you.

240

Pretty soon I am telling you not only what to do with food, but what to do ALL of the time. Smile and nod. Present yourself well. Suck in that fat stomach, dammit! God, you are such a fat cow!!!! When mealtimes come around I tell you what to do. I make a plate of lettuce seem like a feast fit for a king. Push the food around. Make it look like you've eaten something. No piece of anything...if you eat, all the control will be broken...do you WANT that?? To revert back to the fat COW you once were?? I force you to stare at magazine models. Those perfect skinned, white teethed, waifish models of perfection staring out at you from those glossy pages. I make you realize that you could never be them. You will always be fat and never will you be as beautiful as they are. When you look in the mirror, I will distort the image. I will show you obesity and hideousness. I will show you a sumo wrestler where in reality there is a starving child. But you must not know this, because if you knew the truth, you might start to eat again and our relationship would come crashing down.

Sometimes you will rebel. Hopefully not often though. You will recognize the small rebellious fiber left in your body and will venture down to the dark kitchen. The cupboard door will slowly open, creaking softly. Your eyes will move over the food that I have kept at a safe distance from you. You will find your hands reaching out, lethargically, like a nightmare, through the darkness to the box of crackers. You shove them in, mechanically, not really tasting but simply relishing in the fact that you are going against me. You reach for another box, then another, then another. Your stomach will become bloated and grotesque, but you will not stop yet. And all the time I am screaming at you to stop, you fat cow, you really have no self control, you are going to get fat.

When it is over you will cling to me again, ask me for advice because you really do not want to get fat. You broke a cardinal rule and ate, and now you want me back. I'll force you into the bathroom, onto your knees, staring into the void of the toilet bowl. Your fingers will be inserted into your throat, and, not without a great deal of pain, your food binge will come up. Over and over this is to be repeated, until you spit up blood and water and you know it is all gone. When you stand up, you will feel dizzy. Don't pass out. Stand up right now. You fat cow you deserve to be in pain!

Maybe the choice of getting rid of the guilt is different. Maybe I chose to make you take laxatives, where you sit on the toilet until the wee hours of the morning, feeling your insides cringe. Or perhaps I just make you hurt yourself, bang your head into the wall until you receive a throbbing headache. Cutting is also effective. I want you to see your blood, to see it fall down your arm, and in that split second you will realize you deserve whatever pain I give you. You are depressed, obsessed, in pain, hurting, reaching out but no one will listen? Who cares?!?!! You are deserving; you brought this upon yourself.

Oh, is this harsh? Do you not want this to happen to you? Am I unfair? I do do things that will help you. I make it possible for you to stop thinking of emotions that cause you stress. Thoughts of anger, sadness, desperation, and loneliness can cease because I take them away and fill your head with the methodic calorie counting. I take away your struggle to fit in with kids your age, the struggle of trying to please everyone as well. Because now, I am your only friend, and I am the only one you need to please.

I have a weak spot. But we must not tell anyone. If you decide to fight back, to reach out to someone and tell them about how I make you live, all hell will break lose. No one must find out, no one can crack this shell that I have covered you with. I have created you, this thin, perfect, achieving child. You are mine and mine alone. Without me, you are nothing. So do not fight back. When others comment, ignore them. Take it into stride, forget about them, forget about everyone that tries to take me away. I am your greatest asset, and I intend to keep it that way.

Sincerely,

Ana

Don't Let It Show
fallingfast13
February 10, 2005 @ 9:41 pm

dont let it show
they can never see
the way what they do
makes me hurt me.
it never lasts
or they might know
what happens to me
dont let it show
dont come to me for answers
dont talk to me at all
because the place im at right now
is the step before the fall.
i dont want it to happen

but of course i know
it always does again
so please dont let it show.
day after day
hope slips through my hand
fixing them before me
dont think i can.
go away now
please let me be
cant you see what you do
makes me hurt me?

xoxo margot

DARE
darkeyed
February 12, 2005 @ 1:47 pm

I don't like drugs. I will never do drugs. For two good reasons

1.) the thought of the consequences if caught with them scares the shit out of me.

2.) I know I would like them too much. I have an addictive nature....to substances that alter your state of consciousness.

Last nite Joe had to go pick up a friend of his who has hit up some hard times and been homeless these past few weeks. Sooo we couldn't hang out cuz he had to leave to get him before I go off work.

Rite after work. Nothing to do....chk cell phone nobody ever calls me on and there is one message. This guy from school that I drank with a couple of times last semester.....iviting me to go hang out with them.

I go...and as soon as I walk through the door the smell of marajuana almost knocks me over....They were drinking when I got there sooo I thought to myself....ohhh they're done....nope.

In this one bedroom three of them were playing guitar then they go into this bathroom and start doing more out of various instruments that I don't know the name of....not kwel...

They weren't even paying any attention to me (not that I want to be the center of attention..but if you invite me over you could at least acknowledge my existence...)

soo since nobody even really noticed that I was there nobody noticed that I just got up and left till about 30 min later when THE GUY WHO invited me calls my cell phone.

I do not answer. I am in the wonderful wal-mart looking at books and wandering around aimlessly bymylself. proud because I didnt stick around that.....

I'm sorry I do not have anything against people who *smoke* just...I just don't want to be around you when you are doing that kind of thing.....

But I will attempt to out drink you till I have no liver....or am left dry heaving into a toilet.

...Everybody has their secret sin....

Maybe Someone Will Read This
XdeadlyXintentionsX
February 10, 2005 @ 12:33 PM

I also wrote these:
Fuck you asshole,
Someday you'll see
All the pain you caused me
With your insults.
Do you like the results?
Just leave me here to cry
Send me off to bleed and die.
I'm drowning in sorrow
And I've become to hollow.
I need to be rescued
Instead of argued.
This is your cue,
Please help me through.
I'm hiding in a hollow tree,
Please come find me.
I can't take living
With all this pain you've been giving.

I need to escape,
Some time to reshape.
Is it too much to ask
For you to take off the mask?
I want to forget my past
Because it leaves me aghast.
But for now just leave me here to cry...
Send me off to bleed and die.

and

Is there someway
that maybe someday
I can be a thing called happy?
I can smile, and mean it,
and these tears can quit
falling every night.
Maybe then I will know what it's like to say
that I've had a good day
and not be lying.
If they knew what I was really like
would they still tell me to take a hike,
or would they perceive me differently?
But what happens when tears the start calling
and they keep on falling
all through the night?
Will someone please come
and make this undone
so I can be happy?

and

I think I hate you
For all you make me do.
The worthlessness you make me feel,
It's as if I'm not real.
I would ask why
You make me cry,
But that just makes
You tell me all my mistakes.
You clearly don't understand,

I'm sick of obeying your every command.
I need to be myself
Instead of just another on the shelf.
You just can't seem to realize
I'm sick of hearing your lies.
I need to break free.
I need to be me.
Is somebody out there?
Does somebody care?
I feel alone and tired,
When will I get what I've aspired?
I'm not ok,
I can't keep living my life this way.
Please, I beseech you,
Lets not argue.

Turtles
deephippie
January 22, 2005 @ 6:37 PM

today as i pondered life i realized if a turtle doesn't have a shell, is he homeless or is he naked?

Conclusion

- "I blog because it's there."

- "I blog because I write much better than I speak."

- "I blog because... - I enjoy the process of writing. - I know that people enjoy reading what I write,"

- "I blog because it's the easiest, most cost-effective way to publish."

- "No, really I blog for the hell of it."

- " I blog because I've met some fantastically weird and interesting people over the internet"

- "I blog because I must. Blogito ergo sum."

- "I blog because I m not a Molly Ivins or a Mary Oliver."

- " I blog because I feel that I have useful information to share and I enjoy sharing it with my customers"

- "I blog because it is the one place I can say what I want to say out loud and without interruption."

- "I blog because I enjoy it. Ultimately, that's the only reason for doing it."

- "I blog because I don't think I really understand something until I write about it."

- " I blog because I like to write, because I have friends that *do* read it, even if they don't respond"

- "I Blog Because I Can."

- "I blog, because inevitably someone else will challenge my will to do so"

- "I blog because I want to have an audience..."

- "Baldur has noted that he only blogs when somebody or something ticks him off"

- "I blog because it's good hearing about everyone's life- and talking about life in general- and not have to worry about being judged."

- " I blog because I get to tinker with the underlying code, host the site at my own house"

- "Operating a popular blog gives people an incentive to approach me with interesting things of their own devising or discovery"

- "I blog because I enjoy doing so. I don't give a flying fig how many comments I have"

- "I blog because my voice matters, and because blogging is a way for me to collaborate with people I've never seen or met"

- "'Why do I blog? Because I've always liked to dance. I'm light on my feet and I like the clunk, clunk of the shoes. Oh, wait a minute ... that's "clog"

- " I blog because its communication between family and friends who aren't close by, and because its communication with friends I'll see during and after work"

- "I blog because it's more communication and interaction between myself and distant friends and family, plus its more communication "stuff""

- " I blog because I am. Actually, I blog because I write enough for the "real" media and simply must get my own thoughts out there."

- "I blog because I'ma writer. That's the whole deal with me. Back in high school I carried a green steno pad everywhere; now I blog. ..."

- "I blog because it helps me release some of my daily stress."

- "I blog because i get bored and i really want to see how i affect people with em."

- "The more people who do this, the greater the likelihood that new ideas and spokesmen for them will coalesce out of the primeval slime. ... "

- "Why do I blog? Because I'm far too egotistical and obsessed with the idea that my life is a movie starring myself."

- "I blog because I find a lot of interesting sites in the course of my travels,"

- "I blog because I want to share my thoughts and knowledge. Feels good!"

- " I blog because it'sa nice way to vent as you say."

- "why do i blog? because i'm an exhibitionist? why else would one put their private thoughts out for the world to see? "

- "I blog because I love it."

- "I like checking my site stats and seeing how many people have surfed through the site, have been exposed to something I wrote. ..."

- " I blog because information is energy. I absorb it, maybe add to it and pass it on."

- "I blog because I enjoy doing it, but I make my living from that job, so I BLOG ONLY WHEN I'M NOT WORKING. ... "

- " I blog because I want to share the latest news with people and some of my thoughts."

- "I blog because I like to blog."

- I think some things in my life are funny and need to be shared."

- "I blog because it's Monday, and there's nothing else to do."

- "none of my IRL friends blog and most of them think that my blog is silly. my mother especially. "

- "I blog because I get so damn mad at the news, and I carry it around inside of me with no place to let it out—"

- "I blog because I get a pinging in my brain when I cruise other blogs that no drug can match."

- " I blog because: a) I've got more opinions than I have column inches to hold them and b) I want to by-pass the editor for some things which I know would get red"

- "I blog because I am a packrat. I hate losing things; ideas, papers, movie ticket stubs, everything. I can't stand to lose things. ... "

- "... I blog because that whole process — reading, discussing, re-reading, and even re-writing — occurs right here in these MozillaWindows on the world. ... "

- "... I blog because I'ma very important confessional poet. I blog because I'm an american artist. I blog because I can; like a dog licking his balls. ... "

- "... 1) I blog because I'ma nob 2) I blog because I'm boring 3) I blog because I'm insecure and maladjusted 4) I blog because I'm narcissistic"

- "and you know what .. who ever is reading this ..... points finger* you should blog too."

- "I blog, therefore I am"

Acknowledgements

First of all, I would like to thank all of the people that have submitted and given their permission to let us user their blogs. To these individuals we extend our deepest gratitude. Thank you, for allowing us to let the world see the daily struggles that you have gone through. Thank you, for sharing your humorous moments of your day. Thank you, for inspiring words. Thank you, we here at Book Of Blogs could not have done this without you.

If you, or someone you know has a blog that you would like for it to be considered for publication in future volumes please visit www.bookofblogs.org. To those who write blogs and to those who read them, thank you!

Peter Wojtowicz
President of Book Of Blogs Inc.
www.bookofblogs.org

Listed below are the people/organizations that made this book possible:

Book Of Blogs Inc. Members:
    Peter Wojtowicz
    Tomasz Wojtowicz
    Robert Wojtowicz
    Wojciech Kalembasa
    Greg Maslowski
    Dave Bieszczad

"Hello world, this is me, I'm a mess, and I have no idea who I am, sorry."
Kelly-Ann

360 Grafix designed our front cover. 360 Grafix specializes in full color business cards, postcards, and flyers. Our mission is simple: we want to provide high quality designs and printing for everyone while making it both convenient and affordable. Please visit www.360grafix.com.

Xanga: provider of weblog and webpage publishing tools for online diaries and journals. www.xanga.com

tBlog: free web log publishing tool and templates that allow users to add calendar, search, link management, voting, and commenting modules to their sites. www.tblog.com

Blogger: offers free weblog publishing and hosting. www.blogger.com

LiveJournal: offering a place to create and keep your own online journal. Also featuring communities. www.livejournal.com